Chinese

Practical Cookery

Chinese

p

This is a Parragon Book
First published in 2000

Parragon
Queen Street House
4 Queen Street
Bath BA1 1HE, UK

ISBN: 0-75254-093-9

Printed in Indonesia

NOTE

Cup measurements in this book are for American cups.
Tablespoons are assumed to be 15ml. Unless otherwise stated,
milk is assumed to be full fat, eggs are medium
and pepper is freshly ground black pepper.

Recipes using uncooked eggs should be
avoided by infants, the elderly, pregnant women and anyone
suffering from an illness

Contents

Introduction 10

Soups

Starters

Poultry

Meat

Fish & Seafood

Noodles

Rice

Introduction

The abundance of Chinese restaurants testify to the fact that Chinese cuisine is hugely popular in the West. This book will show you how to recreate authentic Chinese dishes in your own home. Along with the more famous Cantonese and Szechuan specialities, there are also less familiar but equally delicious recipes from other regions for you to try.

There can be few places in the world nowadays that are unfamiliar with Chinese cuisine. It first became known in the West with the arrival of Chinese workers in the United States during the Gold rush years and today there are Chinese restaurants from San Francisco to Helsinki and from Sydney to Edinburgh. Home-cooked Chinese food is a more recent phenomenon – at least, in the Western kitchen – but, once the ingredients and the wok became easily available and people realized how quick and easy it is to prepare, it soon became popular.

Besides being quite delicious, which is undoubtedly its most attractive characteristic, Chinese food is both healthy and economic. Carbohydrates, such as rice, which release energy slowly and are recommended by nutritionists as an important part of a healthy diet, are served at every meal. Vegetables, too, play a starring role and they are cooked in ways, such as stir-frying and steaming, which preserve most

of their vitamins and minerals. With a few exceptions, high-cholesterol, high-fat ingredients, such as dairy products and red meat, are either absent altogether or are served sparingly.

To a considerable extent, the distinctive flavours of Chinese food resulted from the need to be economical. Bulky but bland foods, such as noodles, were served in relatively large amounts to satisfy the appetite. Expensive ingredients, such as meat and fish, could be used in only small quantities, so they had to

be prepared in ways that made the most of them – combined with herbs, spices and other flavourings. As a result, Chinese cuisine probably has the largest repertoire of any in the world. Fuel was scarce, so 'fast food' was a necessity, resulting in the art of stir-frying in which ingredients are tossed in a round-based, cast iron wok over a high heat to cook in a short time. This preserves their flavour, colour, texture and nutrients. Steaming, also a favourite Chinese cooking technique, similarly results in flavoursome, attractive and nutritious dishes. Bamboo baskets are stacked one above another over a single heat source, thus saving fuel.

A desire for balance and harmony has permeated all aspects of Chinese life since the days of Confucius and this applies to food as well as everything else. Spicy dishes are complemented by sweet-and-sour ones, dry-cooked dishes are balanced with those bathed in sauce, meat is matched with seafood. Dishes are chosen to complement each other in texture, flavour and colour and it is not considered correct to serve more than one dish with the same main ingredient or to cook them using the same technique. Consciously or unconsciously, Chinese cooks, from the housewife to the professional chef, all work to this ancient Taoist principle of Yin and Yang in which balance and contrast are the key. Mealtimes, too, are a time of harmony, when the family – often three generations – gather and share a selection of different dishes, as well as their daily news.

Regional Cooking

China is a huge country and the terrain and climate vary dramatically from one region to another. The crops grown and the livestock raised are equally diverse, giving rise to distinctive regional culinary traditions.

The North

Beijing has been the capital of China for about 1,000 years and, as befits such an important city, its culinary tradition is venerable. The Emperor's chief chef was a highly respected figure whose responsibilities included maintaining the health of the Imperial family through a careful balance of herbs, spices and other ingredients, not simply creating appetizing dishes. Each newly appointed chef considered it a matter of honour to outdo his predecessors and there was also much rivalry with visiting chefs who accompanied dignitaries from other provinces when they came to Beijing. As a result, Beijing cuisine, which still tends to be called Peking in culinary circles, is varied and elegant. It has also been influenced by the Moslem culinary traditions of Central Asia through a number of Tartar invasions. Sesame seeds and the oil and paste made from them, which now feature in the cooking of all regions of China, were originally introduced by the Tartars. The popularity of lamb, rather than pork, unique to the Northern provinces, is probably also a result of Moslem influences. Outside the city, the cooking is simpler and lacks the light-handed touch that is characteristic of Beijing. Sauces and dips tend to be strongly flavoured and leeks, onions and garlic are popular vegetables. Mongolian or chrysanthemum fire pot dishes – a kind of stock-based fondue – are a speciality.

Wheat, rather than rice, is the staple ingredient in Northern Chinese cuisine and it is used to make noodles, dumplings, pancakes and steamed buns. The climate can be quite harsh, but produce in this region includes pak choi, onions, grapes and peaches. Freshwater fish, especially carp, are popular in the area around the Huang Ho River and prawns (shrimp) and other seafood are abundant in the coastal regions. Drying, smoking and pickling are typical preserving techniques.

The South

The first Chinese emigrants came from Kwangtung in the nineteenth century, so this is probably the best-known style of Chinese cuisine in the West. The capital of the province, Canton, was the first major trading port in the country and so was open to many foreign influences. However,

Regional Cooking

probably the most important influence, from the culinary point of view, was internal. In 1644 the Ming dynasty was overthrown and the Imperial Household, together with its retinue of chefs, fled to Canton from Beijing. This has resulted in a style of cooking that is renowned for its variety, sophistication and excellence.

Steaming is a characteristic technique in Southern China and small fish, little parcels of meat or patties and, above all, dumplings are often cooked this way. Dim sum, which literally means 'to please the heart' are a Cantonese speciality. These small, steamed, filled dumplings are as popular in the West as they are in China, but there, they are never served as an appetizer. Rather, they are eaten as snacks at teahouses in the morning or afternoon. In fact, an alternative way of saying going to a dim sum restaurant is going out for morning tea.

Char siu roasting is another Cantonese technique. No kind of roasting is common in Chinese homes, which often do not have ovens, but this method is popular in restaurants. Meat is seasoned and marinated well and then roasted at a very high temperature for a short time. This results in the marinade becoming encrusted on the meat in a crisp outer layer, while the inside remains succulent and juicy. Only very tender cuts of meat, particularly pork, can be prepared in this way.

Agricultural produce in this semi-tropical region is abundant and varied. Vegetables are often simply stir-fried and served plain or just with oyster sauce. They may also be combined with meat or fish. Spinach, pak choi and dried mushrooms feature widely. Fresh fruit, frequently served on its own as a dessert, may also be combined with meat or fish in sweet-and-sour dishes. Fish and seafood, particularly abalone, crab, lobster, prawns (shrimp) and scallops, are plentiful. They are usually stir-fried or steamed, often flavoured with ginger, and cooking meat with fish is typically Cantonese. Generally, food is not highly spiced, as the Cantonese prefer to enjoy the natural flavours of the ingredients. Light soy sauce is a popular flavouring and other typical sauces include hoisin, oyster, black bean and plum.

The East

The delta of the Yangtse River makes this one of the most fertile regions in China. The abundant produce includes broccoli, spring onions (scallions), sweet potatoes, pak choi, soya beans, tea, wheat, rice, maize and nuts and the region is well known for its superb vegetarian dishes, noodles and dumplings. Freshwater fish are found in the many streams and lakes, especially in Kiangsu, which also has a long tradition of deep-sea fishing.

The provinces that comprise this region each have a particular style of cooking, but all are characterized by their richness. The vast cosmopolitan city of Shanghai has assimilated many influences from both other parts of China and abroad. Its cuisine is unusual in that it features dairy products and uses lavish quantities of lard. Shanghai dishes are typically rich, sweet and beautifully presented. The school of cooking in the surrounding area is known as Kiangche, the name being an amalgamation of the two provinces of Kiangsu and Chekiang. Duck, ham and fish dishes are specialities, often prepared with piquant spices. This region produces the best rice wine in the country. It is one of the most prosperous parts of China and has a long gourmet tradition. In Fukien to the South, the cuisine is less sophisticated, relying mainly on fish and a wealth of fresh produce. It is strongly influenced by neighbouring Kwangtung.

The West

Surrounded by mountains, Szechuan has a mild, humid climate and rich fertile soil. Its cuisine is most noted for its robust, richly coloured dishes flavoured with hot spices, such as chillies and Szechuan peppercorns. Strongly flavoured ingredients, such as garlic, ginger, onions, leeks and sesame seed paste are typical and hot pickles are a speciality. Food preservation techniques, for which Western China is famous, include smoking, drying, salting and pickling. Yunnan, to the South of Szechuan, produces superb cured, smoked raw ham.

Szechuan cooking is traditionally described as having seven kinds of flavours - sweet, salty, sour, bitter, fragrant, sesame and hot - based respectively on honey or sugar, soy sauce, vinegar, onions or leeks, garlic or ginger, sesame seeds and, finally, chillies. Methods of cooking are varied, ranging from dry-frying with very little oil and no additional liquid to cooking in a clear, well-flavoured broth, which is then reduced to make a thick rich sauce. Deep-fried, paper-wrapped parcels of marinated meat or fish are a Szechuan speciality.

Basic Recipes

Chinese Stock

This basic stock is used in Chinese cooking not only as the basis for soup-making, but also whenever liquid is required instead of plain water.

MAKES 2.5L/4½ PINTS/10 CUPS

750 g/1 lb 10 oz chicken pieces

750 g/1 lb 10 oz pork spare ribs

3.75 litres/6½ pints/15 cups cold water

3-4 pieces ginger root, crushed

3-4 spring onions (scallions), each tied into a knot

3-4 tbsp Chinese rice wine or dry sherry

1 Trim off any excess fat from the chicken and spare ribs; chop them into large pieces.

2 Place the chicken and pork in a large pan with the water; add the ginger and spring onion (scallion) knots.

3 Bring to the boil, and skim off the scum. Reduce the heat and simmer uncovered for at least 2-3 hours.

4 Strain the stock, discarding the chicken, pork, ginger and spring onions (scallions); add the wine and return to the boil, simmer for 2-3 minutes.

5 Refrigerate the stock when cool; it will keep for up to 4-5 days. Alternatively, it can be frozen in small containers and be defrosted as required.

Fresh Chicken Stock

MAKES 1.75 LITRES/3 PINTS/7½ CUPS

1 kg/2 lb 4 oz chicken, skinned

2 celery sticks

1 onion

2 carrots

1 garlic clove

few sprigs of fresh parsley

2 litres/3½ pints/9 cups water

salt and pepper

1 Put all the ingredients into a large saucepan.

2 Bring to the boil. Skim away surface scum using a large flat spoon. Reduce the heat to a gentle simmer, partially cover, and cook for 2 hours. Allow to cool.

3 Line a sieve (strainer) with clean muslin (cheesecloth) and place over a large jug or bowl. Pour the stock through the sieve (strainer). The cooked chicken can be used in another recipe. Discard the other solids. Cover the stock and chill.

4 Skim away any fat that forms before using. Store in the refrigerator for 3-4 days, until required, or freeze in small batches.

Fresh Vegetable Stock

This can be kept chilled for up to three days or frozen for up to three months. Salt is not added when cooking the stock: it is better to season it according to the dish in which it its to be used.

MAKES 1.5 LITRES/2¾ PINTS/6¼ CUPS

250 g/9 oz shallots

1 large carrot, diced

1 celery stalk, chopped

½ fennel bulb

1 garlic clove

1 bay leaf

a few fresh parsley and tarragon sprigs

2 litres/ 3½ pints/8¾ cups water

pepper

1 Put all the ingredients in a large saucepan and bring to the boil.

2 Skim off the surface scum with a flat spoon and reduce to a gentle simmer. Partially cover and cook for 45 minutes. Leave to cool.

3 Line a sieve (strainer) with clean muslin (cheesecloth) and put over a large jug or bowl. Pour the stock through the sieve (strainer). Discard the herbs and vegetables.

4 Cover and store in small quantities in the refrigerator for up to three days.

Fresh Lamb Stock

MAKES 1.75 LITRES/3 PINTS/7½ CUPS

about 1 kg/2 lb 4 oz bones from a cooked
  joint or raw chopped lamb bones

2 onions, studded with 6 cloves, or sliced or
chopped coarsely

2 carrots, sliced

1 leek, sliced

1-2 celery sticks, sliced

1 Bouquet Garni

about 2.25 litres/4 pints/2 quarts water

1 Chop or break up the bones and place
in a large saucepan with the other
ingredients.

2 Bring to the boil and remove any
scum from the surface with a
perforated spoon. Cover and simmer
gently for 3-4 hours. Strain the stock and
leave to cool.

3 Remove any fat from the surface and
chill. If stored for more than 24 hours
the stock must be boiled every day, cooled
quickly and chilled again. The stock may
be frozen for up to 2 months; place in a
large plastic bag and seal, leaving at least
2.5 cm/1 inch of headspace to allow for
expansion.

Fresh Fish Stock

MAKES 1.75 LITRES/3 PINTS/7½ CUPS

1 head of a cod or salmon, etc, plus the
  trimmings, skin and bones or just the
  trimmings, skin and bones

1-2 onions, sliced

1 carrot, sliced

1-2 celery sticks, sliced

good squeeze of lemon juice

1 Bouquet Garni or 2 fresh or dried bay
  leaves

1 Wash the fish head and trimmings
and place in a saucepan. Cover with
water and bring to the boil.

2 Remove any scum with a perforated
spoon, then add the remaining
ingredients. Cover and simmer for about
30 minutes.

3 Strain and cool. Store in ther
refrigerator and use within 2 days.

Cornflour (cornstarch) Paste

Cornflour (cornstarch) paste is made by
mixing 1 part cornflour (cornstarch)
with about 1½ parts of cold water. Stir
until smooth. The paste is used to thicken
sauces.

Plain rice

Use long-grain rice or patna rice, or
better still, try fragrant Thai rice

SERVES 4

250 g/9 oz long-grain rice

about 250 ml/9 fl oz/1 cup cold water

pinch of salt

½ tsp oil (optional)

1 Wash and rinse the rice just once.
Place the rice in a saucepan and add
enough water so that there is no more
than 2 cm/³/₄ inch of water above the
surface of the rice.

2 Bring to the boil, add salt and oil (if
using), and stir to prevent the rice
sticking to the bottom of the pan.

3 Reduce the heat to very, very low,
cover and cook for 15-20 minutes.

4 Remove from the heat and let stand,
covered, for 10 minutes or so. Fluff up
the rice with a fork or spoon before
serving.

Fresh Coconut Milk

To make it from fresh grated coconut,
place about 250 g/9 oz grated coconut
in a bowl, pour over about 600 ml/1 pint
of boiling water to just cover and leave to
stand for 1 hour. Strain through muslin,
squeezing hard to extract as much 'thick'
milk as possible. If you require coconut
cream, leave to stand then skim the
'cream' from the surface for use.
Unsweetened desiccated coconut can also
be used in the same quantities.

How to Use This Book

Each recipe contains a wealth of useful information, including a breakdown of nutritional quantities, preparation and cooking times, and level of difficulty. All of this information is explained in detail below.

The nutritional information provided for each recipe is per serving or per portion. Optional ingredients, variations or serving suggestions have not been included in the calculations.

The number of chef's hats represents the difficulty of each recipe, ranging from easy (1 chef's hat) to difficult (5 chef's hats).

This amount of time represents the preparation of ingredients, including cooling, chilling and soaking times.

This represents the cooking time.

The ingredients for each recipe are listed in the order that they are used.

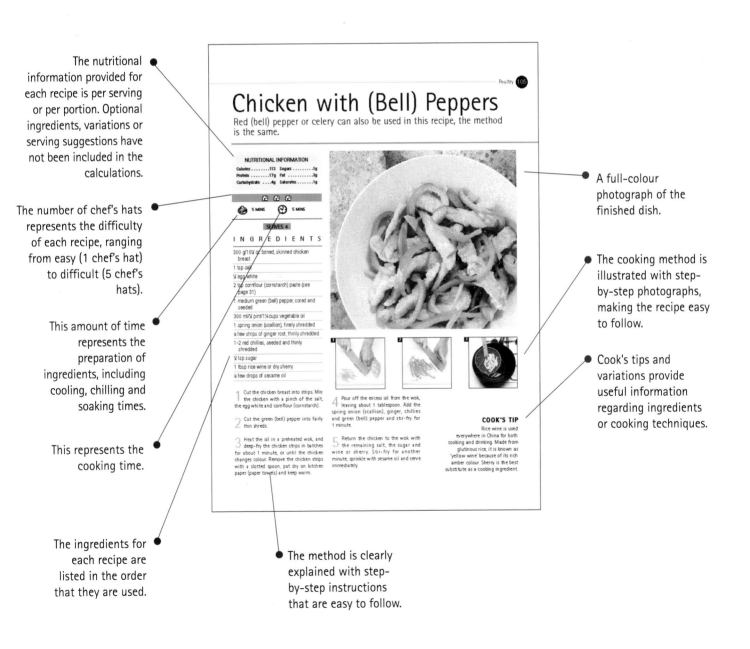

Chicken with (Bell) Peppers

Red (bell) pepper or celery can also be used in this recipe, the method is the same.

Poultry 105

NUTRITIONAL INFORMATION

Calories 113   Sugars 1g
Protein . . . . .17g   Fat 3g
Carbohydrate . . . . .4g   Saturates 1g

5 MINS   5 MINS

SERVES 4

INGREDIENTS

300 g/10½ oz boned, skinned chicken breast

1 tsp salt

¼ egg white

2 tsp cornflour (cornstarch) paste (see page 31)

1 medium green (bell) pepper, cored and seeded

300 ml/½ pint/1¼ cups vegetable oil

1 spring onion (scallion), finely shredded

a few strips of ginger root, thinly shredded

1–2 red chillies, seeded and thinly shredded

¼ tsp sugar

1 tbsp rice wine or dry sherry

a few drops of sesame oil

1 Cut the chicken breast into strips. Mix the chicken with a pinch of the salt, the egg white and cornflour (cornstarch).

2 Cut the green (bell) pepper into fairly thin shreds.

3 Heat the oil in a preheated wok, and deep-fry the chicken strips in batches for about 1 minute, or until the chicken changes colour. Remove the chicken strips with a slotted spoon, pat dry on kitchen paper (paper towels) and keep warm.

4 Pour off the excess oil from the wok, leaving about 1 tablespoon. Add the spring onion (scallion), ginger, chillies and green (bell) pepper and stir-fry for 1 minute.

5 Return the chicken to the wok with the remaining salt, the sugar and wine or sherry. Stir-fry for another minute, sprinkle with sesame oil and serve immediately.

COOK'S TIP
Rice wine is used everywhere in China for both cooking and drinking. Made from glutinous rice, it is known as 'yellow wine' because of its rich amber colour. Sherry is the best substitute as a cooking ingredient.

A full-colour photograph of the finished dish.

The cooking method is illustrated with step-by-step photographs, making the recipe easy to follow.

Cook's tips and variations provide useful information regarding ingredients or cooking techniques.

The method is clearly explained with step-by-step instructions that are easy to follow.

Soups

Soup is an integral part of the Chinese meal but is rarely served as a starter as it is in the Western world. Instead, soup is usually served between courses to clear the palate and act as a beverage throughout the meal. The soup is usually presented in a large tureen in the centre of the table for people to help themselves as the meal progresses.

The soups in this chapter combine a range of flavours and textures. There are thicker soups, thin clear consommés, and those which are served with wontons, dumplings, noodles or even rice in them. Ideally the soup should be made with fresh stock, but if this is unavailable, use a stock cube and reduce the amount of seasonings otherwise the soup will be too salty. It is always worth making your own Chinese Stock (see page 14) if you have time.

Sweetcorn & Lentil Soup

This pale-coloured soup is made with sweetcorn and green lentils, and is similar in style to the traditional crab and sweetcorn soup.

NUTRITIONAL INFORMATION

Calories	171	Sugars	9g
Protein	5g	Fat	2g
Carbohydrate	30g	Saturates	0.3g

 5 MINS   30 MINS

SERVES 4

INGREDIENTS

25 g/1 oz/2 tbsp green lentils

1 litre/1¾ pints/4 cups vegetable stock

1 cm/½ inch piece ginger root, chopped finely

2 tsp soy sauce

1 tsp sugar

1 tbsp cornflour (cornstarch)

3 tbsp dry sherry

325 g/11½ oz can sweetcorn

1 egg white

1 tsp sesame oil

salt and pepper

TO GARNISH

spring onion (scallion), cut into strips

red chilli, cut into strips

1 Wash the lentils in a sieve (strainer). Place in a saucepan with the stock, ginger root, soy sauce and sugar. Bring to the boil and boil rapidly, uncovered, for 10 minutes. Skim off any froth on the surface. Reduce the heat, cover and simmer for 15 minutes.

2 Mix the cornflour (cornstarch) with the sherry in a small bowl. Add the sweetcorn with the liquid from the can and cornflour (cornstarch) mixture to the saucepan. Simmer for 2 minutes.

3 Whisk the egg white lightly with the sesame oil. Pour the egg mixture into the soup in a thin stream, remove from the heat and stir. The egg white will form white strands. Season with salt and pepper to taste.

4 Pour into 4 warmed soup bowls and garnish with strips of spring onion (scallion) and red chilli. Serve the soup immediately.

COOK'S TIP

To save time use a 425 g/15 oz can of green lentils instead of dried ones. Place the lentils and sweetcorn in a large saucepan with the stock and flavourings, bring to the boil and simmer for 2 minutes, then continue the recipe from step 2 as above.

Seafood & Tofu Soup

Use prawn (shrimp), squid or scallops, or a combination of all three in this healthy soup.

NUTRITIONAL INFORMATION

Calories 97   Sugars 0g
Protein . . . . .17g   Fat 2g
Carbohydrate . . . .3g   Saturates 0.4g

3½ HOURS   10 MINS

SERVES 4

INGREDIENTS

250 g/9 oz seafood: peeled prawns (shrimp), squid, scallops, etc., defrosted if frozen

½ egg white, lightly beaten

1 tbsp cornflour (cornstarch) paste (see page 15)

1 cake tofu (bean curd)

700 ml/1¼ pints/3 cups Chinese Stock (see page 14)

1 tbsp light soy sauce

salt and pepper

fresh coriander (cilantro) leaves, to garnish (optional)

1 Small prawns (shrimp) can be left whole; larger ones should be cut into smaller pieces; cut the squid and scallops into small pieces.

2 If raw, mix the prawns (shrimp) and scallops with the egg white and cornflour (cornstarch) paste to prevent them from becoming tough when they are cooked. Cut the cake of tofu into about 24 small cubes.

3 Bring the stock to a rolling boil. Add the tofu and soy sauce, bring back to the boil and simmer for 1 minute.

4 Stir in the seafood, raw pieces first, pre-cooked ones last. Bring back to the boil and simmer for just 1 minute.

5 Adjust the seasoning to taste and serve, garnished with coriander (cilantro) leaves, if liked.

COOK'S TIP

Tofu, also known as bean curd, is made from puréed yellow soya beans, which are very high in protein. Although almost tasteless, tofu absorbs the flavours of other ingredients. It is widely available in supermarkets, and Oriental and health-food stores.

Spinach & Tofu Soup

This is a very colourful and delicious soup. If spinach is not in season, watercress or lettuce can be used instead.

NUTRITIONAL INFORMATION

Calories	33	Sugar	.........1g
Protein	.........4g	Fat	...........2g
Carbohydrate	....1g	Saturates	.....0.2g

3½ HOURS   10 MINS

SERVES 4

INGREDIENTS

1 cake tofu (bean curd)

125 g/4½ oz spinach leaves without stems

700 ml/1¼ pints/3 cups Chinese Stock or water

1 tbsp light soy sauce

salt and pepper

1 Using a sharp knife, cut the tofu into small pieces about 5 mm (¼ inch) thick.

2 Wash the spinach leaves thoroughly under cold, running water and drain thoroughly.

3 Cut the spinach leaves into small pieces or shreds, discarding any discoloured leaves and tough stalks. (If possible, use fresh young spinach leaves, which have not yet developed tough ribs. Otherwise, it is important to cut out all the ribs and stems for this soup.) Set the spinach aside until required.

4 In a preheated wok or large frying pan (skillet), bring the Chinese stock or water to a rolling boil.

5 Add the tofu (bean curd) cubes and light soy sauce, bring back to the boil and simmer for about 2 minutes over a medium heat.

6 Add the shredded spinach leaves and simmer for 1 more minute, stirring gently. Skim the surface of the soup to make it clear, adjust the seasoning to taste.

7 Transfer the spinach and tofu (bean curd) soup to a warm soup tureen or individual serving bowls and serve with chopsticks, to pick up the pieces of food and a broad, shallow spoon for drinking the soup.

COOK'S TIP

Soup is an integral part of a Chinese meal; it is usually presented in a large bowl placed in the centre of the table, and consumed as the meal progresses. It serves as a refresher between different dishes and as a beverage throughout the meal.

Chinese Cabbage Soup

This is a piquant soup, which is slightly sweet-and-sour in flavour.
It can be served as a hearty meal or appetizer.

NUTRITIONAL INFORMATION

Calories 65	Sugars 7g
Protein 3g	Fat 0.5g
Carbohydrate 11g	Saturates 0.1g

 5 MINS   30 MINS

SERVES 4

INGREDIENTS

450 g/1 lb pak choi

600 ml/1 pint/2½ cups vegetable stock

1 tbsp rice wine vinegar

1 tbsp light soy sauce

1 tbsp caster (superfine) sugar

1 tbsp dry sherry

1 fresh red chilli, thinly sliced

1 tbsp cornflour (cornstarch)

2 tbsp water

1 Wash the pak choi thoroughly under cold running water, rinse and drain. Pat dry on kitchen paper (paper towels).

2 Trim the stems of the pak choi and shred the leaves.

3 Heat the vegetable stock in a large saucepan. Add the pak choi and cook for 10–15 minutes.

4 Mix together the rice wine vinegar, soy sauce, caster (superfine) sugar and sherry in a small bowl. Add this mixture to the stock, together with the sliced chilli.

5 Bring to the boil, lower the heat and cook for 2–3 minutes.

6 Blend the cornflour (cornstarch) with the water to form a smooth paste.

7 Gradually stir the cornflour (cornstarch) mixture into the soup. Cook, stirring constantly, until it thickens. Cook for a further 4–5 minutes.

8 Ladle the Chinese cabbage soup into individual warm serving bowls and serve immediately.

COOKS TIP

Pak choi, also known as bok choi or spoon cabbage, has long, white leaf stalks and fleshy, spoon-shaped, shiny green leaves. There are a number of varieties available, which differ mainly in size rather than flavour.

Hot & Sour Soup

This well-known soup from Peking is unusual in that it is thickened. The 'hot' flavour is achieved by the addition of plenty of black pepper.

NUTRITIONAL INFORMATION

Calories 124   Sugars 1g
Protein ....5g   Fat 8g
Carbohydrate ....8g   Saturates 1g

 3½ HOURS   25 MINS

SERVES 4

INGREDIENTS

2 tbsp cornflour (cornstarch)

4 tbsp water

2 tbsp light soy sauce

3 tbsp rice wine vinegar

½ tsp ground black pepper

1 small fresh red chilli, finely chopped

1 egg

2 tbsp vegetable oil

1 onion, chopped

850 ml/1½ pints/3¾ cups chicken or beef consommé

1 open-cap mushroom, sliced

50 g/1¾ oz skinless chicken breast, cut into very thin strips

1 tsp sesame oil

1 In a mixing bowl, blend the cornflour (cornstarch) with the water to form a smooth paste.

2 Add the soy sauce, rice wine vinegar and black pepper.

3 Finely chop the red chilli and add to the ingredients in the bowl. Mix well.

4 Break the egg into a separate bowl and beat well. Set aside while you cook the other ingredients.

5 Heat the oil in a preheated wok and fry the onion for 1–2 minutes until softened.

6 Stir in the consommé, mushroom and chicken and bring to the boil. Cook for about 15 minutes or until the chicken is tender.

7 Gradually pour the cornflour (cornstarch) mixture into the soup and cook, stirring constantly, until it thickens.

8 As you are stirring, gradually drizzle the egg into the soup, to create threads of egg.

9 Pour the hot and sour soup into a warm tureen or individual serving bowls, sprinkle with the sesame oil and serve immediately.

Vegetarian Hot & Sour Soup

This popular soup is easy to make and very filling. It can be eaten as a meal on its own or served as an appetizer before a light menu.

NUTRITIONAL INFORMATION

Calories . . . . .61 Sugars 1g
Protein . . . . .5g Fat 2g
Carbohydrate . . . .8g Saturates 0.2g

30 MINS 10 MINS

SERVES 4

I N G R E D I E N T S

4 Chinese dried mushrooms
 (if unavailable, use open-cup
 mushrooms)

125 g/4½ oz firm tofu (bean curd)

60 g/2 oz/1 cup canned bamboo
 shoots

600 ml/1 pint/2½ cups vegetable stock
 or water

60 g/2 oz/⅓ cup peas

1 tbsp dark soy sauce

2 tbsp white wine vinegar

2 tbsp cornflour (cornstarch)

salt and pepper

sesame oil, to serve

1 Place the Chinese dried mushrooms in a small bowl and cover with warm water. Leave to soak for about 20–25 minutes.

2 Drain the mushrooms and squeeze out the excess water, reserving this. Remove the tough centres and cut the mushrooms into thin shreds. Shred the tofu (bean curd) and bamboo shoots.

3 Bring the stock or water to the boil in a large saucepan. Add the mushrooms, tofu (bean curd), bamboo shoots and peas. Simmer for 2 minutes.

4 Mix together the soy sauce, vinegar and cornflour (cornstarch) with 2 tablespoons of the reserved mushroom liquid.

5 Stir the soy sauce and cornflour (cornstarch) mixture into the soup with the remaining mushroom liquid. Bring to the boil and season with salt and plenty of pepper. Simmer for 2 minutes.

6 Serve in warmed bowls with a few drops of sesame oil sprinkled over the top of each.

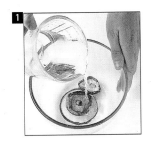

COOK'S TIP

If you use open-cup mushrooms instead of dried mushrooms, add an extra 150 ml/ ¼ pint/⅔ cup vegetable stock or water to the soup, as these mushrooms do not need soaking.

Lettuce & Tofu Soup

This is a delicate, clear soup of shredded lettuce and small chunks of tofu (bean curd) with sliced carrot and spring onion (scallion).

NUTRITIONAL INFORMATION

Calories . . . . .113 Sugars 2g
Protein . . . . .5g Fat 8g
Carbohydrate . . . .3g Saturates 1g

 5 MINS   15 MINS

SERVES 4

INGREDIENTS

200 g/7 oz tofu (bean curd)

2 tbsp vegetable oil

1 carrot, sliced thinly

1 cm/½ inch piece ginger root,
cut into thin shreds

3 spring onions (scallions), sliced
diagonally

1.2 litres/2 pints/5 cups vegetable stock

2 tbsp soy sauce

2 tbsp dry sherry

1 tsp sugar

125 g/4½ oz/1½ cups cos (romaine) lettuce,
shredded

salt and pepper

1 Using a sharp knife, cut the tofu (bean curd) into small cubes.

2 Heat the vegetable oil in a preheated wok or large saucepan, add the tofu (bean curd) and stir-fry until browned. Remove with a perforated spoon and drain on kitchen paper (paper towels).

3 Add the carrot, ginger root and spring onions (scallions) to the wok or saucepan and stir-fry for 2 minutes.

4 Add the vegetable stock, soy sauce, sherry and sugar. Stir well to mix all the ingredients. Bring to the boil and simmer for 1 minute.

5 Add the cos (romaine) lettuce to the wok or saucepan and stir until it has just wilted.

6 Return the tofu (bean curd) to the pan to reheat. Season with salt and pepper to taste and serve the soup immediately in warmed bowls.

COOK'S TIP

For a prettier effect, score grooves along the length of the carrot with a sharp knife before slicing. This will create a flower effect as the carrot is cut into rounds. You could also try slicing the carrot on the diagonal to make longer slices.

Noodle & Mushroom Soup

This soup is very quickly and easily put together, and is cooked so that each ingredient can still be tasted in the finished dish.

NUTRITIONAL INFORMATION

Calories	74	Sugars 1g
Protein	........13g	Fat 3g
Carbohydrate	....9g	Saturates 0.4g

4 HOURS   10 MINS

SERVES 4

I N G R E D I E N T S

15 g/½ oz/¼ cup dried Chinese mushrooms or 125 g/4½ oz/1⅓ cups field or chestnut (crimini) mushrooms

1 litre/1¾ pints/4 cups hot Fresh Vegetable Stock (page 14)

125 g/4½ oz thread egg noodles

2 tsp sunflower oil

3 garlic cloves, crushed

2.5 cm/1 inch piece ginger, shredded finely

½ tsp mushroom ketchup

1 tsp light soy sauce

125 g/4½ oz/2 cups bean sprouts

coriander (cilantro) leaves, to garnish

1 Soak the dried Chinese mushrooms, if using, for at least 30 minutes in 300 ml/½ pint/1¼ cups of the hot vegetable stock. Remove the stalks and discard, then slice the mushrooms. Reserve the stock.

2 Cook the noodles for 2–3 minutes in boiling water. Drain, rinse and set aside until required.

3 Heat the oil over a high heat in a wok or large, heavy frying pan (skillet). Add the garlic and ginger, stir and add the mushrooms. Stir over a high heat for 2 minutes.

4 Add the remaining vegetable stock with the reserved stock and bring to the boil. Add the mushroom ketchup and soy sauce and mix well.

5 Stir in the bean sprouts and cook until tender. Serve over the noodles, garnished with coriander (cilantro) leaves.

COOK'S TIP

Dried mushrooms are highly fragrant and add a special flavour to Chinese dishes. There are many different varieties but Shiitake are the best. Although not cheap, a small amount will go a long way and they will keep indefinitely in an airtight jar.

Mushroom Noodle Soup

A light, refreshing clear soup of mushrooms, cucumber and small pieces of rice noodles, flavoured with soy sauce and a touch of garlic.

NUTRITIONAL INFORMATION

Calories ....84 Sugars 1g
Protein ....1g Fat 8g
Carbohydrate ....3g Saturates 1g

 5 MINS   10 MINS

SERVES 4

INGREDIENTS

125 g/4½ oz flat or open-cup mushrooms

½ cucumber

2 spring onions (scallions)

1 garlic clove

2 tbsp vegetable oil

25 g/1 oz/¼ cup Chinese rice noodles

¾ tsp salt

1 tbsp soy sauce

1 Wash the mushrooms and pat dry on kitchen paper (paper towels). Slice thinly. Do not remove the peel as this adds more flavour.

2 Halve the cucumber lengthways. Scoop out the seeds, using a teaspoon, and slice the cucumber thinly.

3 Chop the spring onions (scallions) finely and cut the garlic clove into thin strips.

4 Heat the vegetable oil in a large saucepan or wok.

5 Add the spring onions (scallions) and garlic to the pan or wok and stir-fry for 30 seconds. Add the mushrooms and stir-fry for 2–3 minutes.

6 Stir in 600 ml/1 pint/2½ cups water. Break the noodles into short lengths and add to the soup. Bring to the boil, stirring occasionally.

7 Add the cucumber slices, salt and soy sauce, and simmer for 2–3 minutes.

8 Serve the mushroom noodle soup in warmed bowls, distributing the noodles and vegetables evenly.

COOK'S TIP

Scooping the seeds out from the cucumber gives it a prettier effect when sliced, and also helps to reduce any bitterness, but if you prefer, you can leave them in.

Wonton Soup

The recipe for the wonton skins makes 24 but the soup requires only half this quantity. The other half can be frozen ready for another time.

NUTRITIONAL INFORMATION

Calories	278	Sugars 2g
Protein	........10g	Fat 5g
Carbohydrate	...50g	Saturates 1g

45 MINS   5 MINS

SERVES 4

INGREDIENTS

WONTON SKINS

1 egg

6 tbsp water

250 g/9 oz/2 cups plain (all-purpose) flour, plus extra for dusting

FILLING

125 g/4½ oz/½ cup frozen chopped spinach, defrosted

15 g/½ oz/1 tbsp pine kernels (nuts), toasted and chopped

25 g/1 oz/¼ cup minced quorn (TVP)

salt

SOUP

600 ml/1 pint/2½ cups vegetable stock

1 tbsp dry sherry

1 tbsp light soy sauce

2 spring onions (scallions), chopped

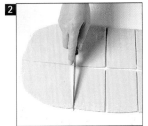

1 To make the wonton skins, beat the egg lightly in a bowl and mix with the water. Stir in the flour to form a stiff dough. Knead lightly, then cover with a damp cloth and leave to rest for 30 minutes.

2 Roll the dough out into a large sheet about 1.5 mm/¼ inch thick. Cut out 24 x 7 cm/3 inch squares. Dust each one lightly with flour. Only 12 squares are required for the soup so freeze the remainder to use on another occasion.

3 To make the filling, squeeze out the excess water from the spinach. Mix the spinach with the pine kernels (nuts) and quorn (TVP) until thoroughly combined. Season with salt.

4 Divide the mixture into 12 equal portions. Using a teaspoon, place one portion in the centre of each square. Seal the wontons by bringing the opposite corners of each square together and squeezing well.

5 To make the soup, bring the vegetable stock, sherry and soy sauce to the boil, add the wontons and boil rapidly for 2–3 minutes. Add the spring onions (scallions) and serve in warmed bowls immediately.

Chicken Wonton Soup

This Chinese-style soup is delicious as a starter to an oriental meal or as a light meal.

NUTRITIONAL INFORMATION

Calories 101	Sugars 0.3g
Protein 14g	Fat 4g
Carbohydrate 3g	Saturates 1g

  15 MINS   10 MINS

SERVES 4-6

INGREDIENTS

FILLING

350 g/12 oz minced (ground) chicken

1 tbsp soy sauce

1 tsp grated, fresh ginger root

1 garlic clove, crushed

2 tsp sherry

2 spring onions (scallions), chopped

1 tsp sesame oil

1 egg white

½ tsp cornflour (cornstarch)

½ tsp sugar

about 35 wonton wrappers

SOUP

1.5 litres/2¾ pints/6 cups chicken stock

1 tbsp light soy sauce

1 spring onion (scallion), shredded

1 small carrot, cut into very thin slices

1 Place all the ingredients for the filling in a large bowl and mix until thoroughly combined.

2 Place a small spoonful of the filling in the centre of each wonton wrapper.

3 Dampen the edges and gather up the wonton wrapper to form a small pouch enclosing the filling.

4 Cook the filled wontons in boiling water for 1 minute or until they float to the top. Remove with a slotted spoon and set aside.

5 Bring the chicken stock to the boil. Add the soy sauce, spring onion (scallion) and carrot.

6 Add the wontons to the soup and simmer gently for 2 minutes. Serve.

COOK'S TIP

Make double quantities of wonton skins and freeze the remainder. Place small squares of baking parchment in between each skin, then place in a freezer bag and freeze. Defrost thoroughly before using.

Clear Chicken & Egg Soup

This tasty chicken soup has the addition of poached eggs, making it both delicious and filling. Use fresh, home-made stock for a better flavour.

NUTRITIONAL INFORMATION

Calories ....138 Sugars 1g
Protein ....16g Fat 7g
Carbohydrate ....1g Saturates 2g

 5 MINS   35 MINS

SERVES 4

I N G R E D I E N T S

1 tsp salt

1 tbsp rice wine vinegar

4 eggs

850 ml/1½ pints/3¾ cups chicken stock

1 leek, sliced

125 g/4½ oz broccoli florets

125 g/4½ oz/1 cup shredded cooked chicken

2 open-cap mushrooms, sliced

1 tbsp dry sherry

dash of chilli sauce

chilli powder, to garnish

VARIATION

You could use 4 dried Chinese mushrooms, rehydrated according to the packet instructions, instead of the open-cap mushrooms, if you prefer.

1 Bring a large saucepan of water to the boil and add the salt and rice wine vinegar.

2 Reduce the heat so that it is just simmering and carefully break the eggs into the water, one at a time. Poach the eggs for 1 minute.

3 Remove the poached eggs with a slotted spoon and set aside.

4 Bring the chicken stock to the boil in a separate pan and add the leek, broccoli, chicken, mushrooms and sherry and season with chilli sauce to taste. Cook for 10–15 minutes.

5 Add the poached eggs to the soup and cook for a further 2 minutes. Carefully transfer the soup and poached eggs to 4 soup bowls. Dust with a little chilli powder and serve immediately.

Chicken Soup with Almonds

This soup can also be made using pheasant breasts. For a really gamey flavour, make game stock from the carcass and use in the soup.

NUTRITIONAL INFORMATION

Calories	219	Sugars	.........2g
Protein	........18g	Fat	..........15g
Carbohydrate	....2g	Saturates	.......2g

10 MINS 20 MINS

SERVES 4

INGREDIENTS

1 large or 2 small boneless skinned chicken breasts

1 tbsp sunflower oil

4 spring onions (scallions), thinly sliced diagonally

1 carrot, cut into julienne strips

700 ml/1¼ pints/3 cups chicken stock

finely grated rind of ½ lemon

40 g/1½ oz/⅓ cup ground almonds

1 tbsp light soy sauce

1 tbsp lemon juice

25 g/1 oz/¼ cup flaked almonds, toasted

salt and pepper

1 Cut each breast into 4 strips lengthways, then slice very thinly across the grain to give shreds of chicken.

2 Heat the oil in a wok, swirling it around until really hot.

3 Add the spring onions (scallions) and cook for 2 minutes, then add the chicken and toss it for 3-4 minutes until sealed and almost cooked through, stirring all the time. Add the carrot strips and stir.

4 Add the stock to the wok and bring to the boil. Add the lemon rind, ground almonds, soy sauce, lemon juice and plenty of seasoning. Bring back to the boil and simmer, uncovered, for 5 minutes, stirring from time to time.

5 Adjust the seasoning, add most of the toasted flaked almonds and continue to cook for a further 1-2 minutes.

6 Serve the soup very hot, in individual bowls, sprinkled with the remaining flaked almonds.

COOK'S TIP

To make game stock, break up a pheasant carcass and place in a pan with 2 litres/3½ pints/8 cups water. Bring to the boil slowly, skimming off any scum. Add 1 bouquet garni, 1 peeled onion and seasoning. Cover and simmer gently for 1½ hours. Strain, and skim any surface fat.

Chicken & Sweetcorn Soup

A hint of chilli and sherry flavour this soup while red (bell) pepper and tomato add colour.

NUTRITIONAL INFORMATION

Calories 199	Sugars 8g
Protein 12g	Fat 8g
Carbohydrate ...19g	Saturates 1g

 5 MINS   20 MINS

SERVES 4

INGREDIENTS

1 skinless, boneless chicken breast, about 175 g/6 oz

2 tbsp sunflower oil

2–3 spring onions (scallions), thinly sliced diagonally

1 small or ½ large red (bell) pepper, thinly sliced

1 garlic clove, crushed

125 g/4½ oz baby sweetcorn (corn-on-the-cob), thinly sliced

1 litre/1¾ pints/4 cups chicken stock

200 g/7 oz can of sweetcorn niblets, well drained

2 tbsp sherry

2–3 tsp bottled sweet chilli sauce

2–3 tsp cornflour (cornstarch)

2 tomatoes, quartered and deseeded, then sliced

salt and pepper

chopped fresh coriander (cilantro) or parsley, to garnish

1 Cut the chicken breast into 4 strips lengthways, then cut each strip into narrow slices across the grain.

2 Heat the oil in a wok or frying pan (skillet), swirling it around until it is really hot.

3 Add the chicken and stir-fry for 3–4 minutes, moving it around the wok until it is well sealed all over and almost cooked through.

4 Add the spring onions (scallions), (bell) pepper and garlic, and stir-fry for 2–3 minutes. Add the sweetcorn and stock and bring to the boil.

5 Add the sweetcorn niblets, sherry, sweet chilli sauce and salt to taste, and simmer for 5 minutes, stirring from time to time.

6 Blend the cornflour (cornstarch) with a little cold water. Add to the soup and bring to the boil, stirring until the sauce is thickened. Add the tomato slices, season to taste and simmer for 1–2 minutes.

7 Serve the chicken and sweetcorn soup hot, sprinkled with chopped coriander (cilantro) or parsley.

Curried Chicken & Corn Soup

Tender cooked chicken strips and baby corn cobs are the main flavours in this delicious clear soup, with just a hint of ginger.

NUTRITIONAL INFORMATION

Calories	206	Sugars	.........5g
Protein	........29g	Fat	..........5g
Carbohydrate	...13g	Saturates	.......1g

5 MINS   30 MINS

SERVES 4

INGREDIENTS

175 g/6 oz can sweetcorn
 (corn), drained

850 ml/1½ pints/3¾ cups
 chicken stock

350 g/12 oz cooked, lean chicken,
 cut into strips

16 baby corn cobs

1 tsp Chinese curry powder

1-cm/½-inch piece fresh root ginger
 (ginger root), grated

3 tbsp light soy sauce

2 tbsp chopped chives

1 Place the canned sweetcorn (corn) in a food processor, together with 150 ml/¼ pint/⅔ cup of the chicken stock and process until the mixture forms a smooth purée.

2 Pass the sweetcorn purée through a fine sieve (strainer), pressing with the back of a spoon to remove any husks.

3 Pour the remaining chicken stock into a large saucepan and add the strips of cooked chicken. Stir in the sweetcorn (corn) purée.

4 Add the baby corn cobs and bring the soup to the boil. Boil the soup for 10 minutes.

5 Add the Chinese curry powder, grated fresh root ginger and light soy sauce and stir well to combine. Cook for a further 10–15 minutes.

6 Stir the chopped chives into the soup.

7 Transfer the curried chicken and corn soup to warm soup bowls and serve immediately.

COOK'S TIP

Prepare the soup up to 24 hours in advance without adding the chicken, cool, cover and store in the refrigerator. Add the chicken and heat the soup through thoroughly before serving.

Chicken Noodle Soup

Quick to make, this hot and spicy soup is hearty and warming. If you like your food really fiery, add a chopped dried or fresh chilli with its seeds.

NUTRITIONAL INFORMATION

Calories	196	Sugars	.........4g
Protein	........16g	Fat	...........11g
Carbohydrate	....8g	Saturates	.......2g

10 MINS   25 MINS

SERVES 4-6

INGREDIENTS

1 sheet of dried egg noodles
  from a 250 g/9 oz pack

1 tbsp oil

4 skinless, boneless
  chicken thighs, diced

1 bunch spring onions (scallions), sliced

2 garlic cloves, chopped

2 cm/¾ inch piece fresh
  ginger root, finely chopped

850 ml/1½ pints/3¾ cups chicken stock

200 ml/7 fl oz/scant 1 cup coconut milk

3 tsp red curry paste

3 tbsp peanut butter

2 tbsp light soy sauce

1 small red (bell) pepper, chopped

60 g/2 oz/½ cup frozen peas

salt and pepper

1 Put the noodles in a shallow dish and soak in boiling water as the packet directs.

2 Heat the oil in a large preheated saucepan or wok.

3 Add the diced chicken to the pan or wok and fry for 5 minutes, stirring until lightly browned.

4 Add the white part of the spring onions (scallions), the garlic and ginger and fry for 2 minutes, stirring.

5 Stir in the chicken stock, coconut milk, red curry paste, peanut butter and soy sauce.

6 Season with salt and pepper to taste. Bring to the boil, stirring, then simmer for 8 minutes, stirring occasionally.

7 Add the red (bell) pepper, peas and green spring onion (scallion) tops and cook for 2 minutes.

8 Add the drained noodles and heat through. Spoon the chicken noodle soup into warmed bowls and serve with a spoon and fork.

VARIATION

Green curry paste can be used instead of red curry paste for a less fiery flavour.

Spicy Chicken Noodle Soup

This filling soup is filled with spicy flavours and bright colours for a really attractive and hearty dish.

NUTRITIONAL INFORMATION

Calories . . . . . . .286 Sugars 21g
Protein . . . . .22g Fat 6g
Carbohydrate . . .37g Saturates 1g

15 MINS   20 MINS

SERVES 4

I N G R E D I E N T S

2 tbsp tamarind paste

4 red chillies, finely chopped

2 cloves garlic, crushed

2.5 cm/1-inch piece Thai ginger, peeled
   and very finely chopped

4 tbsp fish sauce

2 tbsp palm sugar or caster (superfine)
   sugar

8 lime leaves, roughly torn

1.2 litres/2 pints/5 cups chicken stock

350 g/12 oz boneless chicken breast

100 g/3½ oz carrots, very thinly sliced

350 g/12 oz sweet potato, diced

100 g/3½ oz baby corn cobs, halved

3 tbsp fresh coriander (cilantro), roughly
   chopped

100 g/3½ oz cherry tomatoes, halved

150 g/5½ oz flat rice noodles

fresh coriander (cilantro), chopped,
   to garnish

1 Preheat a large wok or frying pan (skillet). Place the tamarind paste, chillies, garlic, ginger, fish sauce, sugar, lime leaves and chicken stock in the wok and bring to the boil, stirring constantly. Reduce the heat and cook for about 5 minutes.

2 Using a sharp knife, thinly slice the chicken. Add the chicken to the wok and cook for a further 5 minutes, stirring the mixture well.

3 Reduce the heat and add the carrots, sweet potato and baby corn cobs to the wok. Leave to simmer, uncovered, for 5 minutes, or until the vegetables are just tender and the chicken is completely cooked through.

4 Stir in the chopped fresh coriander (cilantro), cherry tomatoes and flat rice noodles.

5 Leave the soup to simmer for about 5 minutes, or until the noodles are tender.

6 Garnish the spicy chicken noodle soup with chopped fresh coriander (cilantro) and serve hot.

Spicy Prawn (Shrimp) Soup

Lime leaves are used as a flavouring in this soup to add tartness.

NUTRITIONAL INFORMATION

Calories 217	Sugars 16g	
Protein 16g	Fat 4g	
Carbohydrate . . .31g	Saturates 1g	

10 MINS   20 MINS

SERVES 4

INGREDIENTS

2 tbsp tamarind paste

4 red chilies, very finely chopped

2 cloves garlic, crushed

2.5 cm/1 inch piece Thai ginger, peeled and
very finely chopped

4 tbsp fish sauce

2 tbsp palm sugar or caster (superfine)
sugar

1.2 litres/2 pints/5 cups fish stock

8 lime leaves

100 g/3½ oz carrots, very thinly sliced

350 g/12 oz sweet potato, diced

100 g/3½ oz/1 cup baby corn cobs, halved

3 tbsp fresh coriander (cilantro), roughly
chopped

100g/3½ oz cherry tomatoes, halved

225 g/8 oz fan-tail prawns (shrimp)

1 Place the tamarind paste, red chillies, garlic, ginger, fish sauce, sugar and fish stock in a preheated wok or large, heavy frying pan (skillet). Roughly tear the lime leaves and add to the wok. Bring to the boil, stirring constantly to blend the flavours.

2 Reduce the heat and add the carrot, sweet potato and baby corn cobs to the mixture in the wok.

3 Leave the soup to simmer, uncovered, for about 10 minutes, or until the vegetables are just tender.

4 Stir the coriander (cilantro), cherry tomatoes and prawns (shrimp) into the soup and heat through for 5 minutes.

5 Transfer the soup to a warm soup tureen or individual serving bowls and serve hot.

COOK'S TIP

Thai ginger or galangal
is a member of the ginger
family, but it is yellow in colour
with pink sprouts. The flavour
is aromatic and less pungent
than ginger.

Crab & Sweetcorn Soup

Crab and sweetcorn are classic ingredients in Chinese cookery. Here egg noodles are added for a filling dish.

NUTRITIONAL INFORMATION

Calories	....	.324
Protein	....	27g
Carbohydrate	...	39g

Sugars	....	.6g
Fat	....	.8g
Saturates	....	.2g

5 MINS   20 MINS

SERVES 4

I N G R E D I E N T S

1 tbsp sunflower oil

1 tsp Chinese five-spice powder

225 g/8 oz carrots, cut into sticks

150 g/5½ oz/½ cup canned or frozen sweetcorn

75 g/2¾ oz/¼ cup peas

6 spring onions (scallions), trimmed and sliced

1 red chilli, deseeded and very thinly sliced

2 x 200 g/7 oz can white crab meat

175 g/6 oz egg noodles

1.7 litres/3 pints/7½ cups fish stock

3 tbsp soy sauce

1 Heat the sunflower oil in a large preheated wok or heavy-based frying pan (skillet).

2 Add the Chinese five-spice powder, carrots, sweetcorn, peas, spring onions (scallions) and red chilli to the wok and cook for about 5 minutes, stirring constantly.

3 Add the crab meat to the wok and stir-fry the mixture for 1 minute, distributing the crab meat evenly.

4 Roughly break up the egg noodles and add to the wok.

5 Pour the fish stock and soy sauce into the mixture in the wok and bring to the boil.

6 Cover the wok or frying pan (skillet) and leave the soup to simmer for 5 minutes.

7 Stir once more, then transfer the soup to a warm soup tureen or individual serving bowls and serve at once.

COOK'S TIP

Chinese five-spice powder is a mixture of star anise, fennel, cloves, cinnamon and Szechuan pepper. It has an unmistakeable flavour. Use it sparingly, as it is very pungent.

Peking Duck Soup

This is a hearty and robustly flavoured soup, containing pieces of duck and vegetables cooked in a rich stock.

NUTRITIONAL INFORMATION

Calories	92	Sugars	........3g
Protein	........8g	Fat	..........5g
Carbohydrate	....3g	Saturates	.......1g

  5 MINS   35 MINS

SERVES 4

INGREDIENTS

125 g/4½ oz lean duck breast meat

225 g/8 oz Chinese leaves (cabbage)

850 ml/1½ pints/3¾ cups chicken or duck stock

1 tbsp dry sherry or rice wine

1 tbsp light soy sauce

2 garlic cloves, crushed

pinch of ground star anise

1 tbsp sesame seeds

1 tsp sesame oil

1 tbsp chopped fresh parsley

1 Remove the skin from the duck breast and finely dice the flesh.

2 Using a sharp knife, shred the Chinese leaves (cabbage).

3 Put the stock in a large saucepan and bring to the boil. Add the sherry or rice wine, soy sauce, diced duck meat and shredded Chinese leaves and stir to mix thoroughly. Reduce the heat and leave to simmer gently for 15 minutes.

4 Stir in the garlic and star anise and cook over a low heat for a further 10–15 minutes, or until the duck is tender.

5 Meanwhile, dry-fry the sesame seeds in a preheated, heavy-based frying pan (skillet) or wok, stirring constantly.

6 Remove the sesame seeds from the pan and stir them into the soup, together with the sesame oil and chopped fresh parsley.

7 Spoon the soup into warm bowls and serve immediately.

VARIATION

If Chinese leaves (cabbage) are unavailable, use leafy green cabbage instead. You may wish to adjust the quantity to taste, as Western cabbage has a stronger flavour and odour than Chinese leaves (cabbage).

Beef & Vegetable Noodle Soup

Thin strips of beef are marinated in soy sauce and garlic to form the basis of this delicious soup. Served with noodles, it is both filling and delicious.

NUTRITIONAL INFORMATION

Calories	186	Sugars	.........1g
Protein	........17g	Fat	...........5g
Carbohydrate	...20g	Saturates	.......1g

35 MINS   20 MINS

SERVES 4

INGREDIENTS

225 g/8 oz lean beef

1 garlic clove, crushed

2 spring onions (scallions), chopped

3 tbsp soy sauce

1 tsp sesame oil

225 g/8 oz egg noodles

850 ml/1½ pints/3¾ cups beef stock

3 baby corn cobs, sliced

½ leek, shredded

125 g/4½ oz broccoli, cut into florets (flowerets)

pinch of chilli powder

1 Using a sharp knife, cut the beef into thin strips and place in a bowl with the garlic, spring onions (scallions), soy sauce and sesame oil.

2 Mix together the ingredients in the bowl, turning the beef to coat. Cover and leave to marinate in the refrigerator for 30 minutes.

3 Cook the noodles in a saucepan of boiling water for 3–4 minutes. Drain the noodles thoroughly and set aside.

4 Put the beef stock in a large saucepan and bring to the boil. Add the beef, together with the marinade, the baby corn, leek and broccoli. Cover and leave to simmer over a low heat for 7–10 minutes, or until the beef and vegetables are tender and cooked through.

5 Stir in the noodles and chilli powder and cook for a further 2–3 minutes.

6 Transfer the soup to bowls and serve immediately.

VARIATION

Vary the vegetables used, or use those to hand.

If preferred, use a few drops of chilli sauce instead of chilli powder, but remember it is very hot!

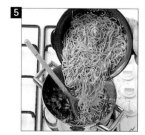

Lamb & Rice Soup

This is a very filling soup, as it contains rice and tender pieces of lamb. Serve before a light main course.

NUTRITIONAL INFORMATION

Calories 116   Sugars 0.2g
Protein . . . . .9g   Fat 4g
Carbohydrate . . .12g   Saturates 2g

5 MINS   35 MINS

SERVES 4

I N G R E D I E N T S

150 g/5½ oz lean lamb

50 g/1¾ oz/¼ cup rice

850 ml/1½ pints/3¾ cups
   lamb stock

1 leek, sliced

1 garlic clove, thinly sliced

2 tsp light soy sauce

1 tsp rice wine vinegar

1 medium open-cap mushroom,
   thinly sliced

salt

1 Using a sharp knife, trim any fat from the lamb and cut the meat into thin strips. Set aside until required.

2 Bring a large pan of lightly salted water to the boil and add the rice. Bring back to the boil, stir once, reduce the heat and cook for 10–15 minutes, until tender.

3 Drain the rice, rinse under cold running water, drain again and set aside until required.

4 Meanwhile, put the lamb stock in a large saucepan and bring to the boil.

5 Add the lamb strips, leek, garlic, soy sauce and rice wine vinegar to the stock in the pan. Reduce the heat, cover and leave to simmer for 10 minutes, or until the lamb is tender and cooked through.

6 Add the mushroom slices and the rice to the pan and cook for a further 2–3 minutes, or until the mushroom is completely cooked through.

7 Ladle the soup into 4 individual warmed soup bowls and serve immediately.

VARIATION

Use a few dried Chinese mushrooms, rehydrated according to the packet instructions and chopped, as an alternative to the open-cap mushroom. Add the Chinese mushrooms with the lamb in step 4.

Chinese Potato & Pork Broth

In this recipe the pork is seasoned with traditional Chinese flavourings – soy sauce, rice wine vinegar and a dash of sesame oil.

NUTRITIONAL INFORMATION

Calories 166	Sugars 2g	
Protein 10g	Fat 5g	
Carbohydrate ...26g	Saturates 1g	

 5 MINS   20 MINS

SERVES 4

I N G R E D I E N T S

1 litre/1¾ pints/4½ cups chicken stock

2 large potatoes, diced

2 tbsp rice wine vinegar

2 tbsp cornflour (cornstarch)

4 tbsp water

125 g/4½ oz pork fillet, sliced

1 tbsp light soy sauce

1 tsp sesame oil

1 carrot, cut into very thin strips

1 tsp ginger root, chopped

3 spring onions (scallions), sliced thinly

1 red (bell) pepper, sliced

225 g/8 oz can bamboo shoots, drained

VARIATION

For extra heat, add 1 chopped red chilli or 1 tsp of chilli powder to the soup in step 5.

1 Add the chicken stock, diced potatoes and 1 tbsp of the rice wine vinegar to a saucepan and bring to the boil. Reduce the heat until the stock is just simmering.

2 Mix the cornflour (cornstarch) with the water then stir into the hot stock.

3 Bring the stock back to the boil, stirring until thickened, then reduce the heat until it is just simmering again.

4 Place the pork slices in a dish and season with the remaining rice wine vinegar, the soy sauce and sesame oil.

5 Add the pork slices, carrot strips and ginger to the stock and cook for 10 minutes. Stir in the spring onions (scallions), red (bell) pepper and bamboo shoots. Cook for a further 5 minutes. Pour the soup into warmed bowls and serve immediately.

Pork & Szechuan Vegetable

Sold in cans, Szechuan preserved vegetable is pickled mustard root which is quite hot and salty, so rinse them in water before use.

NUTRITIONAL INFORMATION

Calories 135	Sugars 1g
Protein 14g	Fat 7g
Carbohydrate 3g	Saturates 2g

  5 MINS   5 MINS

SERVES 4

I N G R E D I E N T S

250 g/9 oz pork fillet

2 tsp cornflour (cornstarch) paste (see page 15)

125 g/4½ oz Szechuan preserved vegetable

700 ml/1¼ pints/3 cups Chinese stock (see page 14) or water

salt and pepper

a few drops sesame oil (optional)

2-3 spring onions (scallions), sliced, to garnish

1 Preheat a wok or large, heavy-based frying pan (skillet).

2 Using a sharp knife, cut the pork across the grain into thin shreds.

3 Mix the pork with the cornflour (cornstarch) paste until the pork is completely coated in the mixture.

4 Thoroughly wash and rinse the Szechuan preserved vegetable, then pat dry on absorbent kitchen paper (paper towels). Cut the Szechuan preserved vegetable into thin shreds the same size as the pork.

5 Pour the Chinese stock or water into the wok or frying pan (skillet) and bring to a rolling boil. Add the pork to the wok and stir to separate the shreds. Return to the boil.

6 Add the shredded Szechuan preserved vegetable and bring back to the boil once more.

7 Adjust the seasoning to taste and sprinkle with sesame oil. Serve hot, garnished with spring onions (scallions).

COOK'S TIP

Szechuan preserved vegetable is actually mustard green root, pickled in salt and chillies. Available in cans from specialist Chinese supermarkets, it gives a crunchy, spicy taste to dishes. Rinse in cold water before use and store in the refrigerator.

Chilli Fish Soup

Chinese mushrooms add an intense flavour to this soup which is unique.
If they are unavailable, use open-cap mushrooms, sliced.

NUTRITIONAL INFORMATION

Calories 166	Sugars 1g
Protein 23g	Fat 7g
Carbohydrate 4g	Saturates 1g

 15 MINS   15 MINS

SERVES 4

INGREDIENTS

15 g/½ oz Chinese dried mushrooms

2 tbsp sunflower oil

1 onion, sliced

100 g/3½ oz/1½ cups mangetout (snow peas)

100 g/3½ oz/1½ cups bamboo shoots

3 tbsp sweet chilli sauce

1.2 litres/2 pints/5 cups fish or vegetable stock

3 tbsp light soy sauce

2 tbsp fresh coriander (cilantro), plus extra to garnish

450 g/1 lb cod fillet, skinned and cubed

COOK'S TIP

Cod is used in this recipe as it is a meaty white fish. For real luxury, use monkfish tail instead.

There are many different varieties of dried mushrooms, but shiitake are best. They are not cheap, but a small amount will go a long way.

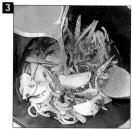

1 Place the mushrooms in a large bowl. Pour over enough boiling water to cover and leave to stand for 5 minutes. Drain the mushrooms thoroughly in a colander. Using a sharp knife, roughly chop the mushrooms.

2 Heat the sunflower oil in a preheated wok or large frying pan (skillet). Add the sliced onion to the wok and stir-fry for 5 minutes, or until softened.

3 Add the mangetout (snow peas), bamboo shoots, chilli sauce, stock and soy sauce to the wok and bring to the boil.

4 Add the coriander (cilantro) and cod and leave to simmer for 5 minutes or until the fish is cooked through.

5 Transfer the soup to warm bowls, garnish with extra coriander (cilantro), if wished, and serve hot.

Shrimp Dumpling Soup

These small dumplings filled with shrimps and pork may be made slightly larger and served as dim sum on their own, if you prefer.

NUTRITIONAL INFORMATION

Calories	311	Sugars	........2g
Protein	........18g	Fat	..........8g
Carbohydrate	...41g	Saturates	.......2g

 20 MINS 10 MINS

SERVES 4

I N G R E D I E N T S

D U M P L I N G S

150 g/5½ oz/1⅜ cups plain (all-purpose) flour

50 ml/2 fl oz/¼ cup boiling water

30 ml/1 fl oz/⅛ cup cold water

1½ tsp vegetable oil

F I L L I N G

125 g/4½ oz minced (ground) pork

125 g/4½ oz cooked peeled shrimp, chopped

50 g/1¾ oz canned water chestnuts, drained, rinsed and chopped

1 celery stick, chopped

1 tsp cornflour (cornstarch)

1 tbsp sesame oil

1 tbsp light soy sauce

S O U P

850 ml/1½ pints/3¾ cups fish stock

50 g/1¾ oz cellophane noodles

1 tbsp dry sherry

chopped chives, to garnish

1 To make the dumplings, mix together the flour, boiling water, cold water and oil in a bowl until a pliable dough is formed.

2 Knead the dough on a lightly floured surface for 5 minutes. Cut the dough into 16 equal sized pieces.

3 Roll the dough pieces into rounds about 7.5 cm/ 3 inches in diameter.

4 Mix the filling ingredients together in a large bowl.

5 Spoon a little of the filling mixture into the centre of each round. Bring the edges of the dough together, scrunching them up to form a 'moneybag' shape. Twist the gathered edges to seal.

6 Pour the fish stock into a large saucepan and bring to the boil.

7 Add the cellophane noodles, dumplings and dry sherry to the pan and cook for 4–5 minutes, until the noodles and dumplings are tender. Garnish with chopped chives and serve immediately.

Prawn (Shrimp) Soup

This soup is an interesting mix of colours and textures. The egg may be made into a flat omelette and added as thin strips if preferred.

NUTRITIONAL INFORMATION

Calories 123	Sugars 0.2g	
Protein 13g	Fat 8g	
Carbohydrate 1g	Saturates 1g	

5 MINS   20 MINS

SERVES 4

I N G R E D I E N T S

2 tbsp sunflower oil

2 spring onions (scallions), thinly sliced diagonally

1 carrot, coarsely grated

125 g/4½ oz large closed cup mushrooms, thinly sliced

1 litre/1¾ pints/4 cups fish or vegetable stock

½ tsp Chinese five-spice powder

1 tbsp light soy sauce

125 g/4½ oz large peeled prawns (shrimp) or peeled tiger prawns (shrimp), defrosted if frozen

½ bunch watercress, trimmed and roughly chopped

1 egg, well beaten

salt and pepper

4 large prawns (shrimp) in shells, to garnish (optional)

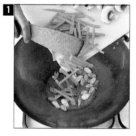
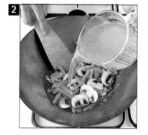

1 Heat the oil in a wok, swirling it around until really hot. Add the spring onions (scallions) and stir-fry for a minute then add the carrots and mushrooms and continue to cook for about 2 minutes.

2 Add the stock and bring to the boil then season to taste with salt and pepper, five-spice powder and soy sauce and simmer for 5 minutes.

3 If the prawns (shrimp) are really large, cut them in half before adding to the wok and simmer for 3-4 minutes.

4 Add the watercress to the wok and mix well, then slowly pour in the beaten egg in a circular movement so that it cooks in threads in the soup. Adjust the seasoning and serve each portion topped with a whole prawn (shrimp).

COOK'S TIP

The large open mushrooms with black gills give the best flavour but they tend to spoil the colour of the soup, making it very dark. Oyster mushrooms can also be used.

Fish & Vegetable Soup

A chunky fish soup with strips of vegetables, all flavoured with ginger and lemon, makes a meal in itself.

NUTRITIONAL INFORMATION

Calories 88   Sugars 1g
Protein ....12g   Fat 3g
Carbohydrate ....3g   Saturates 0.5g

 40 MINS   20 MINS

SERVES 4

INGREDIENTS

250 g/9 oz white fish fillets (cod, halibut, haddock, sole etc)

½ tsp ground ginger

½ tsp salt

1 small leek, trimmed

2-4 crab sticks, defrosted if frozen (optional)

1 tbsp sunflower oil

1 large carrot, cut into julienne strips

8 canned water chestnuts, thinly sliced

1.2 litres/2 pints/5 cups fish or vegetable stock

1 tbsp lemon juice

1 tbsp light soy sauce

1 large courgette (zucchini), cut into julienne strips

black pepper

COOK'S TIP

To skin fish, place the fillet skin-side down and insert a sharp, flexible knife at one end between the flesh and the skin. Hold the skin tightly at the end and push the knife along, keeping the blade flat against the skin.

1 Remove any skin from the fish and cut into cubes, about 2.5 cm/1 inch. Combine the ground ginger and salt and use to rub into the pieces of fish. Leave to marinate for at least 30 minutes.

2 Meanwhile, divide the green and white parts of the leek. Cut each part into 2.5 cm/1 inch lengths and then into julienne strips down the length of each piece, keeping the two parts separate. Slice the crab sticks into 1 cm/ ½ inch pieces.

3 Heat the oil in the wok, swirling it around so it is really hot. Add the white part of the leek and stir-fry for a couple of minutes, then add the carrots and water chestnuts and continue to cook for 1-2 minutes, stirring thoroughly.

4 Add the stock and bring to the boil, then add the lemon juice and soy sauce and simmer for 2 minutes.

5 Add the fish and continue to cook for about 5 minutes until the fish begins to break up a little, then add the green part of the leek and the courgettes (zucchini) and simmer for about 1 minute. Add the sliced crab sticks, if using, and season to taste with black pepper. Simmer for a further minute or so and serve piping hot.

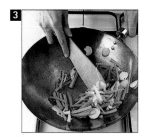

Oriental Fish Soup

This is a deliciously different fish soup which can be made quickly and easily in a microwave.

NUTRITIONAL INFORMATION

Calories . . . . .105 Sugars 1g
Protein . . . . .13g Fat 5g
Carbohydrate . . . .1g Saturates 1g

20 MINS   10 MINS

SERVES 4

INGREDIENTS

1 egg

1 tsp sesame seeds, toasted

1 celery stick, chopped

1 carrot, cut into julienne strips

4 spring onions (scallions), sliced on the diagonal

1 tbsp oil

60 g/2 oz/1½ cups fresh spinach

850 ml/1½ pints/3½ cups hot vegetable stock

4 tsp light soy sauce

250 g/9 oz haddock, skinned and cut into small chunks

salt and pepper

VARIATION

Instead of topping the soup with omelette shreds, you could pour the beaten egg, without the sesame seeds, into the hot stock at the end of the cooking time. The egg will set in pretty strands to give a flowery look.

1 Beat the egg with the sesame seeds and seasoning. Lightly oil a plate and pour on the egg mixture. Cook on HIGH power for 1½ minutes until just setting in the centre. Leave to stand for a few minutes then remove from the plate. Roll up the egg and shred thinly.

2 Mix together the celery, carrot, spring onions (scallions) and oil. Cover and cook on HIGH power for 3 minutes.

3 Wash the spinach thoroughly under cold, running water. Cut off and discard any long stalks and drain well. Shred the spinach finely.

4 Add the hot stock, soy sauce, haddock and spinach to the vegetable mixture. Cover and cook on HIGH power for 5 minutes. Stir the soup and season to taste. Serve in warmed bowls with the shredded egg scattered over.

Fish Soup with Wontons

This soup is topped with small wontons filled with prawns (shrimp), making it both very tasty and satisfying.

NUTRITIONAL INFORMATION

Calories	115	Sugars	0g
Protein	16g	Fat	5g
Carbohydrate	1g	Saturates	1g

 10 MINS   15 MINS

SERVES 4

I N G R E D I E N T S

125 g/4½ oz large, cooked, peeled prawns (shrimp)

1 tsp chopped chives

1 small garlic clove, finely chopped

1 tbsp vegetable oil

12 wonton wrappers

1 small egg, beaten

850 ml/1½ pints/3¾ cups fish stock

175 g/6 oz white fish fillet, diced

dash of chilli sauce

sliced fresh red chilli and chives, to garnish

1 Roughly chop a quarter of the prawns (shrimp) and mix together with the chopped chives and garlic.

2 Heat the oil in a preheated wok or large frying pan (skillet) until it is really hot.

3 Stir-fry the prawn (shrimp) mixture for 1–2 minutes. Remove from the heat and set aside to cool completely.

4 Spread out the wonton wrappers on a work surface (counter). Spoon a little of the prawn (shrimp) filling into the centre of each wrapper. Brush the edges of the wrappers with beaten egg and press the edges together, scrunching them to form a 'moneybag' shape. Set aside while you are preparing the soup.

5 Pour the fish stock into a large saucepan and bring to the boil. Add the diced white fish and the remaining prawns (shrimp) and cook for 5 minutes.

6 Season to taste with the chilli sauce. Add the wontons and cook for a further 5 minutes.

7 Spoon into warmed serving bowls, garnish with sliced red chilli and chives and serve immediately.

VARIATION

Replace the prawns (shrimp) with cooked crabmeat for an alternative flavour.

Three-Flavour Soup

Ideally, use raw prawns (shrimp) in this soup. If that is not possible, add ready-cooked ones at the very last stage.

NUTRITIONAL INFORMATION

Calories 117	Sugars 0g
Protein 20g	Fat 3g
Carbohydrate 2g	Saturates 1g

3½ HOURS   10 MINS

SERVES 4

INGREDIENTS

125 g/4½ oz skinned, boned chicken breast

125 g/4½ oz raw peeled prawns (shrimp)

salt

½ egg white, lightly beaten

2 tsp cornflour (cornstarch) paste (see page 15)

125 g/4½ oz honey-roast ham

700 ml/1¼ pints/3 cups Chinese Stock (see page 14) or water

finely chopped spring onions (scallions), to garnish

1 Using a sharp knife or meat cleaver, thinly slice the chicken into small shreds. If the prawns (shrimp) are large, cut each in half lengthways, otherwise leave them whole.

2 Place the chicken and prawns (shrimps) in a bowl and mix with a pinch of salt, the egg white and cornflour (cornstarch) paste until well coated. Set aside until required.

3 Cut the honey-roast ham into small thin slices roughly the same size as the chicken pieces.

4 In a preheated wok or large, heavy frying pan (skillet), bring the Chinese stock or water to a rolling boil and add the chicken, the raw prawns (shrimp) and the ham.

5 Bring the soup back to the boil, and simmer for 1 minute.

6 Adjust the seasoning to taste, then pour the soup into four warmed individual serving bowls, garnish with the spring onions (scallions) and serve immediately.

COOK'S TIP

Soups such as this are improved enormously in flavour if you use a well-flavoured stock. Either use a stock cube, or find time to make Chinese Stock. Better still, make double quantities and freeze some for future use.

Crab & Ginger Soup

Two classic ingredients in Chinese cooking are blended together in this recipe for a special soup.

NUTRITIONAL INFORMATION

Calories	32	Sugars	.........1g
Protein	.........6g	Fat	..........0.4g
Carbohydrate	....1g	Saturates	.......0g

10 MINS   25 MINS

SERVES 4

INGREDIENTS

1 carrot

1 leek

1 bay leaf

850 ml/1½ pints/3¾ cups fish stock

2 medium-sized cooked crabs

2.5-cm/1-inch piece fresh root ginger (ginger root), grated

1 tsp light soy sauce

½ tsp ground star anise

salt and pepper

1 Using a sharp knife, chop the carrot and leek into small pieces and place in a large saucepan with the bay leaf and fish stock.

2 Bring the mixture in the saucepan to the boil.

3 Reduce the heat, cover and leave to simmer for about 10 minutes, or until the vegetables are nearly tender.

4 Remove all of the meat from the cooked crabs. Break off and reserve the claws, break the joints and remove the meat, using a fork or skewer.

5 Add the crabmeat to the pan of fish stock, together with the ginger, soy sauce and star anise and bring to the boil. Leave to simmer for about 10 minutes, or until the vegetables are tender and the crab is heated through.

6 Season the soup then ladle into a warmed soup tureen or individual serving bowls and garnish with crab claws. Serve immediately.

VARIATION

If fresh crabmeat is unavailable, use drained canned crabmeat or thawed frozen crabmeat instead.

Starters

This chapter contains a range of old favourites and traditional Chinese dishes, and there is sure to be something to suit every occasion. One of the advantages of these dishes is that they can be prepared well in advance. The Chinese usually serve a selection of appetizers together as an assorted hors d'oeuvres.

Remember not to have more than one type of the same food. The ingredients should be chosen for their harmony and balance in colour, aroma, texture and flavour. A suitable selection might contain Crispy Seaweed, Sesame Prawn Toasts, Spare Ribs and Spring Rolls. Many of these dishes would also make an attractive addition to a buffet.

Pancake Rolls

This classic *dim sum* dish is adaptable to almost any filling of your choice. Here the traditional mixture of pork and pak choi is used.

NUTRITIONAL INFORMATION

Calories	488	Sugars	........19g
Protein	........16g	Fat	.........24g
Carbohydrate	...55g	Saturates	.......4g

20 MINS   20 MINS

SERVES 4

INGREDIENTS

4 tsp vegetable oil

1-2 garlic cloves, crushed

225 g/8 oz minced (ground) pork

225/8 oz pak choi, shredded

4½ tsp light soy sauce

½ tsp sesame oil

8 spring roll skins, 25 cm/10 inches square, thawed if frozen

oil, for deep-frying

CHILLI SAUCE

60 g/2 oz/¼ cup caster (superfine) sugar

50 ml/2 fl oz/¼ cup rice vinegar

2 tbsp water

2 red chillies, finely chopped

1 Heat the oil in a preheated wok. Add the garlic and stir-fry for 30 seconds. Add the pork and stir-fry for 2–3 minutes, until lightly coloured.

2 Add the pak choi, soy sauce and sesame oil to the wok and stir-fry for 2–3 minutes. Remove from the heat and set aside to cool.

3 Spread out the spring roll skins on a work surface (counter) and spoon 2 tablespoons of the pork mixture along one edge of each. Roll the skin over once and

fold in the sides. Roll up completely to make a sausage shape, brushing the edges with a little water to seal. Set the pancake rolls aside for 10 minutes to seal firmly.

4 To make the chilli sauce, heat the sugar, vinegar and water in a small saucepan, stirring until the sugar dissolves. Bring the mixture to the boil and boil rapidly until a light syrup forms. Remove from the heat and stir in the

chopped red chillies. Leave the sauce to cool before serving.

5 Heat the oil for deep-frying in a wok until almost smoking. Reduce the heat slightly and fry the pancake rolls, in batches if necessary, for 3–4 minutes, until golden brown. Remove from the oil with a slotted spoon and drain on absorbent kitchen paper (paper towels). Serve with the chilli sauce.

Filled Cucumber Cups

These attractive little cups would make an impressive appetizer at a dinner party.

NUTRITIONAL INFORMATION

Calories 256   Sugars 7g
Protein ....10g   Fat 21g
Carbohydrate ....8g   Saturates 4g

     10 MINS   0 MINS

SERVES 4

INGREDIENTS

1 cucumber

4 spring onions (scallions),
  chopped finely

4 tbsp lime juice

2 small red chillies, deseeded and
  chopped finely

3 tsp sugar

150 g/5½ oz/1¼ cups ground roasted
  peanuts

¼ tsp salt

3 shallots, sliced finely and deep-fried,
  to garnish

1 Wash the cucumber thoroughly and pat dry with absorbent kitchen paper (paper towels).

2 To make the cucumber cups, cut the ends off the cucumber, and divide it into 3 equal lengths. Mark a line around the centre of each one as a guide.

3 Make a zigzag cut all the way around the centre of each section, always pointing the knife towards the centre of the cucumber.

4 Pull apart the two halves. Scoop out the centre of each cup with a melon baller or teaspoon, leaving a base on the bottom of each cup.

5 Put the spring onions (scallions), lime juice, red chillies, sugar, ground roasted peanuts and salt in a bowl and mix well to combine.

6 Divide the filling evenly between the 6 cucumber cups and arrange on a serving plate.

7 Garnish the cucumber cups with the deep-fried shallots and serve.

COOK'S TIP

Cherry tomatoes can also be hollowed out very simply with a melon baller and filled with this mixture. The two look very pretty arranged together on a serving dish.

Little Golden Parcels

These little parcels will draw admiring gasps from your guests, but they are fairly simple to prepare.

NUTRITIONAL INFORMATION

Calories 320   Sugars 1g
Protein . . . . .6g   Fat 21g
Carbohydrate . . .28g   Saturates 5g

 35 MINS   35 MINS

SERVES 4

INGREDIENTS

1 garlic clove, crushed

1 tsp chopped coriander (cilantro) root

1 tsp pepper

250 g/9 oz/1 cup boiled mashed potato

175 g/6 oz/1 cup water chestnuts, chopped finely

1 tsp grated ginger root

2 tbsp ground roasted peanuts

2 tsp light soy sauce

½ tsp salt

½ tsp sugar

30 wonton sheets, defrosted

1 tsp cornflour (cornstarch), made into a paste with a little water

vegetable oil, for deep-frying

fresh chives, to garnish

sweet chilli sauce, to serve

VARIATION

If wonton sheets are not available, use spring roll sheets or filo pastry, and cut the large squares down to about 10 cm/ 4 inches square.

1 Mix together all the ingredients except the wonton sheets, cornflour (cornstarch) and oil.

2 Keeping the remainder of the wonton sheets covered with a damp cloth, lay 4 sheets out on a work surface (counter). Put a teaspoonful of the mixture on each. Make a line of the cornflour (cornstarch) paste around each sheet, about 1 cm/ ½ inch from the edge.

3 Bring all four corners to the centre and press together to form little bags. Repeat with all the wonton sheets.

4 Heat 5 cm/2 inches of the oil in a pan until a light haze appears on top and fry the parcels, in batches of 3, until golden brown. Remove and drain on paper towels. Tie a chive around the neck of each bag to garnish, and serve with a sweet chilli sauce for dipping.

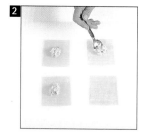

Stuffed Courgettes (Zucchini)

Hollow out some courgettes (zucchini), fill them with a spicy beef mixture and bake them in the oven for a delicious side dish.

NUTRITIONAL INFORMATION

Calories 208	Sugars 3g	
Protein 12g	Fat 9g	
Carbohydrate ...20g	Saturates 4g	

45 MINS   35 MINS

SERVES 4

INGREDIENTS

8 medium courgettes (zucchini)

1 tbsp sesame or vegetable oil

1 garlic clove, crushed

2 shallots, chopped finely

1 small red chilli, deseeded and chopped finely

250 g/9 oz/1 cup lean minced (ground) beef

1 tbsp fish sauce or mushroom ketchup

1 tbsp chopped fresh coriander (cilantro) or basil

2 tsp cornflour (cornstarch), blended with a little cold water

90 g/3 oz/½ cup cooked long-grain rice

salt and pepper

TO GARNISH

sprigs of fresh coriander (cilantro) or basil

carrot slices

1 Slice the courgettes (zucchini) in half horizontally and scoop out a channel down the middle, discarding all the seeds. Sprinkle with salt and set aside for 15 minutes.

2 Heat the oil in a wok or frying pan (skillet) and add the garlic, shallots and chilli. Stir-fry for 2 minutes, until golden. Add the minced (ground) beef and stir-fry briskly for about 5 minutes. Stir in the fish sauce or mushroom ketchup, the chopped coriander (cilantro) or basil and the blended cornflour (cornstarch), and cook for 2 minutes, stirring until thickened. Season with salt and pepper, then remove from the heat.

3 Rinse the courgettes (zucchini) in cold water and arrange them in a greased shallow ovenproof dish, cut side uppermost. Mix the cooked rice into the minced (ground) beef, then use this mixture to stuff the courgettes (zucchini).

4 Cover with foil and bake in a preheated oven at 190°C/375°F/Gas Mark 5 for 20–25 minutes, removing the foil for the last 5 minutes of cooking time.

5 Serve at once, garnished with sprigs of fresh coriander (cilantro) or basil, and carrot slices.

Aubergine Dipping Platter

Dipping platters are a very sociable dish, bringing together all the diners at the table.

NUTRITIONAL INFORMATION

Calories . . . . .81 Sugars 4g
Protein . . . . .4g Fat 5g
Carbohydrate . . . .5g Saturates 1g

 15 MINS   10 MINS

SERVES 4

I N G R E D I E N T S

1 aubergine (eggplant), peeled and cut into 2.5 cm/1 inch cubes

3 tbsp sesame seeds, roasted in a dry pan over a low heat

1 tsp sesame oil

grated rind and juice of ½ lime

1 small shallot, diced

1 tsp sugar

1 red chilli, deseeded and sliced

125 g/4½ oz/1¼ cups broccoli florets

2 carrots, cut into matchsticks

125 g/4½ oz/8 baby corn, cut in half lengthways

2 celery stalks, cut into matchsticks

1 baby red cabbage, cut into 8 wedges, the leaves of each wedge held together by the core

salt and pepper

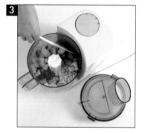  

1 Cook the diced aubergine (eggplant) in a saucepan of boiling water for 7–8 minutes.

2 Meanwhile, grind the sesame seeds with the oil in a food processor or pestle and mortar.

3 Add the aubergine (eggplant), lime rind and juice, shallot, ½ tsp salt, pepper, sugar and chilli in that order to the sesame seeds. Process, or chop and mash by hand, until smooth.

4 Adjust the seasoning to taste then spoon the dip into a bowl.

5 Serve the aubergine (eggplant) dipping platter surrounded by the broccoli, carrots, baby corn, celery and red cabbage.

VARIATION

You can vary the selection of vegetables depending on your preference or whatever you have at hand. Other vegetables you could use are cauliflower florets and cucumber sticks.

Aubergine (Eggplant) Satay

Aubergines (eggplants) and mushrooms are grilled on skewers and served with a satay sauce.

NUTRITIONAL INFORMATION

Calories ....155 Sugars 2g
Protein ....4g Fat 14g
Carbohydrate ....3g Saturates 3g

2¼ HOURS   25 MINS

SERVES 4

INGREDIENTS

2 aubergines (eggplants), cut into 2.5 cm/
  1 inch pieces

175 g/6 oz small chestnut mushrooms

MARINADE

1 tsp cumin seeds

1 tsp coriander seeds

2.5 cm/1 inch piece ginger root, grated

2 garlic cloves, crushed lightly

½ stalk lemon grass, chopped roughly

4 tbsp light soy sauce

8 tbsp sunflower oil

2 tbsp lemon juice

PEANUT SAUCE

½ tsp cumin seeds

½ tsp coriander seeds

3 garlic cloves

1 small onion, puréed in a food processor or
  chopped very finely by hand

1 tbsp lemon juice

1 tsp salt

½ red chilli, deseeded and sliced

125 ml/4 fl oz/½ cup coconut milk

250 g/9 oz/1 cup crunchy peanut butter

250 ml/8 fl oz/1 cup water

1 Thread the vegetables on to eight metal or pre-soaked wooden skewers.

2 For the marinade, grind the cumin and coriander seeds, ginger, garlic and lemon grass. Stir-fry over a high heat until fragrant. Remove from the heat and add the remaining marinade ingredients. Place the skewers in a dish and spoon the marinade over. Leave to marinate for at least 2 hours and up to 8 hours.

3 To make the sauce, grind the cumin and coriander seeds with the garlic. Add all the ingredients except the water. Transfer to a pan and stir in the water. Bring to the boil and cook until thick.

4 Cook the skewers under a preheated very hot grill (broiler) for 15–20 minutes. Brush with the marinade frequently and turn once. Serve with the peanut sauce.

Spinach Meatballs

Balls of pork mixture are coated in spinach and steamed before being served with a sesame and soy sauce dip.

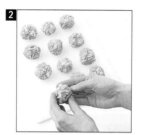

NUTRITIONAL INFORMATION

Calories ..:.....137 Sugars 2g
Protein ....13g Fat 7g
Carbohydrate ....6g Saturates 2g

 20 MINS   25 MINS

SERVES 4

I N G R E D I E N T S

125 g/4½ oz pork

1 small egg

1-cm/½-inch piece fresh root ginger (ginger root), chopped

1 small onion, finely chopped

1 tbsp boiling water

25 g/1 oz canned bamboo shoots, drained, rinsed and chopped

2 slices smoked ham, chopped

2 tsp cornflour (cornstarch)

450 g/1 lb fresh spinach

2 tsp sesame seeds

S A U C E

150 ml/¼ pint/⅔ cup vegetable stock

½ tsp cornflour (cornstarch)

1 tsp cold water

1 tsp light soy sauce

½ tsp sesame oil

1 tbsp chopped chives

1 Mince (grind) the pork very finely in a food processor. Lightly beat the egg in a bowl and stir into the pork.

2 Put the ginger and onion in a separate bowl, add the boiling water and let stand for 5 minutes. Drain and add to the pork mixture with the bamboo shoots, ham and cornflour (cornstarch). Mix thoroughly and roll into 12 balls.

3 Wash the spinach and remove the stalks. Blanch in boiling water for 10 seconds, drain well then slice into very thin strips and mix with the sesame seeds. Roll the meatballs in the mixture to coat.

4 Place the meatballs on a heatproof plate in the base of a steamer. Cover and steam for 8–10 minutes, until cooked through and tender.

5 Meanwhile, make the sauce. Put the stock in a saucepan and bring to the boil. Mix together the cornflour (cornstarch) and water to a smooth paste and stir it into the stock. Stir in the soy sauce, sesame oil and chives. Transfer the cooked meatballs to a warm plate and serve with the sauce.

Crispy Wontons

Mushroom-filled crispy wontons are served on skewers with a dipping sauce flavoured with chillies.

NUTRITIONAL INFORMATION

Calories ....302 Sugars 1g
Protein ....3g Fat 25
Carbohydrate ...15g Saturates 6g

45 MINS   20 MINS

SERVES 4

INGREDIENTS

8 wooden skewers, soaked in cold water for 30 minutes

1 tbsp vegetable oil

1 tbsp chopped onion

1 small garlic clove, chopped

½ tsp chopped ginger root

60 g/2 oz/½ cup flat mushrooms, chopped

16 wonton skins

vegetable oil, for deep-frying

salt

SAUCE

2 tbsp vegetable oil

2 spring onions (scallions), shredded thinly

1 red and 1 green chilli, deseeded and shredded thinly

3 tbsp light soy sauce

1 tbsp vinegar

1 tbsp dry sherry

pinch of sugar

1 Heat the vegetable oil in a preheated wok or frying pan (skillet).

2 Add the onion, garlic and ginger root to the wok or pan and stir-fry for 2 minutes. Stir in the mushrooms and fry for a further 2 minutes. Season well with salt and leave to cool.

3 Place 1 teaspoon of the cooled mushroom filling in the centre of each wonton skin.

4 Bring two opposite corners of each wonton skin together to cover the mixture and pinch together to seal. Repeat with the remaining corners.

5 Thread 2 wontons on to each skewer. Heat enough oil in a large saucepan to deep-fry the wontons in batches until golden and crisp. Do not overheat the oil or the wontons will brown on the outside before they are properly cooked inside. Remove the wontons with a perforated spoon and drain on absorbent kitchen paper (paper towels).

6 To make the sauce, heat the vegetable oil in a small saucepan until quite hot or until a small cube of bread dropped in the oil browns in a few seconds. Put the spring onions (scallions) and chillies in a bowl and pour the hot oil slowly on top. Mix in the remaining ingredients.

7 Transfer the crispy wontons to a serving dish and serve with the dipping sauce.

Tofu (Bean Curd) Tempura

Crispy coated vegetables and tofu (bean curd) accompanied by a sweet, spicy dip give a real taste of the Orient in this Japanese-style dish.

NUTRITIONAL INFORMATION

Calories 582   Sugars 10g
Protein ....16g   Fat 27g
Carbohydrate ...65g   Saturates 4g

15 MINS   20 MINS

SERVES 4

I N G R E D I E N T S

125 g/4½ oz baby courgettes (zucchini)

125 g/4½ oz baby carrots

125 g/4½ oz baby corn cobs

125 g/4½ oz baby leeks

2 baby aubergines (eggplants)

225 g/8 oz tofu (bean curd)

vegetable oil, for deep-frying

julienne strips of carrot, root ginger and
   baby leek to garnish

noodles, to serve

B A T T E R

2 egg yolks

300 ml/½ pint/1¼ cups water

225 g/8 oz/2 cups plain (all-purpose) flour

D I P P I N G   S A U C E

5 tbsp mirin or dry sherry

5 tbsp Japanese soy sauce

2 tsp clear honey

1 garlic clove, crushed

1 tsp grated root ginger

1 Slice the courgettes (zucchini) and carrots in half lengthways. Trim the corn. Trim the leeks at both ends. Quarter the aubergines (eggplants). Cut the tofu (bean curd) into 2.5 cm/1 inch cubes.

2 To make the batter, mix the egg yolks with the water. Sift in 175 g/6 oz/1½ cups of the flour and beat with a balloon whisk to form a thick batter. Don't worry if there are any lumps. Heat the oil for deep-frying to 180°C/350°F or until a cube of bread browns in 30 seconds.

3 Place the remaining flour on a large plate and toss the vegetables and tofu (bean curd) until lightly coated.

4 Dip the tofu (bean curd) in the batter and deep-fry for 2-3 minutes, until lightly golden. Drain on kitchen paper (paper towels) and keep warm.

5 Dip the vegetables in the batter and deep-fry, a few at a time, for 3-4 minutes, until golden. Drain and place on a warmed serving plate.

6 To make the dipping sauce, mix all the ingredients together. Serve with the vegetables and tofu (bean curd), accompanied with noodles and garnished with julienne strips of vegetables.

Son-in-Law Eggs

This recipe is supposedly so called because it is an easy dish for a son-in-law to cook to impress his new mother-in-law!

NUTRITIONAL INFORMATION

Calories 229   Sugars 8g
Protein . . . . .9g   Fat 18g
Carbohydrate . . . .8g   Saturates 3g

15 MINS   15 MINS

SERVES 4

I N G R E D I E N T S

6 eggs, hard-boiled (hard-cooked)
   and shelled

4 tbsp sunflower oil

1 onion, sliced thinly

2 fresh red chillies, sliced

2 tbsp sugar

1 tbsp water

2 tsp tamarind pulp

1 tbsp liquid seasoning, such
   as Maggi

rice, to serve

1 Prick the hard-boiled (hard-cooked) eggs 2 or 3 times with a cocktail stick (toothpick).

2 Heat the sunflower oil in a wok and fry the eggs until crispy and golden. Drain on absorbent kitchen paper (paper towels).

3 Halve the eggs lengthways and put on a serving dish.

4 Reserve one tablespoon of the oil, pour off the rest, then heat the tablespoonful in the wok. Cook the onion and chillies over a high heat until golden and slightly crisp. Drain on kitchen paper (paper towels).

5 Heat the sugar, water, tamarind pulp and liquid seasoning in the wok and simmer for 5 minutes until thickened.

6 Pour the sauce over the eggs and spoon over the onion and chillies. Serve immediately with rice.

COOK'S TIP

Tamarind pulp is sold in oriental stores, and is quite sour. If it is not available, use twice the amount of lemon juice in its place.

Vegetable Spring Rolls

There are many different versions of spring rolls throughout the Far East, a vegetable filling being the classic.

NUTRITIONAL INFORMATION

Calories	189	Sugars	.........4g
Protein	.........2g	Fat	..........16g
Carbohydrate	....11g	Saturates	.......5g

10 MINS   15 MINS

SERVES 4

I N G R E D I E N T S

225 g/8 oz carrots

1 red (bell) pepper

1 tbsp sunflower oil, plus extra for frying

75 g/2¾ oz/¾ cup bean sprouts

finely grated zest and juice of 1 lime

1 red chilli, deseeded and very finely chopped

1 tbsp soy sauce

½ tsp arrowroot

2 tbsp chopped fresh coriander (cilantro)

8 sheets filo pastry

25 g/1 oz butter

2 tsp sesame oil

TO SERVE

chilli sauce

spring onion (scallion) tassels

1 Using a sharp knife, cut the carrots into thin sticks. Deseed the (bell) pepper and cut into thin slices.

2 Heat the sunflower oil in a large preheated wok.

3 Add the carrot, red (bell) pepper and bean sprouts and cook, stirring, for 2 minutes, or until softened. Remove the wok from the heat and toss in the lime zest and juice, and the red chilli.

4 Mix the soy sauce with the arrowroot. Stir the mixture into the wok, return to the heat and cook for 2 minutes or until the juices thicken.

5 Add the chopped fresh coriander (cilantro) to the wok and mix well.

6 Lay the sheets of filo pastry out on a board. Melt the butter and sesame oil and brush each sheet with the mixture.

7 Spoon a little of the vegetable filling at the top of each sheet, fold over each long side, and roll up.

8 Add a little oil to the wok and cook the spring rolls in batches, for 2–3 minutes, or until crisp and golden.

9 Transfer the spring rolls to a serving dish, garnish and serve hot with chilli dipping sauce.

Crispy Seaweed

This tasty Chinese starter is not all that it seems – the 'seaweed' is in fact pak choi which is then fried, salted and tossed with pine kernels.

NUTRITIONAL INFORMATION

Calories	214	Sugars	........14g
Protein	.........6g	Fat	..........15g
Carbohydrate	...15g	Saturates	.......2g

  10 MINS · 5 MINS

SERVES 4

I N G R E D I E N T S

1 kg/2 lb 4 oz pak choi

groundnut oil, for deep-frying (about 850 ml/1½ pints/3¾ cups)

1 tsp salt

1 tbsp caster (superfine) sugar

50 g/1¾ oz/2½ tbsp toasted pine kernels (nuts)

1 Rinse the pak choi leaves under cold running water and then pat dry thoroughly with absorbent kitchen paper (paper towels).

2 Discarding any tough outer leaves, roll each pak choi leaf up, then slice

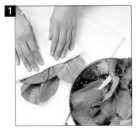  

COOK'S TIP

The tough, outer leaves of pak choi are discarded as these will spoil the overall taste and texture of the dish.

Use savoy cabbage instead of the pak choi if it is unavailable, drying the leaves thoroughly before frying.

through thinly so that the leaves are finely shredded. Alternatively, use a food processor to shred the pak choi.

3 Heat the groundnut oil in a large wok or heavy-based frying pan (skillet).

4 Carefully add the shredded pak choi leaves to the wok or frying pan (skillet) and fry for about 30 seconds or until they shrivel up and become crispy

(you will probably need to do this in several batches, depending on the size of the wok).

5 Remove the crispy seaweed from the wok with a slotted spoon and drain on absorbent kitchen paper (paper towels).

6 Transfer the crispy seaweed to a large bowl and toss with the salt, sugar and pine kernels (nuts). Serve immediately.

Money Bags

These traditional steamed dumplings can be eaten on their own or dipped in a mixture of soy sauce, sherry and slivers of ginger root.

NUTRITIONAL INFORMATION

Calories	315	Sugars	.........3g
Protein	.........8g	Fat	...........8g
Carbohydrate	...56g	Saturates	.......1g

45 MINS   20 MINS

SERVES 4

INGREDIENTS

3 Chinese dried mushrooms
(if unavailable, use thinly sliced
open-cup mushrooms)

250 g/9 oz/2 cups plain (all-purpose) flour

1 egg, beaten

75 ml/3 fl oz/⅓ cup water

1 tsp baking powder

¾ tsp salt

2 tbsp vegetable oil

2 spring onions (scallions), chopped

90 g/3 oz/½ cup sweetcorn kernels

½ red chilli, deseeded and chopped

1 tbsp brown bean sauce

1 Place the dried mushrooms in a small bowl, cover with warm water and leave to soak for 20–25 minutes.

2 To make the wrappers, sift the plain (all-purpose) flour into a bowl. Add the beaten egg and mix in lightly. Stir in the water, baking powder and salt. Mix to make a soft dough.

3 Knead the dough lightly on a floured board. Cover with a damp tea towel (dish cloth) and set aside for 5–6 minutes. This allows the baking powder time to activate, so that the dumplings swell when steaming.

4 Drain the mushrooms, squeezing them dry. Remove the tough centres and chop the mushrooms.

5 Heat the vegetable oil in a wok or large frying pan (skillet) and stir-fry the mushrooms, spring onions (scallions), sweetcorn and chilli for 2 minutes.

6 Stir in the brown bean sauce and remove from the heat.

7 Roll the dough into a large sausage and cut into 24 even-sized pieces. Roll each piece out into a thin round and place a teaspoonful of the filling in the centre. Gather up the edges to a point, pinch together and twist to seal.

8 Stand the dumplings in an oiled steaming basket. Place over a saucepan of simmering water, cover and steam for 12–14 minutes before serving.

Vegetable Dim Sum

Dim sum are small Chinese parcels which may be filled with any variety of fillings, steamed or fried and served with a dipping sauce.

NUTRITIONAL INFORMATION

Calories 295   Sugars 1g
Protein . . . . .5g   Fat 22g
Carbohydrate . . .20g   Saturates 6g

15 MINS   15 MINS

SERVES 4

I N G R E D I E N T S

2 spring onions (scallions), chopped

25 g/1 oz green beans, chopped

½ small carrot, finely chopped

1 red chilli, chopped

25 g/1 oz/⅓ cup bean sprouts, chopped

25 g/1 oz/⅓ cup button mushrooms, chopped

25 g/1 oz/¼ cup unsalted cashew nuts, chopped

1 small egg, beaten

2 tbsp cornflour (cornstarch)

1 tsp light soy sauce

1 tsp hoisin sauce

1 tsp sesame oil

32 wonton wrappers

oil, for deep-frying

1 tbsp sesame seeds

1 Mix all of the vegetables together in a bowl. Add the nuts, egg, cornflour (cornstarch), soy sauce, hoi-sin sauce and sesame oil to the bowl. Mix well.

2 Lay the wonton wrappers out on a chopping board and spoon small quantities of the mixture into the centre of each. Gather the wrapper around the filling at the top, to make little parcels, leaving the top open.

3 Heat the oil for deep-frying in a wok to 180°C/350°F or until a cube of bread browns in 30 seconds. Fry the wontons, in batches, for 1–2 minutes or until golden brown. Drain on kitchen paper (paper towels) and keep warm whilst frying the remaining wontons.

4 Sprinkle the sesame seeds over the wontons. Serve the vegetable dim sum with a soy or plum dipping sauce.

COOK'S TIP

If preferred, arrange the wontons on a heatproof plate and then steam in a steamer for 5-7 minutes for a healthier cooking method.

Spicy Sweetcorn Fritters

Cornmeal can be found in most supermarkets or health food shops.
Yellow in colour, it acts as a binding agent in this recipe.

NUTRITIONAL INFORMATION

Calories 213	Sugars 6g	
Protein 5g	Fat 8g	
Carbohydrate . . .30g	Saturates 1g	

5 MINS   15 MINS

SERVES 4

I N G R E D I E N T S

225 g/8 oz/¾ cup canned or frozen
  sweetcorn

2 red chillies, deseeded and very finely
  chopped

2 cloves garlic, crushed

10 lime leaves, very finely chopped

2 tbsp fresh coriander (cilantro),
  chopped

1 large egg

75 g/2¾ oz/½ cup cornmeal

100 g/3½ oz fine green beans, very finely
  sliced

groundnut oil, for frying

1 Place the sweetcorn, chillies, garlic, lime leaves, coriander (cilantro), egg and cornmeal in a large mixing bowl, and stir to combine.

2 Add the green beans to the ingredients in the bowl and mix well, using a wooden spoon.

3 Divide the mixture into small, evenly sized balls. Flatten the balls of mixture between the palms of your hands to form rounds.

4 Heat a little groundnut oil in a preheated wok or large frying pan (skillet) until really hot. Cook the fritters, in batches, until brown and crispy on the outside, turning occasionally.

5 Leave the fritters to drain on absorbent kitchen paper (paper towels) while frying the remaining fritters.

6 Transfer the fritters to warm serving plates and serve immediately.

COOK'S TIP

Kaffir lime leaves are dark green, glossy leaves that have a lemony-lime flavour. They can be bought from specialist Asian stores either fresh or dried. Fresh leaves impart the most delicious flavour.

Deep-Fried Chilli Corn Balls

These small corn balls have a wonderful hot and sweet flavour, offset by the pungent coriander (cilantro).

NUTRITIONAL INFORMATION

Calories	248	Sugars 6g
Protein	.........6g	Fat 12
Carbohydrate	...30g	Saturates 5g

  15 MINS 30 MINS

SERVES 4

INGREDIENTS

6 spring onions (scallions), sliced

3 tbsp fresh coriander (cilantro), chopped

225 g/8 oz canned sweetcorn

1 tsp mild chilli powder

1 tbsp sweet chilli sauce

25 g/1 oz/¼ cup desiccated (shredded) coconut

1 egg

75 g/2¾ oz/⅓ cup polenta (cornmeal)

oil, for deep-frying

extra sweet chilli sauce, to serve

1 In a large bowl, mix together the spring onions (scallions), coriander (cilantro), sweetcorn, chilli powder, chilli sauce, coconut, egg and polenta (cornmeal) until well blended.

2 Cover the bowl with cling film (plastic wrap) and leave to stand for about 10 minutes.

3 Heat the oil for deep-frying in a large preheated wok or frying pan (skillet) to 180°C/350°F or until a cube of bread browns in 30 seconds.

4 Carefully drop spoonfuls of the chilli and polenta (cornmeal) mixture into the hot oil. Deep-fry the chilli corn balls, in batches, for 4–5 minutes or until crispy and a deep golden brown colour.

5 Remove the chilli corn balls with a slotted spoon, transfer to absorbent kitchen paper (paper towels) and leave to drain thoroughly.

6 Transfer the chilli corn balls to serving plates and serve with an extra sweet chilli sauce for dipping.

COOK'S TIP

For safe deep-frying in a round-bottomed wok, place it on a wok rack so that it rests securely. Only half-fill the wok with oil. Never leave the wok unattended over a high heat.

Aspagarus Parcels

These small parcels are ideal as part of a main meal and irresistible as a quick snack with extra plum sauce for dipping.

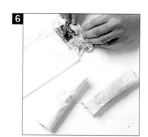

NUTRITIONAL INFORMATION

Calories 194	Sugars 2g	
Protein 3g	Fat 16g	
Carbohydrate 11g	Saturates 4g	

 5 MINS   25 MINS

SERVES 4

I N G R E D I E N T S

100 g/3½ oz fine tip asparagus

1 red (bell) pepper, deseeded and thinly sliced

50 g/1¾ oz/½ cup bean sprouts

2 tbsp plum sauce

1 egg yolk

8 sheets filo pastry

oil, for deep-frying

1 Place the asparagus, (bell) pepper and beansprouts in a large mixing bowl.

2 Add the plum sauce to the vegetables and mix until well-combined.

3 Beat the egg yolk and set aside until required.

4 Lay the sheets of filo pastry out on to a clean work surface (counter).

5 Place a little of the asparagus and red (bell) pepper filling at the top end of each filo pastry sheet. Brush the edges of the filo pastry with a little of the beaten egg yolk.

6 Roll up the filo pastry, tucking in the ends and enclosing the filling like a spring roll. Repeat with the remaining filo sheets.

7 Heat the oil for deep-frying in a large preheated wok. Carefully cook the parcels, 2 at a time, in the hot oil for 4–5 minutes or until crispy.

8 Remove the parcels with a slotted spoon and leave to drain on absorbent kitchen paper (paper towels).

9 Transfer the parcels to warm serving plates and serve immediately.

COOK'S TIP

Be sure to use fine-tipped asparagus as it is more tender than the larger stems.

Chicken Spring Rolls

A cucumber dipping sauce tastes perfect with these delicious spring rolls, filled with chicken and fresh, crunchy vegetables.

NUTRITIONAL INFORMATION

Calories 367   Sugars 18g
Protein . . . . .13g   Fat 21g
Carbohydrate . . .32g   Saturates 3g

 10 MINS   25 MINS

SERVES 4

INGREDIENTS

2 tbsp vegetable oil

4 spring onions (scallions), trimmed and sliced very finely

1 carrot, cut into matchstick pieces

1 small green or red (bell) pepper, cored, deseeded and sliced finely

60 g/2 oz/⅔ cup button mushrooms, sliced

60 g/2 oz/1 cup bean-sprouts

175 g/6 oz/1 cup cooked chicken, shredded

1 tbsp light soy sauce

1 tsp sugar

2 tsp cornflour (cornstarch), blended in 2 tbsp cold water

12 × 20 cm/8 inch spring roll wrappers

oil for deep-frying

salt and pepper

spring onion (scallion) brushes to garnish

SAUCE

50 ml/2 fl oz/¼ cup light malt vinegar

60 g/2 oz/¼ cup light muscovado sugar

½ tsp salt

5 cm/2 inch piece of cucumber, peeled and chopped finely

4 spring onions (scallions), trimmed and sliced finely

1 small red or green chilli, deseeded and chopped very finely

1 Stir-fry the spring onions (scallions), carrot and (bell) pepper for 2–3 minutes. Add the mushrooms, bean-sprouts and chicken and cook for 2 minutes. Season. Mix the soy sauce, sugar and blended cornflour (cornstarch). Add to the wok and stir-fry for 1 minute. Leave to cool slightly. Spoon the chicken and vegetable mixture on to the spring roll wrappers. Dampen the edges and roll them up to enclose the filling completely.

2 To make the sauce, heat the vinegar, water, sugar and salt in a pan. Boil for 1 minute. Combine the cucumber, spring onions (scallions) and chilli and pour over the vinegar mixture. Leave to cool.

3 Heat the oil and fry the rolls until crisp and golden brown. Drain on paper towels, garnish with spring onion (scallion) brushes and serve with the cucumber dipping sauce.

Pot Sticker Dumplings

These dumplings obtain their name from the fact that they would stick to the pot when steamed if they were not fried crisply enough initially.

NUTRITIONAL INFORMATION

Calories	345	Sugar	.........3g
Protein	........13g	Fat	..........17g
Carbohydrate	...36g	Saturates	.......2g

50 MINS   25 MINS

SERVES 4

INGREDIENTS

DUMPLINGS

175 g/6 oz/1½ cups plain (all-purpose) flour

pinch of salt

3 tbsp vegetable oil

6–8 tbsp boiling water

oil, for deep-frying

125 ml/4 fl oz/½ cup water, for steaming

sliced spring onions (scallions) and chives, to garnish

soy sauce or hoisin sauce, to serve

FILLING

150 g/5½ oz lean chicken, very finely chopped

25 g/1 oz canned bamboo shoots, drained and chopped

2 spring onions (scallions), finely chopped

½ small red (bell) pepper, seeded and finely chopped

½ tsp Chinese curry powder

1 tbsp light soy sauce

1 tsp caster (superfine) sugar

1 tsp sesame oil

1 To make the dumplings, mix together the flour and salt in a bowl. Make a well in the centre, add the oil and water and mix well to form a soft dough. Knead the dough on a lightly floured surface,

wrap in cling film (plastic wrap) and let stand for 30 minutes. Meanwhile, mix all of the filling ingredients together in a large bowl.

2 Divide the dough into 12 equal-sized pieces and roll each piece into a 12.5-cm/5-inch round. Spoon a portion of the filling on to one half of each round. Fold the dough over the filling to form a 'pasty', pressing the edges together to seal.

3 Pour a little oil into a frying pan (skillet) and cook the dumplings, in batches, until browned and slightly crisp.

4 Return all of the dumplings to the pan and add about 125 ml/4 fl oz/½ cup water. Cover and steam for 5 minutes, or until the dumplings are cooked through. Remove with a slotted spoon and garnish with spring onions (scallions) and chives. Serve with soy sauce or hoisin sauce.

Chinese Omelette

This is a fairly filling omelette, as it contains chicken and prawns (shrimp). It is cooked as a whole omelette and then sliced for serving.

NUTRITIONAL INFORMATION

Calories 309	Sugars 0g	
Protein 34g	Fat 19g	
Carbohydrate ...0.2g	Saturates 5g	

    5 MINS   5 MINS

SERVES 4

INGREDIENTS

8 eggs

225 g/8 oz/2 cups cooked chicken, shredded

12 tiger prawns (jumbo shrimp), peeled and deveined

2 tbsp chopped chives

2 tsp light soy sauce

dash of chilli sauce

2 tbsp vegetable oil

1 Lightly beat the eggs in a large mixing bowl.

2 Add the shredded chicken and tiger prawns (jumbo shrimp) to the eggs, mixing well.

3 Stir in the chopped chives, light soy sauce and chilli sauce, mixing well to combine all the ingredients.

4 Heat the vegetable oil in a large preheated frying pan (skillet) over a medium heat.

5 Add the egg mixture to the frying pan (skillet), tilting the pan to coat the base completely.

6 Cook over a medium heat, gently stirring the omelette with a fork, until

the surface is just set and the underside is a golden brown colour.

7 When the omelette is set, slide it out of the pan, with the aid of a palette knife (spatula).

8 Cut the Chinese omelette into squares or slices and serve immediately. Alternatively, serve the omelette as a main course for two people.

VARIATION

You could add extra flavour to the omelette by stirring in 3 tablespoons of finely chopped fresh coriander (cilantro) or 1 teaspoon of sesame seeds with the chives in step 3.

Honeyed Chicken Wings

Chicken wings are ideal for a starter as they are small and perfect for eating with the fingers.

NUTRITIONAL INFORMATION

Calories 131   Sugars 4g
Protein . . . . .10g   Fat 8g
Carbohydrate . . . .4g   Saturates 2g

 5 MINS   40 MINS

SERVES 4

I N G R E D I E N T S

450 g/1 lb chicken wings

2 tbsp peanut oil

2 tbsp light soy sauce

2 tbsp hoisin sauce

2 tbsp clear honey

2 garlic cloves, crushed

1 tsp sesame seeds

M A R I N A D E

1 dried red chilli

½–1 tsp chilli powder

½–1 tsp ground ginger

finely grated rind of 1 lime

1 To make the marinade, crush the dried chilli in a pestle and mortar. Mix together the crushed dried chilli, chilli powder, ground ginger and lime rind in a small mixing bowl.

2 Thoroughly rub the spice mixture into the chicken wings with your fingertips. Set aside for at least 2 hours to allow the flavours to penetrate the chicken wings.

3 Heat the peanut oil in a large wok or frying pan (skillet).

4 Add the chicken wings and fry, turning frequently, for about 10–12 minutes, until golden and crisp. Drain off any excess oil.

5 Add the soy sauce, hoisin sauce, honey, garlic and sesame seeds to the wok, turning the chicken wings to coat.

6 Reduce the heat and cook for 20–25 minutes, turning the chicken wings frequently, until completely cooked through. Serve hot.

COOK'S TIP

Make the dish in advance and freeze the chicken wings. Defrost thoroughly, cover with foil and heat right through in a moderate oven.

Bang-Bang Chicken

The cooked chicken meat is tenderized by being beaten with a rolling pin, hence the name for this very popular Szechuan dish.

NUTRITIONAL INFORMATION

Calories 82	Sugars 1g
Protein 13g	Fat 3g
Carbohydrate 2g	Saturates 1g

🕒 1¼ HOURS   🕐 40 MINS

SERVES 4

I N G R E D I E N T S

1 litre/1¾ pints/4 cups water

2 chicken quarters (breast half and leg)

1 cucumber, cut into matchstick shreds

S A U C E

2 tbsp light soy sauce

1 tsp sugar

1 tbsp finely chopped spring onions
  (scallions), plus extra to garnish

1 tsp red chilli oil

¼ tsp pepper

1 tsp white sesame seeds

2 tbsp peanut butter, creamed with a little
  sesame oil, plus extra to garnish

1 Bring the water to a rolling boil in a wok or a large saucepan. Add the chicken pieces, reduce the heat, cover and cook for 30-35 minutes.

2 Remove the chicken from the wok or pan and immerse in a bowl of cold water for at least 1 hour to cool it, ready for shredding.

3 Remove the chicken pieces, drain and dry on absorbent kitchen paper (paper towels). Take the meat off the bone.

4 On a flat surface, pound the chicken with a rolling pin, then tear the meat into shreds with 2 forks. Mix the chicken with the shredded cucumber and arrange in a serving dish.

5 To serve, mix together all the sauce ingredients until thoroughly combined and pour over the chicken and cucumber in the serving dish. Sprinkle some sesame seeds and chopped spring onions (scallions) over the sauce and serve.

COOK'S TIP

Take the time to tear the chicken meat into similar-sized shreds, to make an elegant-looking dish. You can do this quite efficiently with 2 forks, although Chinese cooks would do it with their fingers.

Sesame Ginger Chicken

Chunks of chicken breast are marinated in a mixture of lime juice, garlic, sesame oil and fresh ginger to give them a great flavour.

NUTRITIONAL INFORMATION

Calories	204	Sugars	.........0g
Protein	........28g	Fat	..........10g
Carbohydrate	....1g	Saturates	.......2g

  2¼ HOURS   10 MINS

SERVES 4

I N G R E D I E N T S

4 wooden satay sticks, soaked in
    warm water

500 g/1 lb 2 oz boneless chicken
    breasts

sprigs of fresh mint, to garnish

M A R I N A D E

1 garlic clove, crushed

1 shallot, chopped very finely

2 tbsp sesame oil

1 tbsp fish sauce or light soy sauce

finely grated rind of 1 lime or
    ½ lemon

2 tbsp lime juice or lemon juice

1 tsp sesame seeds

2 tsp finely grated fresh ginger root

2 tsp chopped fresh mint

salt and pepper

1 To make the marinade, put the crushed garlic, chopped shallot, sesame oil, fish sauce or soy sauce, lime or lemon rind and juice, sesame seeds, grated ginger root and chopped mint into a large non-metallic bowl. Season with a little salt and pepper and mix together until all the ingredients are thoroughly combined.

2 Remove the skin from the chicken breasts and cut the flesh into chunks.

3 Add the chicken to the marinade, stirring to coat the chicken completely in the mixture. Cover with cling film (plastic wrap) and chill in the refrigerator for at least 2 hours so that the flavours are absorbed.

4 Thread the chicken on to wooden satay sticks. Place them on the rack of a grill (broiler) pan and baste with the marinade.

5 Place the kebabs under a preheated grill (broiler) for about 8–10 minutes. Turn them frequently, basting them with the remaining marinade.

6 Serve the chicken skewers at once, garnished with sprigs of fresh mint.

COOK'S TIP

The kebabs taste delicious if dipped into an accompanying bowl of hot chilli sauce.

Steamed Duck Buns

The dough used in this recipe may also be wrapped around chicken, pork or prawns (shrimp), or sweet fillings as an alternative.

NUTRITIONAL INFORMATION

Calories	307	Sugars	........11g
Protein	........17g	Fat	...........6g
Carbohydrate	...50g	Saturates	.......1g

1½ HOURS   1 HOUR

SERVES 4

INGREDIENTS

DUMPLING DOUGH

300 g/10½ oz/2⅔ cups plain (all-purpose) flour

15 g/½ oz dried yeast

1 tsp caster (superfine) sugar

2 tbsp warm water

175 ml/6 fl oz/¾ cup warm milk

FILLING

300 g/10½ oz duck breast

1 tbsp light brown sugar

1 tbsp light soy sauce

2 tbsp clear honey

1 tbsp hoisin sauce

1 tbsp vegetable oil

1 leek, finely chopped

1 garlic clove, crushed

1-cm/½-inch piece fresh root ginger (ginger root), grated

1 Place the duck breast in a large bowl. Mix together the light brown sugar, soy sauce, honey and hoisin sauce. Pour the mixture over the duck and marinate for 20 minutes.

2 Remove the duck from the marinade and cook on a rack set over a roasting tin (pan) in a preheated oven, at 200°C/400°F/Gas Mark 6, for 35–40 minutes, or until cooked through. Leave to cool, remove the meat from the bones and cut into small cubes.

3 Heat the vegetable oil in a preheated wok or frying pan (skillet) until really hot.

4 Add the leek, garlic and ginger to the wok and fry for 3 minutes. Mix with the duck meat.

5 Sift the plain (all-purpose) flour into a large bowl. Mix the yeast, caster (superfine) sugar and warm water in a separate bowl and leave in a warm place for 15 minutes.

6 Pour the yeast mixture into the flour, together with the warm milk, mixing to form a firm dough. Knead the dough on a floured surface for 5 minutes. Roll into a sausage shape, 2.5 cm/1 inch in diameter. Cut into 16 pieces, cover and let stand for 20–25 minutes.

7 Flatten the dough pieces into 10-cm/4-inch rounds. Place a spoonful of filling in the centre of each, draw up the sides to form a 'moneybag' shape and twist to seal.

8 Place the dumplings on a clean, damp tea towel (dish cloth) in the base of a steamer, cover and steam for 20 minutes. Serve immediately.

Beef Satay

In this dish, strips of beef are threaded on to skewers, grilled (broiled) and served with a spicy peanut sauce.

NUTRITIONAL INFORMATION

Calories . . . . .314 Sugars 8g
Protein . . . . .32g Fat 16g
Carbohydrate . . .10g Saturates 4g

  2¼ HOURS   15 MINS

SERVES 6

INGREDIENTS

4 boneless, skinned chicken breasts or
  750 g/1 lb 10 oz rump steak, trimmed

MARINADE

1 small onion, finely chopped

1 garlic clove, crushed

2.5 cm/1 inch piece ginger root, peeled
  and grated

2 tbsp dark soy sauce

2 tsp chilli powder

1 tsp ground coriander

2 tsp dark brown sugar

1 tbsp lemon or lime juice

1 tbsp vegetable oil

SAUCE

300 ml/½ pint/1¼ cups coconut milk

4 tbsp/⅓ cup crunchy peanut butter

1 tbsp fish sauce

1 tsp lemon or lime juice

salt and pepper

1 Using a sharp knife, trim any fat from the chicken or beef then cut into thin strips, about 7 cm/3 inches long.

2 To make the marinade, place all the ingredients in a shallow dish and mix well. Add the chicken or beef strips and turn in the marinade until well coated.

Cover with cling film (plastic wrap) and leave to marinate for 2 hours orovernight in the refrigerator.

3 Remove the meat from the marinade and thread the pieces, concertina style, on pre-soaked bamboo or thin wooden skewers.

4 Grill (broil) the chicken and beef satays for 8-10 minutes, turning and brushing occasionally with the marinade, until cooked through.

5 Meanwhile, to make the sauce, mix the coconut milk with the peanut butter, fish sauce and lemon or lime juice in a saucepan. Bring to the boil and cook for 3 minutes. Season to taste.

6 Transfer the sauce to a serving bowl and serve with the cooked satays.

Pork with Chilli & Garlic

Any leftovers from this dish can be used for a number of other dishes, for example stir-fries.

NUTRITIONAL INFORMATION

Calories ....137 Sugars 0.1g
Protein ....16g Fat 8g
Carbohydrate ....1g Saturates 2g

🍲 5 HOURS   🕐 35 MINS

SERVES 4

INGREDIENTS

500 g/1 lb 2 oz leg of pork, boned but not skinned

SAUCE

1 tsp finely chopped garlic

1 tsp finely chopped spring onions (scallions)

2 tbsp light soy sauce

1 tsp red chilli oil

½ tsp sesame oil

sprig of fresh coriander (cilantro), to garnish (optional)

1 Place the pork, tied together in one piece, in a large saucepan, add enough cold water to cover, and bring to a rolling boil over a medium heat.

2 Using a slotted spoon, skim off the scum that rises to the surface, cover the pan with a lid and simmer gently for 25-30 minutes.

3 Leave the meat in the liquid to cool, under cover, for at least 1-2 hours.

4 Lift out the meat with 2 slotted spoons and leave to cool completely, skin-side up, for 2-3 hours.

5 To serve, cut off the skin, leaving a very thin layer of fat on top like a

ham joint. Cut the meat in small thin slices across the grain, and arrange on a plate in an overlapping pattern.

6 In a small bowl, mix together the sauce ingredients, and pour the sauce evenly over the pork.

7 Garnish the pork with a sprig of fresh coriander (cilantro), if wished, and serve at once.

COOK'S TIP

This is a very simple dish, but beautifully presented. Make sure you slice the meat as thinly and evenly as possible to make an elegantly arranged dish.

Pork Dim Sum

These small steamed parcels are traditionally served as an appetizer and are very adaptable to your favourite fillings.

NUTRITIONAL INFORMATION

Calories	478	Sugars	.........3g
Protein	........33g	Fat	..........29g
Carbohydrate	...21g	Saturates	.......9g

 10 MINS   15 MINS

SERVES 4

INGREDIENTS

400 g/14 oz minced (ground) pork

2 spring onions (scallions), chopped

50 g/1¾ oz canned bamboo shoots, drained, rinsed and chopped

1 tbsp light soy sauce

1 tbsp dry sherry

2 tsp sesame oil

2 tsp caster (superfine) sugar

1 egg white, lightly beaten

4½ tsp cornflour (cornstarch)

24 wonton wrappers

1 Place the minced (ground) pork, spring onions (scallions), bamboo shoots, soy sauce, dry sherry, sesame oil, caster (superfine) sugar and beaten egg white in a large mixing bowl and mix until all the ingredients are thoroughly combined.

2 Stir in the cornflour (cornstarch), mixing until thoroughly incorporated with the other ingredients.

3 Spread out the wonton wrappers on a work surface (counter). Place a spoonful of the pork and vegetable mixture in the centre of each wonton wrapper and lightly brush the edges of the wrappers with water.

4 Bring the sides of the wrappers together in the centre of the filling, pinching firmly together.

5 Line a steamer with a clean, damp tea towel (dish cloth) and arrange the wontons inside.

6 Cover and steam for 5–7 minutes, until the dim sum are cooked through. Serve immediately.

COOK'S TIP

Bamboo steamers are designed to rest on the sloping sides of a wok above the water. They are available in a range of sizes.

Pork Sesame Toasts

This classic Chinese appetizer is also a great nibble for serving at parties – but be sure to make plenty!

NUTRITIONAL INFORMATION

Calories	674	Sugars	.........2g
Protein	........33g	Fat	..........46g
Carbohydrate	...33g	Saturates	.......7g

 5 MINS   35 MINS

SERVES 4

INGREDIENTS

250 g/9 oz lean pork

250 g/9 oz/⅔ cup uncooked peeled prawns (shrimp), deveined

4 spring onions (scallions), trimmed

1 garlic clove, crushed

1 tbsp chopped fresh coriander (cilantro) leaves and stems

1 tbsp fish sauce

1 egg

8–10 slices of thick-cut white bread

3 tbsp sesame seeds

150 ml/¼ pint/⅔ cup vegetable oil

salt and pepper

TO GARNISH

sprigs of fresh coriander (cilantro)

red (bell) pepper, sliced finely

1 Put the pork, prawns (shrimp), spring onions (scallions), garlic, coriander (cilantro), fish sauce, egg and seasoning into a food processor or blender. Process for a few seconds until the ingredients are finely chopped. Transfer the mixture to a bowl. Alternatively, chop the pork, prawns (shrimp) and spring onions (scallions) very finely, and mix with the garlic, coriander (cilantro), fish sauce, beaten egg and seasoning until all the ingredients are well combined.

2 Spread the pork and prawn (shrimp) mixture thickly over the bread so that it reaches right up to the edges. Cut off the crusts and slice each piece of bread into 4 squares or triangles.

3 Sprinkle the topping liberally with sesame seeds.

4 Heat the oil in a wok or frying pan (skillet). Fry a few pieces of the bread, topping side down first so that it sets the egg, for about 2 minutes or until golden brown. Turn the pieces over to cook on the other side, about 1 minute.

5 Drain the pork and prawn (shrimp) toasts and place them on kitchen paper (paper towels). Fry the remaining pieces. Serve garnished with sprigs of fresh coriander (cilantro) and strips of red (bell) pepper.

Barbecue Spare Ribs

This is a simplified version of the half saddle of pork ribs seen hanging in the windows of Cantonese restaurants.

NUTRITIONAL INFORMATION

Calories	271	Sugars	.........4g
Protein	........13g	Fat	..........22g
Carbohydrate	....5g	Saturates	.......8g

 6½ HOURS 50 MINS

SERVES 4

I N G R E D I E N T S

500 g/1 lb 2 oz pork finger spare ribs

1 tbsp sugar

1 tbsp light soy sauce

1 tbsp dark soy sauce

3 tbsp hoi-sin sauce

1 tbsp rice wine or dry sherry

4-5 tbsp water or Chinese Stock (see page 14)

mild chilli sauce, to dip

coriander (cilantro) leaves, to garnish

1 Using a sharp knife, trim off any excess fat from the spare ribs and cut into pieces. Place the ribs in a baking dish.

2 Mix together the sugar, light and dark soy sauce, hoi-sin sauce and wine. Pour over the ribs in the baking dish. Turn to coat the ribs thoroughly in the mixture and leave to marinate for about 2-3 hours.

3 Add the water or Chinese stock to the ribs and spread them out in the dish. Roast in a preheated hot oven for 15 minutes.

4 Turn the ribs over, lower the oven temperature and cook for 30-35 minutes longer.

5 To serve, chop each rib into 3-4 small, bite-sized pieces with a large knife or Chinese cleaver and arrange neatly on a serving dish.

6 Pour the sauce from the baking dish over the spare ribs and garnish with a few coriander (cilantro) leaves. Place some mild chilli sauce into a small dish and serve with the ribs as a dip. Serve immediately.

COOK'S TIP

Finger ribs are specially small, thin ribs. Ask your local butcher to cut some if you can't find the right size in the supermarket. Don't throw away any trimmings from the ribs – they can be used for soup or stock.

Spicy Salt & Pepper Prawns

For best results, use raw tiger prawns (shrimp) in their shells. They are 7-10 cm/3-4 inches long, and you should get 18-20 per 500 g/1 lb 2 oz.

NUTRITIONAL INFORMATION

Calories 160   Sugars 0.2g
Protein . . . . .17g   Fat 10g
Carbohydrate . . .0.5g   Saturates 1g

35 MINS   20 MINS

SERVES 4

INGREDIENTS

250-300 g/9-10½ oz raw prawns (shrimp) in their shells, defrosted if frozen

1 tbsp light soy sauce

1 tsp Chinese rice wine or dry sherry

2 tsp cornflour (cornstarch)

vegetable oil, for deep-frying

2-3 spring onions (scallions), to garnish

SPICY SALT AND PEPPER

1 tbsp salt

1 tsp ground Szechuan peppercorns

1 tsp five-spice powder

1 Pull the soft legs off the prawns (shrimp), but keep the body shell on. Dry well on absorbent kitchen paper (paper towels).

2 Place the prawns (shrimp) in a bowl with the soy sauce, rice wine or sherry and cornflour (cornstarch). Turn the prawns (shrimp) to coat thoroughly in the mixture and leave to marinate for about 25-30 minutes.

3 To make the Spicy Salt and Pepper, mix the salt, ground Szechuan peppercorns and five-spice powder together. Place in a dry frying pan (skillet) and stir-fry for about 3-4 minutes over a low heat, stirring constantly to prevent the spices burning on the bottom of the pan. Remove from the heat and allow to cool.

4 Heat the vegetable oil in a preheated wok or large frying pan (skillet) until smoking, then deep-fry the prawns (shrimp) in batches until golden brown. Remove the prawns (shrimp) from the wok with a slotted spoon and drain on kitchen paper (paper towels).

5 Place the spring onions (scallions) in a bowl, pour on 1 tablespoon of the hot oil and leave for 30 seconds. Serve the prawns (shrimp) garnished with the spring onions (scallions), and with the Spicy Salt and Pepper as a dip.

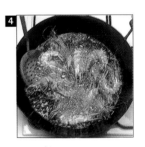

COOK'S TIP

The roasted spice mixture made with Szechuan peppercorns is used throughout China as a dip for deep-fried food. The peppercorns are sometimes roasted first and then ground. Dry-frying is a way of releasing the flavours of the spices.

Prawn (Shrimp) Parcels

These small prawn (shrimp) bites are packed with the flavour of lime and coriander (cilantro) for a quick and tasty starter.

NUTRITIONAL INFORMATION

Calories	305	Sugars	........2g
Protein	........15g	Fat	..........21g
Carbohydrate	...14g	Saturates	.......8g

 15 MINS ⏱ 20 MINS

SERVES 4

I N G R E D I E N T S

1 tbsp sunflower oil

1 red (bell) pepper, deseeded and very thinly sliced

75 g/2¾ oz/¾ cup beansprouts

finely grated zest and juice of 1 lime

1 red chili, deseeded and very finely chopped

1 cm/½ inch piece of root ginger, peeled and grated

225 g/8 oz peeled prawns (shrimp)

1 tbsp fish sauce

½ tsp arrowroot

2 tbsp chopped fresh coriander (cilantro)

8 sheets filo pastry

25 g/1 oz/2 tbsp butter

2 tsp sesame oil

oil, for frying

spring onion (scallion) tassels, to garnish

chilli sauce, to serve

1 Heat the sunflower oil in a large preheated wok. Add the red (bell) pepper and beansprouts and stir-fry for 2 minutes, or until the vegetables have softened.

2 Remove the wok from the heat and toss in the lime zest and juice, red chilli, ginger and prawns (shrimp), stirring well.

3 Mix the fish sauce with the arrowroot and stir the mixture into the wok juices. Return the wok to the heat and cook, stirring, for 2 minutes, or until the juices thicken. Toss in the coriander (cilantro) and mix well.

4 Lay the sheets of filo pastry out on a board. Melt the butter and sesame oil and brush each pastry sheet with the mixture.

5 Spoon a little of the prawn (shrimp) filling on to the top of each sheet, fold over each end, and roll up to enclose the filling.

6 Heat the oil in a large wok. Cook the parcels, in batches, for 2–3 minutes, or until crisp and golden. Garnish with spring onion (scallion) tassels and serve hot with a chilli dipping sauce.

COOK'S TIP

If using cooked prawns (shrimp), cook for 1 minute only otherwise the prawns (shrimp) will toughen.

Fat Horses

A mixture of meats is flavoured with coconut milk, fish sauce and coriander (cilantro) in this curious sounding dish.

NUTRITIONAL INFORMATION

Calories	195	Sugars	.........1g
Protein	........23g	Fat	...........11g
Carbohydrate	....1g	Saturates	.......6g

 10 MINS   30 MINS

SERVES 4

I N G R E D I E N T S

25 g/1 oz/2 tbsp creamed coconut

125 g/4½ oz lean pork

125 g/4½ oz chicken breast, skin removed

125 g/4½ oz/½ cup canned crab meat, drained

2 eggs

2 garlic cloves, crushed

4 spring onions (scallions), trimmed and chopped

1 tbsp fish sauce

1 tbsp chopped fresh coriander (cilantro) leaves and stems

1 tbsp dark muscovado sugar

salt and pepper

TO GARNISH

finely sliced white radish (mooli) or turnip

chives

red chilli

sprigs of fresh coriander (cilantro)

1 Mix the coconut with 3 tbsp of hot water. Stir to dissolve the coconut.

2 Put the pork, chicken and crab meat into a food processor or blender and process for 10–15 seconds until minced (ground), or chop them finely by hand and put in a mixing bowl.

3 Add the coconut mixture to the food processor or blender with the eggs, garlic, spring onions (scallions), fish sauce, coriander (cilantro) and sugar. Season to taste and process for a few more seconds. Alternatively, mix these ingredients into the chopped pork, chicken and crab meat.

4 Grease 6 ramekin dishes with a little butter. Spoon in the minced (ground) mixture, levelling the surface. Place them in a steamer, then set the steamer over a pan of gently boiling water. Cook until set – about 30 minutes.

5 Lift out the dishes and leave to cool for a few minutes. Run a knife around the edge of each dish, then invert on to warmed plates. Serve garnished with finely sliced white radish (mooli) or turnip, chives, red chilli and sprigs of fresh coriander (cilantro).

Chilli Fish Cakes

These small fish cakes are quick to make and are delicious served with a chilli dip.

NUTRITIONAL INFORMATION

Calories 164   Sugars 1g
Protein ....23g   Fat 6g
Carbohydrate ....6g   Saturates 1g

  5 MINS   40 MINS

SERVES 4

INGREDIENTS

450 g/1 lb cod fillets, skinned

2 tbsp fish sauce

2 red chillies, deseeded and very finely chopped

2 cloves garlic, crushed

10 lime leaves, very finely chopped

2 tbsp fresh coriander (cilantro), chopped

1 large egg

25 g/1 oz/¼ cup plain (all-purpose) flour

100 g/3½ oz fine green beans, very finely sliced

groundnut oil, for frying

chilli dip, to serve

1 Using a sharp knife, roughly cut the cod fillets into bite-sized pieces.

2 Place the cod in a food processor together with the fish sauce, chillies, garlic, lime leaves, coriander (cilantro), egg and flour. Process until finely chopped and turn out into a large mixing bowl.

3 Add the green beans to the cod mixture and combine.

4 Divide the mixture into small balls. Flatten the balls between the palms of your hands to form rounds.

5 Heat a little oil in a preheated wok or large frying pan (skillet). Fry the fish cakes on both sides until brown and crispy on the outside.

6 Transfer the fish cakes to serving plates and serve hot with a chilli dip.

VARIATION

Almost any kind of fish fillets and seafood can used in this recipe, try haddock, crab meat or lobster.

Sweet & Sour Prawns

Prawns (shrimp) are marinated in a soy sauce mixture then coated in a light batter, fried and served with a delicious sweet-and-sour dip.

NUTRITIONAL INFORMATION

Calories	294	Sugars	........11g
Protein	........14g	Fat	..........12g
Carbohydrate	...34g	Saturates	.......2g

40 MINS   20 MINS

SERVES 4

INGREDIENTS

16 large raw prawns (shrimp), peeled

1 tsp grated fresh root ginger

1 garlic clove, crushed

2 spring onions (scallions), sliced

2 tbsp dry sherry

2 tsp sesame oil

1 tbsp light soy sauce

vegetable oil, for deep-frying

shredded spring onion (scallion),
  to garnish

BATTER

4 egg whites

4 tbsp cornflour (cornstarch)

2 tbsp plain (all-purpose) flour

SAUCE

2 tbsp tomato purée (paste)

3 tbsp white wine vinegar

4 tsp light soy sauce

2 tbsp lemon juice

3 tbsp light brown sugar

1 green (bell) pepper, seeded and cut into
  thin matchsticks

½ tsp chilli sauce

300 ml/½ pint/1¼ cups vegetable stock

2 tsp cornflour (cornstarch)

1 Using tweezers, devein the prawns (shrimp), then flatten them with a large knife.

2 Place the prawns (shrimp) in a dish and add the ginger, garlic, spring onions (scallions), dry sherry, sesame oil and soy sauce. Cover with cling film (plastic wrap) and leave to marinate for 30 minutes.

3 Make the batter by beating the egg whites until thick. Fold in the cornflour (cornstarch) and plain (all-purpose) flour to form a light batter.

4 Place all of the sauce ingredients in a saucepan and bring to the boil. Reduce the heat and leave to simmer for 10 minutes.

5 Remove the prawns (shrimp) from the marinade and dip them into the batter to coat.

6 Heat the vegetable oil in a preheated wok or large frying pan (skillet) until almost smoking. Reduce the heat and fry the prawns (shrimp) for 3–4 minutes, until crisp and golden brown.

7 Garnish the prawns (shrimp) with shredded spring onion (scallion) and serve with the sauce.

Poultry

Second to pork, poultry is one of the most popular foods throughout China. It also plays an important symbolic role in Chinese cooking. The cockerel symbolizes the male, positiveness and aggression while the duck represents happiness and fidelity. Being uniformly tender, poultry is ideal for Chinese cooking methods which rely on the rapid

cooking of small, even-sized pieces of meat. Poultry can be cut into wafer-thin slices, thin matchstick strips or cubes, and can be quickly cooked without any loss of moisture or tenderness. This chapter contains dishes which are stir-fried, braised, steamed and roasted and contains old favourites, as well as more unusual dishes.

Chicken Chop Suey

Chop suey is a well known and popular dish based on bean sprouts and soy sauce with a meat or vegetable flavouring.

NUTRITIONAL INFORMATION

Calories	337	Sugars	.........7g
Protein	........32g	Fat	..........18g
Carbohydrate	...14g	Saturates	.......3g

🍲 25 MINS   🕐 15 MINS

SERVES 4

I N G R E D I E N T S

4 tbsp light soy sauce

2 tsp light brown sugar

500 g/1 lb 2 oz skinless, boneless chicken breasts

3 tbsp vegetable oil

2 onions, quartered

2 garlic cloves, crushed

350 g/12 oz bean sprouts

3 tsp sesame oil

1 tbsp cornflour (cornstarch)

3 tbsp water

425 ml/¾ pint/2 cups chicken stock

shredded leek, to garnish

VARIATION

This recipe may be made with strips of lean steak, pork or with mixed vegetables. Change the type of stock accordingly.

1 Mix the soy sauce and sugar together, stirring until the sugar has dissolved.

2 Trim any fat from the chicken and cut into thin strips. Place the meat in a shallow dish and spoon the soy mixture over them, turning to coat. Marinate in the refrigerator for 20 minutes.

3 Heat the oil in a wok and stir-fry the chicken for 2–3 minutes, until golden brown. Add the onions and garlic and cook for a further 2 minutes. Add the bean sprouts, cook for 4–5 minutes, then add the sesame oil.

4 Mix the cornflour (cornstarch) and water to form a smooth paste. Pour the stock into the wok, add the cornflour (cornstarch) paste and bring to the boil, stirring until the sauce is thickened and clear. Serve, garnished with shredded leek.

Cashew Chicken

Yellow bean sauce is available from large supermarkets. Try to buy a chunky sauce rather than a smooth sauce for texture.

NUTRITIONAL INFORMATION

Calories 398   Sugars 2g
Protein . . . . .31g   Fat 27g
Carbohydrate . . . .8g   Saturates 4g

 10 MINS   🕐 15 MINS

SERVES 4

I N G R E D I E N T S

450 g/1 lb boneless chicken breasts

2 tbsp vegetable oil

1 red onion, sliced

175 g/6 oz/1½ cups flat mushrooms, sliced

100 g/3½ oz/⅓ cup cashew nuts

75 g/2¾ oz jar yellow bean sauce

fresh coriander (cilantro), to garnish

egg fried rice or plain boiled rice, to serve

1 Using a sharp knife, remove the excess skin from the chicken breasts, if desired. Cut the chicken into small, bite-sized chunks.

2 Heat the vegetable oil in a preheated wok or frying pan (skillet).

3 Add the chicken to the wok and stir-fry for 5 minutes.

4 Add the red onion and mushrooms to the wok and continue to stir-fry for a further 5 minutes.

5 Place the cashew nuts on a baking tray (cookie sheet) and toast under a preheated medium grill (broiler) until just browning – toasting nuts brings out their flavour.

6 Toss the toasted cashew nuts into the wok together with the yellow bean sauce and heat through.

7 Allow the sauce to bubble for 2–3 minutes.

8 Transfer the chop suey to warm serving bowls and garnish with fresh coriander (cilantro). Serve hot with egg fried rice or plain boiled rice.

VARIATION

Chicken thighs could be used instead of the chicken breasts for a more economical dish.

Lemon Chicken

This is on everyone's list of favourite Chinese dishes, and it is so simple to make. Serve with stir-fried vegetables for a truly delicious meal.

NUTRITIONAL INFORMATION

Calories	272	Sugars	.........1g
Protein	........36g	Fat	...........11g
Carbohydrate	....5g	Saturates	.......2g

5 MINS   15 MINS

SERVES 4

I N G R E D I E N T S

vegetable oil, for deep-frying

650 g/1 lb 7 oz skinless, boneless chicken, cut into strips

lemon slices and shredded spring onion (scallion), to garnish

S A U C E

1 tbsp cornflour (cornstarch)

6 tbsp cold water

3 tbsp fresh lemon juice

2 tbsp sweet sherry

½ tsp caster (superfine) sugar

1 Heat the oil for deep-frying in a preheated wok or frying pan (skillet) to 180°C/350°F or until a cube of bread browns in 30 seconds.

2 Reduce the heat and stir-fry the chicken strips for 3–4 minutes, until cooked through.

3 Remove the chicken with a slotted spoon, set aside and keep warm. Drain the oil from the wok.

4 To make the sauce, mix the cornflour (cornstarch) with 2 tablespoons of the water to form a paste.

5 Pour the lemon juice and remaining water into the mixture in the wok.

6 Add the sweet sherry and caster (superfine) sugar and bring to the boil, stirring until the sugar has completely dissolved.

7 Stir in the cornflour (cornstarch) mixture and return to the boil. Reduce the heat and simmer, stirring constantly, for 2-3 minutes, until the sauce is thickened and clear.

8 Transfer the chicken to a warm serving plate and pour the sauce over the top.

9 Garnish the chicken with the lemon slices and shredded spring onion (scallion) and serve immediately.

COOK'S TIP

If you would prefer to use chicken portions rather than strips, cook them in the oil, covered, over a low heat for about 30 minutes, or until cooked through.

Stir-Fried Ginger Chicken

The oranges add colour and piquancy to this refreshing dish, which complements the chicken well.

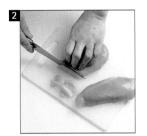

NUTRITIONAL INFORMATION

Calories	289	Sugars	........15g
Protein	........20g	Fat	...........9g
Carbohydrate	...17g	Saturates	.......2g

5 MINS   20 MINS

SERVES 4

I N G R E D I E N T S

2 tbsp sunflower oil

1 onion, sliced

175 g/6 oz carrots, cut into thin sticks

1 clove garlic, crushed

350 g/12 oz boneless skinless chicken breasts

2 tbsp fresh ginger, peeled and grated

1 tsp ground ginger

4 tbsp sweet sherry

1 tbsp tomato purée (tomato paste)

1 tbsp demerara sugar

100 ml/3½ fl oz/⅓ cup orange juice

1 tsp cornflour (cornstarch)

1 orange, peeled and segmented

fresh snipped chives, to garnish

1 Heat the oil in a large preheated wok. Add the onion, carrots and garlic and stir-fry over a high heat for 3 minutes or until the vegetables begin to soften.

2 Slice the chicken into thin strips. Add to the wok with the fresh and ground ginger. Stir-fry for a further 10 minutes, or until the chicken is well cooked through and golden in colour.

3 Mix together the sherry, tomato purée (tomato paste), sugar, orange juice and cornflour (cornstarch) in a bowl. Stir the mixture into the wok and heat through until the mixture bubbles and the juices start to thicken.

4 Add the orange segments and carefully toss to mix.

5 Transfer the stir-fried chicken to warm serving bowls and garnish with freshly snipped chives. Serve immediately.

COOK'S TIP

Make sure that you do not continue cooking the dish once the orange segments have been added in step 4, otherwise they will break up.

Kung Po Chicken

In this recipe, cashew nuts are used but peanuts, walnuts or almonds can be substituted, if preferred.

NUTRITIONAL INFORMATION

Calories	294	Sugars	.........3g
Protein	........21g	Fat	..........18g
Carbohydrate	...10g	Saturates	.......4g

10 MINS   5 MINS

SERVES 4

INGREDIENTS

250-300 g/9-10½ oz chicken meat, boned and skinned

¼ tsp salt

⅓ egg white

1 tsp cornflour (cornstarch) paste (see page 15)

1 medium green (bell) pepper, cored and seeded

4 tbsp vegetable oil

1 spring onion (scallion), cut into short sections

a few small slices of ginger root

4-5 small dried red chillies, soaked, seeded and shredded

2 tbsp crushed yellow bean sauce

1 tsp rice wine or dry sherry

125 g/4½ oz roasted cashew nuts

a few drops of sesame oil

boiled rice, to serve

1 Cut the chicken into small cubes about the size of sugar lumps. Place the chicken in a small bowl and mix with a pinch of salt, the egg white and the cornflour (cornstarch) paste, in that order.

2 Cut the green (bell) pepper into cubes or triangles about the same size as the chicken pieces.

3 Heat the oil in a wok, add the chicken and stir-fry for 1 minute. Remove with a slotted spoon and keep warm.

4 Add the spring onion (scallion), ginger, chillies and green (bell) pepper. Stir-fry for 1 minute, then add the chicken with the yellow bean sauce and wine. Blend well and stir-fry for another minute. Finally stir in the cashew nuts and sesame oil. Serve hot with boiled rice.

VARIATION

Any nuts can be used in place of the cashew nuts, if preferred. The important point is the crunchy texture, which is very much a feature of Szechuan cooking.

Green Chicken Stir-Fry

Tender chicken is mixed with a selection of spring greens and flavoured with yellow bean sauce in this crunchy stir-fry.

NUTRITIONAL INFORMATION

Calories	297	Sugars	.........5g
Protein	........30g	Fat	..........16g
Carbohydrate	....8g	Saturates	.......3g

🥔 5 MINS   🕐 15 MINS

SERVES 4

INGREDIENTS

2 tbsp sunflower oil

450 g/1 lb skinless, boneless chicken breasts

2 cloves garlic, crushed

1 green (bell) pepper

100 g/3½ oz/1½ cups mangetout (snow peas)

6 spring onions (scallions), sliced, plus extra to garnish

225 g/8 oz spring greens or cabbage, shredded

160 g/5¾ oz jar yellow bean sauce

50 g/1¾ oz/3 tbsp roasted cashew nuts

1 Heat the sunflower oil in a large preheated wok.

2 Slice the chicken into thin strips and add to the wok together with the garlic. Stir-fry for about 5 minutes or until the chicken is sealed on all sides and beginning to turn golden.

3 Using a sharp knife, deseed the green (bell) pepper and cut into thin strips.

4 Add the mangetout (snow peas), spring onions (scallions), green (bell) pepper strips and spring greens or cabbage to the wok. Stir-fry for a further 5 minutes or until the vegetables are just tender.

5 Stir in the yellow bean sauce and heat through for about 2 minutes or until the mixture starts to bubble.

6 Scatter the roasted cashew nuts into the wok.

7 Transfer the stir-fry to warm serving plates and garnish with extra spring onions (scallions), if desired. Serve the stir-fry immediately.

COOK'S TIP

Do not add salted cashew nuts to this dish otherwise the dish will be too salty.

Orange Chicken Stir-Fry

Chicken thighs are inexpensive, meaty portions which are readily available. Although not as tender as breast, it is perfect for stir-frying.

NUTRITIONAL INFORMATION

Calories 267   Sugars 11g
Protein . . . . .23g   Fat 11g
Carbohydrate . . .15g   Saturates 2g

10 MINS   15 MINS

SERVES 4

I N G R E D I E N T S

3 tbsp sunflower oil

350 g/12 oz boneless chicken thighs, skinned and cut into thin strips

1 onion, sliced

1 clove garlic, crushed

1 red (bell) pepper, deseeded and sliced

75 g/2¾ oz/1¼ cups mangetout (snow peas)

4 tbsp light soy sauce

4 tbsp sherry

1 tbsp tomato purée (tomato paste)

finely grated rind and juice of 1 orange

1 tsp cornflour (cornstarch)

2 oranges

100 g/3½ oz/1 cup bean sprouts

cooked rice or noodles, to serve

1 Heat the oil in a large preheated wok. Add the chicken and stir-fry for 2–3 minutes or until sealed on all sides.

2 Add the onion, garlic, (bell) pepper and mangetout (snow peas) to the wok. Stir-fry for a further 5 minutes, or until the vegetables are just tender and the chicken is completely cooked through.

3 Mix together the soy sauce, sherry, tomato purée (tomato paste), orange rind and juice and the cornflour (cornstarch). Add to the wok and cook, stirring, until the juices start to thicken.

4 Using a sharp knife, peel and segment the oranges. Add the segments to the mixture in the wok with the bean sprouts and heat through for a further 2 minutes.

5 Transfer the stir-fry to serving plates and serve at once with cooked rice or noodles.

COOK'S TIP

Bean sprouts are sprouting mung beans and are a regular ingredient in Chinese cooking. They require very little cooking and may even be eaten raw, if wished.

Chilli Coconut Chicken

This tasty dish combines the flavours of lime, peanut, coconut and chilli. You'll find coconut cream in most supermarkets or delicatessens.

NUTRITIONAL INFORMATION

Calories	348	Sugars	.........2g
Protein	........36g	Fat	..........21g
Carbohydrate	....3g	Saturates	.......8g

 4 MINS   15 MINS

SERVES 4

I N G R E D I E N T S

150 ml/¼ pint/⅔ cup hot chicken stock

25 g/1 oz/⅓ cup coconut cream

1 tbsp sunflower oil

8 skinless, boneless chicken thighs,
  cut into long, thin strips

1 small red chilli, sliced thinly

4 spring onions (scallions),
  sliced thinly

4 tbsp smooth or crunchy peanut butter

finely grated rind and juice of 1 lime

1 fresh red chilli and spring onion (scallion)
  tassel, to garnish

boiled rice, to serve

1 Pour the chicken stock into a measuring jug or small bowl. Crumble the coconut cream into the chicken stock and stir the mixture until the coconut cream dissolves.

2 Heat the oil in a preheated wok or large heavy pan.

3 Add the chicken strips and cook, stirring, until the chicken turns a golden colour.

4 Stir in the chopped red chilli and spring onions (scallions) and cook gently for a few minutes.

5 Add the peanut butter, coconut cream and chicken stock mixture, lime rind, lime juice and simmer, uncovered, for about 5 minutes, stirring frequently to prevent the mixture sticking to the base of the wok or pan.

6 Transfer the chilli coconut chicken to a warm serving dish, garnish with the red chilli and spring onion (scallion) tassel and serve with boiled rice.

COOK'S TIP

Serve jasmine rice with this spicy dish. It has a fragrant aroma that is well-suited to the flavours in this dish.

Chicken with Black Bean Sauce

This tasty chicken stir-fry is quick and easy to make and is full of fresh flavours and crunchy vegetables.

NUTRITIONAL INFORMATION

Calories	205	Sugars	.........4g
Protein	........25g	Fat	..........9g
Carbohydrate	....6g	Saturates	.......2g

 40 MINS 10 MINS

SERVES 4

I N G R E D I E N T S

425 g/15 oz chicken breasts,
  sliced thinly

pinch of salt

pinch of cornflour (cornstarch)

2 tbsp oil

1 garlic clove, crushed

1 tbsp black bean sauce

1 each small red and green (bell) pepper,
  cut into strips

1 red chilli, chopped finely

75 g/2¾ oz/1 cup mushrooms, sliced

1 onion, chopped

6 spring onions (scallions), chopped

salt and pepper

S E A S O N I N G

½ tsp salt

½ tsp sugar

3 tbsp chicken stock

1 tbsp dark soy sauce

2 tbsp beef stock

2 tbsp rice wine

1 tsp cornflour (cornstarch), blended
  with a little rice wine

1 Put the chicken strips in a bowl. Add a pinch of salt and a pinch of cornflour (cornstarch) and cover with water. Leave to stand for 30 minutes.

2 Heat 1 tablespoon of the oil in a wok or deep-sided frying pan (skillet) and stir-fry the chicken for 4 minutes.

3 Remove the chicken to a warm serving dish and clean the wok.

4 Add the remaining oil to the wok and add the garlic, black bean sauce, green and red (bell) peppers, chilli, mushrooms, onion and spring onions (scallions). Stir-fry for 2 minutes then return the chicken to the wok.

5 Add the seasoning ingredients, fry for 3 minutes and thicken with a little of the cornflour (cornstarch) blend. Serve with fresh noodles.

Szechuan Chilli Chicken

In China, the chicken pieces are chopped through the bone for this dish, but if you do not possess a cleaver, use filleted chicken meat.

NUTRITIONAL INFORMATION

Calories 218	Sugars 4g	
Protein 23g	Fat 9g	
Carbohydrate 8g	Saturates 2g	

45 MINS   15 MINS

SERVES 4

I N G R E D I E N T S

500 g/1 lb 2 oz chicken thighs

¼ tsp pepper

1 tbsp sugar

2 tsp light soy sauce

1 tsp dark soy sauce

1 tbsp rice wine or dry sherry

2 tsp cornflour (cornstarch)

2-3 tbsp vegetable oil

1-2 garlic cloves, crushed

2 spring onions (scallions), cut into short sections, with the green and white parts separated

4-6 small dried red chillies, soaked and seeded

2 tbsp crushed yellow bean sauce

about 150 ml/¼ pint/⅔ cup Chinese Stock (see page 14) or water

1 Cut or chop the chicken thighs into bite-sized pieces and marinate with the pepper, sugar, soy sauce, wine and cornflour (cornstarch) for 25-30 minutes.

2 Heat the oil in a pre-heated wok and stir-fry the chicken for about 1–2 minutes until lightly brown. Remove with a slotted spoon, transfer to a warm dish and reserve. Add the garlic, the white parts of the spring onions (scallions), the chillies and yellow bean sauce to the wok and stir-fry for about 30 seconds.

3 Return the chicken to the wok, stirring constantly for about 1-2 minutes, then add the stock or water, bring to the boil and cover. Braise over a medium heat for 5-6 minutes, stirring once or twice. Garnish with the green parts of the spring onions (scallions) and serve immediately.

COOK'S TIP

One of the striking features of Szechuan cooking is the quantity of chillies used. Food generally in this region is much hotter than elsewhere in China – people tend to keep a string of dry chillies hanging from the eaves of their houses.

Cumin-Spiced Chicken

Cumin seeds are more frequently associated with Indian cooking, but they are used in this Chinese recipe for their earthy flavour.

NUTRITIONAL INFORMATION

Calories	245	Sugars	.........9g
Protein	........28g	Fat	..........10g
Carbohydrate	....11g	Saturates	.......2g

 5 MINS   15 MINS

SERVES 4

INGREDIENTS

450 g/1 lb boneless, skinless chicken breasts

2 tbsp sunflower oil

1 clove garlic, crushed

1 tbsp cumin seeds

1 tbsp grated fresh ginger root

1 red chilli, deseeded and sliced

1 red (bell) pepper, deseeded and sliced

1 green (bell) pepper, deseeded and sliced

1 yellow (bell) pepper, deseeded and sliced

100 g/3½ oz/1 cup bean sprouts

350 g/12 oz pak choi or other green leaves

2 tbsp sweet chilli sauce

3 tbsp light soy sauce

deep-fried crispy ginger, to garnish (see Cook's Tip)

COOK'S TIP

To make the deep-fried ginger garnish, peel and thinly slice a large piece of root ginger. Carefully lower the slices of ginger into a wok or small pan of hot oil and cook for about 30 seconds. Transfer to kitchen paper and leave to drain thoroughly.

1 Using a sharp knife, slice the chicken breasts into thin strips.

2 Heat the oil in a large preheated wok.

3 Add the chicken to the wok and stir-fry for 5 minutes.

4 Add the garlic, cumin seeds, ginger and chilli to the wok, stirring to mix.

5 Add all the (bell) peppers to the wok and stir-fry for a further 5 minutes.

6 Toss in the bean sprouts and pak choi together with the sweet chilli sauce and soy sauce and continue to cook until the pak choi leaves start to wilt.

7 Transfer to warm serving bowls and garnish with deep-fried ginger (see Cook's Tip).

Spicy Peanut Chicken

This quick dish has many variations, but this version includes the classic combination of peanuts, chicken and chillies.

NUTRITIONAL INFORMATION

Calories	342	Sugars	.........3g
Protein	........25g	Fat	..........24g
Carbohydrate	....6g	Saturates	.......5g

5 MINS   10 MINS

SERVES 4

INGREDIENTS

300 g/10½ oz skinless, boneless
    chicken breast

2 tbsp peanut oil

125 g/4½ oz/1 cup shelled peanuts

1 fresh red chilli, sliced

1 green (bell) pepper, seeded and
    cut into strips

fried rice, to serve

SAUCE

150 ml/¼ pint/⅔ cup chicken stock

1 tbsp Chinese rice wine or
    dry sherry

1 tbsp light soy sauce

1½ tsp light brown sugar

2 garlic cloves, crushed

1 tsp grated fresh root ginger

1 tsp rice wine vinegar

1 tsp sesame oil

1 Trim any fat from the chicken and cut the meat into 2.5-cm/1-inch cubes. Set aside until required.

2 Heat the peanut oil in a preheated wok or frying pan (skillet).

3 Add the peanuts to the wok and stir-fry for 1 minute. Remove the peanuts with a slotted spoon and set aside.

4 Add the chicken to the wok and cook for 1–2 minutes.

5 Stir in the chilli and green (bell) pepper and cook for 1 minute. Remove from the wok with a slotted spoon and set aside.

6 Put half of the peanuts in a food processor and process until almost smooth. If necessary, add a little stock to form a softer paste. Alternatively, place them in a plastic bag and crush them with a rolling pin.

7 To make the sauce, add the chicken stock, Chinese rice wine or dry sherry, light soy sauce, light brown sugar, crushed garlic cloves, grated fresh root ginger and rice wine vinegar to the wok.

8 Heat the sauce without boiling and stir in the peanut purée, remaining peanuts, chicken, sliced red chilli and green (bell) pepper strips. Mix well until all the ingredients are thoroughly combined.

9 Sprinkle the sesame oil into the wok, stir and cook for 1 minute. Transfer the spicy peanut chicken to a warm serving dish and serve hot with fried rice.

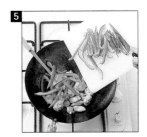

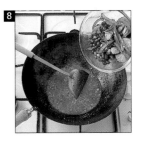

Yellow Bean Chicken

Ready-made yellow bean sauce is available from large supermarkets and Chinese food stores. It is made from yellow soya beans and is quite salty.

NUTRITIONAL INFORMATION

Calories 234   Sugars 1g
Protein ....26g   Fat 12g
Carbohydrate ....6g   Saturates 2g

25 MINS   10 MINS

SERVES 4

INGREDIENTS

450 g/1 lb skinless, boneless chicken breasts

1 egg white, beaten

1 tbsp cornflour (cornstarch)

1 tbsp rice wine vinegar

1 tbsp light soy sauce

1 tsp caster (superfine) sugar

3 tbsp vegetable oil

1 garlic clove, crushed

1-cm/½-inch piece fresh root ginger, grated

1 green (bell) pepper, seeded and diced

2 large mushrooms, sliced

3 tbsp yellow bean sauce

yellow or green (bell) pepper strips, to garnish

1 Trim any fat from the chicken and cut the meat into 2.5-cm/1-inch cubes.

2 Mix the egg white and cornflour (cornstarch) in a shallow bowl. Add the chicken and turn in the mixture to coat. Set aside for 20 minutes.

3 Mix the rice wine vinegar, soy sauce and caster (superfine) sugar in a bowl.

4 Remove the chicken from the egg white mixture.

5 Heat the oil in a preheated wok, add the chicken and stir-fry for 3–4 minutes, until golden brown. Remove the chicken from the wok with a slotted spoon, set aside and keep warm.

6 Add the garlic, ginger, (bell) pepper and mushrooms to the wok and stir-fry for 1–2 minutes.

7 Add the yellow bean sauce and cook for 1 minute. Stir in the vinegar mixture and return the chicken to the wok. Cook for 1–2 minutes and serve hot, garnished with (bell) pepper strips.

VARIATION

Black bean sauce would work equally well with this recipe. Although this would affect the appearance of the dish, as it is much darker in colour, the flavours would be compatible.

Peppered Chicken

Crushed mixed peppercorns coat tender, thin strips of chicken which are cooked with green and red (bell) peppers for a really colourful dish.

NUTRITIONAL INFORMATION

Calories	.219	Sugars	.6g
Protein	22g	Fat	.10g
Carbohydrate	.11g	Saturates	.2g

 5 MINS 15 MINS

SERVES 4

INGREDIENTS

2 tbsp tomato ketchup

2 tbsp soy sauce

450 g/1 lb boneless, skinless chicken breasts

2 tbsp crushed mixed peppercorns

2 tbsp sunflower oil

1 red (bell) pepper

1 green (bell) pepper

175 g/6 oz/2½ cups sugar snap peas

2 tbsp oyster sauce

1 Mix the tomato ketchup with the soy sauce in a bowl.

2 Using a sharp knife, slice the chicken into thin strips.

3 Toss the chicken in the tomato ketchup and soy sauce mixture until the chicken is well coated.

4 Sprinkle the crushed peppercorns on to a plate. Dip the coated chicken in the peppercorns until evenly coated.

5 Heat the sunflower oil in a preheated wok or large frying pan (skillet), until the oil is smoking.

6 Add the chicken to the wok and stir-fry for 5 minutes.

7 Using a sharp knife, deseed and slice the (bell) peppers.

8 Add the (bell) peppers to the wok together with the sugar snap peas and stir-fry for a further 5 minutes.

9 Add the oyster sauce and allow to bubble for 2 minutes. Transfer the peppered chicken to serving bowls and serve immediately.

VARIATION

Use mangetout (snow peas) instead of the sugar snap peas, if you prefer.

Chicken & Corn Sauté

This quick and healthy dish is stir-fried, which means you need use only the minimum of fat.

NUTRITIONAL INFORMATION

Calories 280	Sugars 7g
Protein 31g	Fat 11g
Carbohydrate 9g	Saturates 2g

 5 MINS   10 MINS

SERVES 4

I N G R E D I E N T S

4 skinless, boneless chicken breasts

250 g/9 oz/1⅓ cups baby sweetcorn (corn-on-the-cob)

250 g/9 oz mangetout (snow peas)

2 tbsp sunflower oil

1 tbsp sherry vinegar

1 tbsp honey

1 tbsp light soy sauce

1 tbsp sunflower seeds

pepper

rice or Chinese egg noodles, to serve

1 Using a sharp knife, slice the chicken breasts into long, thin strips.

2 Cut the baby sweetcorn in half lengthways and top and tail the mangetout (snow peas).

3 Heat the sunflower oil in a preheated wok or a wide frying pan (skillet).

4 Add the chicken and fry over a fairly high heat, stirring, for 1 minute.

5 Add the baby sweetcorn and mangetout (snow peas) and stir-fry over a moderate heat for 5–8 minutes, until evenly cooked. The vegetables should still be slightly crunchy.

 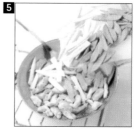 

6 Mix together the sherry vinegar, honey and soy sauce in a small bowl.

7 Stir the vinegar mixture into the pan with the sunflower seeds.

8 Season well with pepper. Cook, stirring, for 1 minute.

9 Serve the chicken & corn sauté hot with rice or Chinese egg noodles.

VARIATION

Rice vinegar or balsamic vinegar makes a good substitute for the sherry vinegar.

Chicken with (Bell) Peppers

Red (bell) pepper or celery can also be used in this recipe, the method is the same.

NUTRITIONAL INFORMATION

Calories 113   Sugars 1g
Protein . . . . .17g   Fat 3g
Carbohydrate . . . .4g   Saturates 1g

 5 MINS   5 MINS

SERVES 4

I N G R E D I E N T S

300 g/10½ oz boned, skinned chicken breast

1 tsp salt

½ egg white

2 tsp cornflour (cornstarch) paste (see page 15)

1 medium green (bell) pepper, cored and seeded

300 ml/½ pint/1¼ cups vegetable oil

1 spring onion (scallion), finely shredded

a few strips of ginger root, thinly shredded

1-2 red chillies, seeded and thinly shredded

½ tsp sugar

1 tbsp rice wine or dry sherry

a few drops of sesame oil

 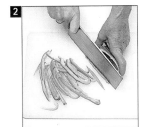 

1 Cut the chicken breast into strips. Mix the chicken with a pinch of the salt, the egg white and cornflour (cornstarch).

2 Cut the green (bell) pepper into fairly thin shreds.

3 Heat the oil in a preheated wok, and deep-fry the chicken strips in batches for about 1 minute, or until the chicken changes colour. Remove the chicken strips with a slotted spoon, pat dry on kitchen paper (paper towels) and keep warm.

4 Pour off the excess oil from the wok, leaving about 1 tablespoon. Add the spring onion (scallion), ginger, chillies and green (bell) pepper and stir-fry for 1 minute.

5 Return the chicken to the wok with the remaining salt, the sugar and wine or sherry. Stir-fry for another minute, sprinkle with sesame oil and serve immediately.

COOK'S TIP

Rice wine is used everywhere in China for both cooking and drinking. Made from glutinous rice, it is known as 'yellow wine' because of its rich amber colour. Sherry is the best substitute as a cooking ingredient.

Braised Chicken

This is a delicious way to cook a whole chicken. It has a wonderful glaze, which is served as a sauce.

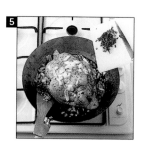

NUTRITIONAL INFORMATION

Calories 294   Sugars 9g
Protein . . . . .31g   Fat 15g
Carbohydrate . . .10g   Saturates 3g

 5 MINS   1¼ HOURS

SERVES 4

I N G R E D I E N T S

1.5 kg/3 lb 5 oz chicken

3 tbsp vegetable oil

1 tbsp peanut oil

2 tbsp dark brown sugar

5 tbsp dark soy sauce

150 ml/¼ pint/⅔ cup water

2 garlic cloves, crushed

1 small onion, chopped

1 fresh red chilli, chopped

celery leaves and chives,
  to garnish

1 Preheat a large wok or large frying pan (skillet).

2 Clean the chicken inside and out with damp kitchen paper (paper towels).

3 Put the vegetable oil and peanut oil in the wok, add the dark brown sugar and heat gently until the sugar caramelizes.

4 Stir the soy sauce into the wok. Add the chicken and turn it in the mixture to coat thoroughly on all sides.

5 Add the water, garlic, onion and chilli. Cover and simmer, turning the chicken occasionally, for about 1 hour, or

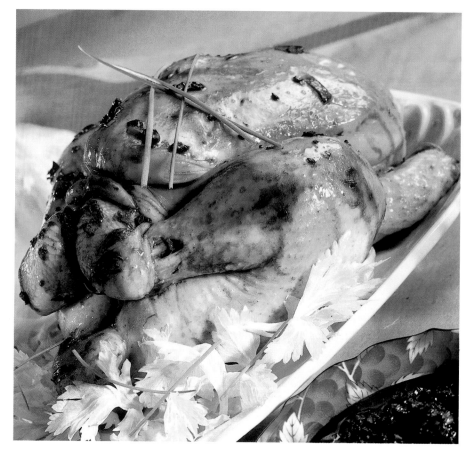

until cooked through. Test by piercing a thigh with the point of a knife or a skewer – the juices will run clear when the chicken is cooked.

6 Remove the chicken from the wok and set aside. Increase the heat and reduce the sauce in the wok until thickened. Transfer the chicken to a serving plate, garnish with celery leaves and chives and serve with the sauce.

COOK'S TIP

For a spicier sauce, add 1 tbsp finely chopped fresh root ginger and 1 tbsp ground Szechuan peppercorns with the chilli in step 5.

Honey & Soy Chicken

Clear honey is often added to Chinese recipes for sweetness. It combines well with the saltiness of the soy sauce.

NUTRITIONAL INFORMATION

Calories	279	Sugars	........10g
Protein	........38g	Fat	...........8g
Carbohydrate	...12g	Saturates	.......2g

 35 MINS   25 MINS

SERVES 4

INGREDIENTS

2 tbsp clear honey

3 tbsp light soy sauce

1 tsp Chinese five-spice powder

1 tbsp sweet sherry

1 clove garlic, crushed

8 chicken thighs

1 tbsp sunflower oil

1 red chilli

100 g/3½ oz/1¼ cups baby corn cobs, halved

8 spring onions (scallions), sliced

150 g/5½ oz/1½ cups bean sprouts

1 Mix together the honey, soy sauce, Chinese five-spice powder, sherry and garlic in a large bowl.

2 Using a sharp knife, make 3 slashes in the skin of each chicken thigh. Brush the honey and soy marinade over the chicken thighs, cover and leave to stand for at least 30 minutes.

3 Heat the oil in a large preheated wok. Add the chicken and cook over a fairly high heat for 12–15 minutes, or until the chicken browns and the skin begins to crispen. Remove the chicken with a slotted spoon and keep warm until required.

4 Using a sharp knife, deseed and very finely chop the chilli.

5 Add the chilli, corn cobs, spring onions (scallions) and bean sprouts to the wok and stir-fry for 5 minutes.

6 Return the chicken to the wok and mix all of the ingredients together until completely heated through. Transfer to serving plates and serve immediately.

COOK'S TIP

Chinese five-spice powder is found in most large supermarkets and is a blend of star anise, fennel seeds, cloves, cinnamon bark and Szechuan pepper.

Peanut Sesame Chicken

Sesame seeds and peanuts give extra crunch and flavour to this stir-fry and the fruit juice glaze gives a lovely shiny coating to the sauce.

NUTRITIONAL INFORMATION

Calories 435   Sugars 10g
Protein ....38g   Fat 26g
Carbohydrate ...14g   Saturates 4g

10 MINS   15 MINS

SERVES 4

I N G R E D I E N T S

2 tbsp vegetable oil

2 tbsp sesame oil

500 g/1 lb 2 oz boneless, skinned chicken breasts, sliced into strips

250 g/9 oz broccoli, divided into small florets

250 g/9 oz baby or dwarf corn, halved if large

1 small red (bell) pepper, cored, seeded and sliced

2 tbsp soy sauce

250 ml/9 fl oz/1 cup orange juice

2 tsp cornflour (cornstarch)

2 tbsp toasted sesame seeds

60 g/2 oz/⅓ cup roasted, shelled, unsalted peanuts

rice or noodles, to serve

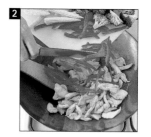

1 Heat the vegetable oil and sesame oil in a large, heavy-based frying pan (skillet) or wok until smoking. Add the chicken strips and stir-fry until browned, about 4-5 minutes.

2 Add the broccoli, corn and red (bell) pepper and stir-fry for a further 1-2 minutes.

3 Meanwhile, mix the soy sauce with the orange juice and cornflour (cornstarch). Stir into the chicken and vegetable mixture, stirring constantly until the sauce has slightly thickened and a glaze develops.

4 Stir in the sesame seeds and peanuts, mixing well. Heat the stir-fry for a further 3-4 minutes.

5 Transfer the stir-fry to a warm serving dish and serve with rice or noodles.

COOK'S TIP

Make sure you use the unsalted variety of peanuts or the dish will be too salty, as the soy sauce adds saltiness.

Chicken Fu-Yung

Although commonly described as an omelette, a fu-yung ('white lotus petals') should use egg whites only to create a very delicate texture.

NUTRITIONAL INFORMATION

Calories	220	Sugars	.........1g
Protein	........16g	Fat	..........14g
Carbohydrate	....7g	Saturates	.......3g

5 MINS   5 MINS

SERVES 4

INGREDIENTS

175 g/6 oz chicken breast fillet, skinned

½ tsp salt

pepper

1 tsp rice wine or dry sherry

1 tbsp cornflour (cornstarch)

3 eggs

½ tsp finely chopped spring onions (scallions)

3 tbsp vegetable oil

125 g/4½ oz green peas

1 tsp light soy sauce

salt

few drops of sesame oil

1 Cut the chicken across the grain into very small, paper-thin slices, using a cleaver. Place the chicken slices in a shallow dish.

2 In a small bowl, mix together ½ teaspoon salt, pepper, rice wine or dry sherry and cornflour (cornstarch).

3 Pour the mixture over the chicken slices in the dish, turning the chicken until well coated.

4 Beat the eggs in a small bowl with a pinch of salt and the spring onions (scallions).

5 Heat the vegetable oil in a preheated wok, add the chicken slices and stir-fry for about 1 minute, making sure that the slices are kept separated.

6 Pour the beaten eggs over the chicken, and lightly scramble until set. Do not stir too vigorously, or the mixture will break up in the oil. Stir the oil from the bottom of the wok so that the foo-yung rises to the surface.

7 Add the peas, light soy sauce and salt to taste and blend well. Transfer to warm serving dishes, sprinkle with sesame oil and serve.

COOK'S TIP

If available, chicken *goujons* can be used for this dish: these are small, delicate strips of chicken which require no further cutting and are very tender.

Crispy Chicken

In this recipe, the chicken is brushed with a syrup and deep-fried until golden. It is a little time consuming, but well worth the effort.

NUTRITIONAL INFORMATION

Calories	283	Sugars	.........8g
Protein	........29g	Fat	..........15g
Carbohydrate	....8g	Saturates	.......3g

15 HOURS   35 MINS

SERVES 4

I N G R E D I E N T S

1.5 kg/3 lb 5 oz oven-ready chicken

2 tbsp clear honey

2 tsp Chinese five-spice powder

2 tbsp rice wine vinegar

850 ml/1½ pints/3 ¾ cups vegetable oil, for deep-frying

chilli sauce, to serve

1 Rinse the chicken inside and out under cold running water and pat dry with kitchen paper (paper towels).

2 Bring a large saucepan of water to the boil and remove from the heat. Place the chicken in the water, cover and set aside for 20 minutes.

3 Remove the chicken from the water and pat dry with absorbent kitchen paper (paper towels). Cool and leave to chill in the refrigerator overnight.

4 To make the glaze, mix the honey, Chinese five-spice powder and rice wine vinegar.

5 Brush some of the glaze all over the chicken and return to the refrigerator for 20 minutes.

6 Repeat this process of glazing and refrigerating the chicken until all of the glaze has been used up. Return the chicken to the refrigerator for at least 2 hours after the final coating.

7 Using a cleaver or heavy kitchen knife, open the chicken out by splitting it through the centre through the breast and then cut each half into 4 pieces.

8 Heat the oil for deep-frying in a wok until almost smoking. Reduce the heat and fry each piece of chicken for 5–7 minutes, until golden and cooked through. Remove from the oil with a slotted spoon and drain on absorbent kitchen paper (paper towels).

9 Transfer to a serving dish and serve hot with a little chilli sauce.

COOK'S TIP

If it is easier, use chicken portions instead of a whole chicken. You could also use chicken legs for this recipe, if you prefer.

Lemon & Sesame Chicken

Sesame seeds have a strong flavour which adds nuttiness to recipes.
They are perfect for coating these thin chicken strips.

NUTRITIONAL INFORMATION

Calories	273	Sugars	.........5g
Protein	........29g	Fat	..........13g
Carbohydrate	....11g	Saturates	.......3g

 10 MINS   10 MINS

SERVES 4

I N G R E D I E N T S

4 boneless, skinless chicken breasts

1 egg white

25 g/1 oz/2 tbsp sesame seeds

2 tbsp vegetable oil

1 onion, sliced

1 tbsp demerara (brown crystal)
   sugar

finely grated zest and juice of
   1 lemon

3 tbsp lemon curd

200 g/7 oz can water chestnuts,
   drained

lemon zest, to garnish

COOK'S TIP

Water chestnuts are
commonly added to Chinese
recipes for their crunchy
texture as they do not have a
great deal of flavour.

1 Place the chicken breasts between 2 sheets of cling film (plastic wrap) and pound with a rolling pin to flatten. Slice the chicken into thin strips.

2 Whisk the egg white until light and foamy. Dip the chicken strips into the egg white, then coat in the sesame seeds.

3 Heat the oil in a wok and stir-fry the onion for 2 minutes until softened.

4 Add the chicken to the wok and stir-fry for 5 minutes, or until the chicken turns golden.

5 Mix the sugar, lemon zest, lemon juice and lemon curd and add to the wok. Allow it to bubble slightly.

6 Slice the water chestnuts thinly, add to the wok and cook for 2 minutes. Garnish with lemon zest and serve hot.

Chicken with Chilli & Basil

Chicken drumsticks are cooked in a delicious sauce and served with deep-fried basil for colour and flavour.

NUTRITIONAL INFORMATION

Calories	196	Sugars	.........2g
Protein	........23g	Fat	..........10g
Carbohydrate	....3g	Saturates	.......2g

 5 MINS   30 MINS

SERVES 4

I N G R E D I E N T S

8 chicken drumsticks

2 tbsp soy sauce

1 tbsp sunflower oil

1 red chilli

100 g/3½ oz carrots, cut into thin sticks

6 celery stalks, cut into sticks

3 tbsp sweet chilli sauce

oil, for frying

about 50 fresh basil leaves

1 Remove the skin from the chicken drumsticks if desired. Make 3 slashes in each drumstick. Brush the drumsticks with the soy sauce.

2 Heat the sunflower oil in a preheated wok and fry the drumsticks for 20 minutes, turning frequently, until they are cooked through.

3 Deseed and finely chop the chilli. Add the chilli, carrots and celery to the wok and cook for a further 5 minutes. Stir in the chilli sauce, cover and allow to bubble gently whilst preparing the basil leaves.

4 Heat a little oil in a heavy based pan. Carefully add the basil leaves – stand well away from the pan and protect

your hand with a tea towel (dish cloth) as they may spit a little. Cook the basil leaves for about 30 seconds or until they begin to curl up but not brown. Leave the leaves to drain on absorbent kitchen paper (paper towels).

5 Arrange the cooked chicken, vegetables and pan juices on to a warm serving plate, garnish with the deep-fried crispy basil leaves and serve immediately.

COOK'S TIP

Basil has a very strong flavour which is perfect with chicken and Chinese flavourings. You could use baby spinach instead of the basil, if you prefer.

Aromatic & Crispy Duck

As it is very time-consuming to make the pancakes, buy ready-made ones from Oriental stores, or use crisp lettuce leaves as the wrapper.

NUTRITIONAL INFORMATION

Calories	169	Sugars	.........1g
Protein	.........7g	Fat	...........11g
Carbohydrate	....7g	Saturates	.......3g

   7 HOURS   5 HOURS

SERVES 4

I N G R E D I E N T S

2 large duckling quarters

1 tsp salt

3-4 pieces star anise

1 tsp Szechuan red peppercorns

1 tsp cloves

2 cinnamon sticks, broken into pieces

2-3 spring onions (scallions), cut into short sections

4-5 small slices ginger root

3-4 tbsp rice wine or dry sherry

vegetable oil, for deep-frying

TO SERVE

12 ready-made pancakes or 12 crisp lettuce leaves

hoisin or plum sauce

¼ cucumber, thinly shredded

3-4 spring onions (scallions), thinly shredded

1 Rub the duck with the salt and arrange the star anise, peppercorns, cloves and cinnamon on top. Sprinkle with the spring onions (scallions), ginger and wine and marinate for at least 3-4 hours.

2 Arrange the duck pieces on a plate that will fit inside a bamboo steamer. Pour some hot water into a wok, place the bamboo steamer on top, sitting on a trivet. Add the duck and cover with the bamboo lid. Steam the duck over a high heat for 2-3 hours, until tender and cooked through. Top up the hot water from time to time as required. Remove the duck and leave to cool for at least 4-5 hours so the duck becomes crispy.

3 Pour off the water and wipe the wok dry. Pour in the oil and heat until smoking. Deep-fry the duck pieces, skin-side down, for 4-5 minutes or until crisp and brown. Remove and drain.

4 To serve, scrape the meat off the bone, place about 1 teaspoon of hoisin or plum sauce on the centre of a pancake (or lettuce leaf), add a few pieces of cucumber and spring onion (scallion) with a portion of the duck meat. Wrap up to form a small parcel and eat with your fingers.

Fruity Duck Stir-Fry

The pineapple and plum sauce add a sweetness and fruity flavour to this colourful recipe which blends well with the duck.

NUTRITIONAL INFORMATION

Calories 241	Sugars 7g
Protein 26g	Fat 8g
Carbohydrate . . .16g	Saturates 2g

🥢 5 MINS   🕐 25 MINS

SERVES 4

I N G R E D I E N T S

4 duck breasts

1 tsp Chinese five-spice powder

1 tbsp cornflour (cornstarch)

1 tbsp chilli oil

225 g/8 oz baby onions, peeled

2 cloves garlic, crushed

100 g/3½ oz/1 cup baby corn cobs

175 g/6 oz/1¼ cups canned pineapple chunks

6 spring onions (scallions), sliced

100 g/3½ oz/1 cup bean sprouts

2 tbsp plum sauce

1 Remove any skin from the duck breasts. Cut the duck into thin slices.

2 Mix the five-spice powder and the cornflour (cornstarch). Toss the duck in the mixture until well coated.

3 Heat the oil in a preheated wok. Stir-fry the duck for 10 minutes, or until just begining to crispen around the edges. Remove from the wok and set aside.

4 Add the onions and garlic to the wok and stir-fry for 5 minutes, or until softened. Add the baby corn cobs and stir-fry for a further 5 minutes. Add the pineapple, spring onions (scallions) and bean sprouts and stir-fry for 3–4 minutes. Stir in the plum sauce.

5 Return the cooked duck to the wok and toss until well mixed. Transfer to warm serving dishes and serve hot.

COOK'S TIP

Buy pineapple chunks in natural juice rather than syrup for a fresher flavour. If you can only obtain pineapple in syrup, rinse it in cold water and drain thoroughly before using.

Duck with Ginger & Lime

Just the thing for a lazy summer day – roasted duck sliced and served with a dressing made of ginger, lime juice, sesame oil and fish sauce.

NUTRITIONAL INFORMATION

Calories	529	Sugars	.........3g
Protein	........38g	Fat	..........41g
Carbohydrate	....3g	Saturates	.......6g

20 MINS   25 MINS

SERVES 4

INGREDIENTS

3 boneless Barbary duck breasts, about 250 g/9 oz each

salt

DRESSING

125 ml/4 fl oz/½ cup olive oil

2 tsp sesame oil

2 tbsp lime juice

grated rind and juice of 1 orange

2 tsp fish sauce

1 tbsp grated ginger root

1 garlic clove, crushed

2 tsp light soy sauce

3 spring onions (scallions), finely chopped

1 tsp sugar

about 250 g/9 oz assorted salad leaves

orange slices, to garnish (optional)

1 Wash the duck breasts, dry on kitchen paper (paper towels), then cut in half. Prick the skin all over with a fork and season well with salt. Place the duck pieces, skin-side down, on a wire rack or trivet over a roasting tin (pan).

2 Cook the duck in a preheated oven for 10 minutes, then turn over and cook for a further 12-15 minutes, or until the duck is cooked, but still pink in the centre, and the skin is crisp.

3 To make the dressing, beat the olive oil and sesame oil with the lime juice, orange rind and juice, fish sauce, grated ginger root, garlic, light soy sauce, spring onions (scallions) and sugar until well blended.

4 Remove the duck from the oven, and allow to cool. Using a sharp knife, cut the duck into thick slices.

5 Add a little of the dressing to moisten and coat the duck.

6 To serve, arrange assorted salad leaves on a serving dish. Top with the sliced duck breasts and drizzle with the remaining salad dressing.

7 Garnish with orange slices, if using, then serve at once.

Barbecued (Grilled) Duckling

The sweet, spicy marinade used in this recipe gives the duckling a subtle flavour of the Orient.

NUTRITIONAL INFORMATION

Calories	249	Sugars	........20g
Protein	........27g	Fat	...........6g
Carbohydrate	...23g	Saturates	.......2g

 6¼ HOURS   30 MINS

SERVES 4

I N G R E D I E N T S

3 cloves garlic, crushed

150 ml/5 fl oz/⅔ cup light soy sauce

5 tbsp light muscovado sugar

2.5 cm/1 inch piece root (fresh) ginger, grated

1 tbsp chopped, fresh coriander (cilantro)

1 tsp five-spice powder

4 duckling breasts

sprig of fresh coriander (cilantro), to garnish (optional)

1 To make the marinade, mix together the garlic, soy sauce, sugar, grated ginger, chopped coriander (cilantro) and five-spice powder in a small bowl until well combined.

2 Place the duckling breasts in a shallow, non-metallic dish and pour over the marinade. Carefully turn over the duckling so that it is fully coated with the marinade on both sides.

3 Cover the bowl with cling film (plastic wrap) and leave to marinate for 1-6 hours, turning the duckling once or twice so that the marinade is fully absorbed.

4 Remove the duckling from the marinade, reserving the marinade for basting.

5 Barbecue (grill) the duckling breasts over hot coals for about 20–30 minutes, turning and basting frequently with the reserved marinade, using a pastry brush.

6 Cut the duckling into slices and transfer to warm serving plates. Serve the barbecued (grilled) duckling garnished with a sprig of fresh coriander (cilantro), if using.

COOK'S TIP

Duckling is quite a fatty meat so there is no need to add oil to the marinade. However, you must remember to oil the barbecue (grill) rack to prevent the duckling from sticking. Oil the barbecue (grill) rack well away from the barbecue (grill) to avoid any danger of a flare-up.

Sweet Mango Chicken

The sweet, scented flavour of mango gives this dish its characteristic sweetness.

NUTRITIONAL INFORMATION

Calories	244	Sugars 18g
Protein	........27g	Fat 7g
Carbohydrate	...2.1g	Saturates 2g

10 MINS   15 MINS

SERVES 4

INGREDIENTS

1 tbsp sunflower oil

6 skinless, boneless chicken thighs

1 ripe mango

2 cloves garlic, crushed

225 g/8 oz leeks, shredded

100 g/3½ oz/1 cup bean sprouts

150 ml/¼ pint/⅔ cup mango juice

1 tbsp white wine vinegar

2 tbsp clear honey

2 tbsp tomato ketchup

1 tsp cornflour (cornstarch)

COOK'S TIP

Mango juice is avaialable in jars from most supermarkets and is quite thick and sweet. If it is unavailable, purée and sieve a ripe mango and add a little water to make up the required quantity.

1 Heat the sunflower oil in a large preheated wok.

2 Cut the chicken into bite-sized cubes, add to the wok and stir-fry over a high heat for 10 minutes, tossing frequently until the chicken is cooked through and golden in colour.

3 Peel and slice the mango and add to the wok with the garlic, leeks and bean sprouts. Stir-fry for a further 2–3 minutes, or until softened.

4 Mix together the mango juice, white wine vinegar, honey, tomato ketchup and cornflour (cornstarch). Pour into the wok and stir-fry for a further 2 minutes, or until the juices start to thicken.

5 Transfer to a warmed serving dish and serve immediately.

Duck in Spicy Sauce

Chinese five-spice powder gives a lovely flavour to this sliced duck, and the chilli adds a little subtle heat.

NUTRITIONAL INFORMATION

Calories ....162 Sugars 2g
Protein ....20g Fat 7g
Carbohydrate ....3g Saturates 2g

🄖 🄖 🄖

 5 MINS   🕐 25 MINS

SERVES 4

INGREDIENTS

1 tbsp vegetable oil

1 tsp grated fresh root ginger

1 garlic clove, crushed

1 fresh red chilli, chopped

350 g/12 oz skinless, boneless duck meat, cut into strips

125 g/4½ oz cauliflower, cut into florets

60 g/2 oz mangetout (snow peas)

60 g/2 oz baby corn cobs, halved lengthways

300 ml/½ pint/1¼ cups chicken stock

1 tsp Chinese five-spice powder

2 tsp Chinese rice wine or dry sherry

1 tsp cornflour (cornstarch)

2 tsp water

1 tsp sesame oil

1 Heat the oil in a wok. Lower the heat slightly, add the ginger, garlic, chilli and duck and stir-fry for 2-3 minutes. Remove from the wok and set aside.

2 Add the vegetables to the wok and stir-fry for 2-3 minutes. Pour off any excess oil from the wok and push the vegetables to one side.

3 Return the duck to the wok and pour in the stock. Sprinkle the Chinese five-spice powder over the top, stir in the wine or sherry and cook over a low heat for 15 minutes, or until the duck is tender.

4 Blend the cornflour (cornstarch) with the water to form a paste and stir into the wok with the sesame oil. Bring to the boil, stirring until the sauce has thickened and cleared. Transfer the duck and spicy sauce to a warm serving dish and serve immediately.

COOK'S TIP

Omit the chilli for a milder dish, or deseed the chilli before adding it to remove some of the heat.

Duck with Leek & Cabbage

Duck is a strongly-flavoured meat which benefits from the added citrus peel to counteract this rich taste.

NUTRITIONAL INFORMATION

Calories ....192 Sugars 5g
Protein ....26g Fat 7g
Carbohydrate ....6g Saturates 2g

10 MINS   40 MINS

SERVES 4

INGREDIENTS

4 duck breasts

350 g/12 oz green cabbage, thinly shredded

225 g/8 oz leeks, sliced

finely grated zest of 1 orange

6 tbsp oyster sauce

1 tsp toasted sesame seeds, to serve

1 Heat a large wok and dry-fry the duck breasts, with the skin on, for about 5 minutes on each side (you may need to do this in 2 batches).

2 Remove the duck breasts from the wok and transfer to a clean board.

3 Using a sharp knife, cut the duck breasts into thin slices.

4 Remove all but 1 tablespoon of the fat from the duck left in the wok; discard the rest.

5 Using a sharp knife, thinly shred the green cabbage.

6 Add the leeks, green cabbage and orange zest to the wok and stir-fry for about 5 minutes, or until the vegetables have softened.

7 Return the duck to the wok and heat through for 2–3 minutes.

8 Drizzle the oyster sauce over the mixture in the wok, toss well until all the ingredients are combined and then heat through.

9 Scatter the stir-fry with toasted sesame seeds, transfer to a warm serving dish and serve hot.

VARIATION

Use Chinese leaves (cabbage) for a lighter, sweeter flavour instead of the green cabbage, if you prefer.

Duck with Lime & Kiwi Fruit

Tender breasts of duck served in thin slices, with a sweet but very tangy lime and wine sauce, full of pieces of kiwi fruit.

NUTRITIONAL INFORMATION

Calories	264	Sugars	.......20g
Protein	........20g	Fat	..........10g
Carbohydrate	...21g	Saturates	.......2g

1¼ HOURS   15 MINS

SERVES 4

INGREDIENTS

4 boneless or part-boned
   duck breasts

grated rind and juice of 2 large limes

2 tbsp sunflower oil

4 spring onions (scallions), thinly
   sliced diagonally

125 g/4½ oz carrots, cut into
   matchsticks

6 tbsp dry white wine

60 g/2 oz/¼ cup white sugar

2 kiwi fruit, peeled, halved and sliced

salt and pepper

parsley sprigs and lime halves tied in knots
   (see Cook's Tip), to garnish

1 Trim any fat from the duck, then prick the skin all over with a fork and lay in a shallow dish. Add half the grated lime and half the juice to the duck breasts, rubbing in thoroughly. Leave to stand in a cool place for at least 1 hour, turning the breasts at least once.

2 Drain the duck breasts, reserving the marinade. Heat 1 tbsp of oil in a wok. Add the duck and fry quickly to seal all over then lower the heat and continue to cook for about 5 minutes, turning several times until just cooked through and well browned all over. Remove and keep warm.

3 Wipe the wok clean with kitchen paper (paper towels) and heat the remaining oil. Add the spring onions (scallions) and carrots and stir-fry for 1 minute, then add the remaining lime marinade, wine and sugar. Bring to the boil and simmer for 2-3 minutes until slightly syrupy.

4 Add the duck breasts to the sauce, season and add the kiwi fruit. Stir-fry for a minute or until really hot and both the duck and kiwi fruit are well coated in the sauce.

5 Cut each duck breast into slices, leaving a 'hinge' at one end, open out into a fan shape and arrange on plates. Spoon the sauce over the duck, sprinkle with the remaining pieces of lime peel, garnish and serve.

COOK'S TIP

To make the garnish, trim a piece off the base of each lime half so they stand upright. Pare off a thin strip of rind from the top of the lime halves, about 5 mm/¼ inch thick, but do not detach it. Tie the strip into a knot with the end bending over the cut surface of the lime.

Duck with Broccoli & Peppers

This is a colourful dish using different coloured (bell) peppers
and broccoli to make it both tasty and appealing to the eye.

NUTRITIONAL INFORMATION

Calories 261	Sugars 3g	
Protein 26g	Fat 13g	
Carbohydrate 11g	Saturates 2g	

🍲 35 MINS   🕐 15 MINS

SERVES 4

INGREDIENTS

1 egg white

2 tbsp cornflour (cornstarch)

450 g/1 lb skinless, boneless duck meat

vegetable oil, for deep-frying

1 red (bell) pepper, seeded and diced

1 yellow (bell) pepper, seeded and diced

125 g/4½ oz small broccoli florets

1 garlic clove, crushed

2 tbsp light soy sauce

2 tsp Chinese rice wine or dry sherry

1 tsp light brown sugar

125 ml/4 fl oz/½ cup chicken stock

2 tsp sesame seeds

1 In a mixing bowl, beat together the egg white and cornflour (cornstarch).

2 Using a sharp knife, cut the duck into 2.5-cm/1-inch cubes and stir into the egg white mixture. Leave to stand for 30 minutes.

3 Heat the oil for deep-frying in a preheated wok or heavy-based frying pan (skillet) until almost smoking.

4 Remove the duck from the egg white mixture, add to the wok and fry in the oil for 4–5 minutes, until crisp. Remove the duck from the oil with a slotted spoon and drain on kitchen paper (paper towels).

5 Add the (bell) peppers and broccoli to the wok and fry for 2–3 minutes. Remove with a slotted spoon and drain on kitchen paper (paper towels).

6 Pour all but 2 tablespoons of the oil from the wok and return to the heat. Add the garlic and stir-fry for 30 seconds. Stir in the soy sauce, Chinese rice wine or sherry, sugar and chicken stock and bring to the boil.

7 Stir in the duck and reserved vegetables and cook for 1–2 minutes.

8 Carefully spoon the duck and vegetables on to a warmed serving dish and sprinkle with the sesame seeds. Serve immediately.

Duck with Mangoes

Use fresh mangoes in this recipe for a terrific flavour and colour. If they are unavailable, use canned mangoes and rinse them before using.

NUTRITIONAL INFORMATION

Calories . . . . . . .235 Sugars 6g
Protein . . . . .23g Fat 14g
Carbohydrate . . . .6g Saturates 2g

5 MINS   35 MINS

SERVES 4

INGREDIENTS

2 medium-size ripe mangoes

300 ml/½ pint/1¼ cups chicken stock

2 garlic cloves, crushed

1 tsp grated fresh root ginger

3 tbsp vegetable oil

2 large skinless duck breasts, about 225 g/8 oz each

1 tsp wine vinegar

1 tsp light soy sauce

1 leek, sliced

freshly chopped parsley, to garnish

1 Peel the mangoes and cut the flesh from each side of the stones (pits). Cut the flesh into strips.

2 Put half of the mango pieces and the chicken stock in a food processor and process until smooth. Alternatively, press half of the mangoes through a fine sieve and mix with the stock.

3 Rub the garlic and ginger over the duck. Heat the vegetable oil in a preheated wok and cook the duck breasts, turning, until sealed. Reserve the oil in the wok and remove the duck.

4 Place the duck on a rack set over a roasting tin (pan) and cook in a preheated oven, at 220°C/425°F/Gas Mark 7, for 20 minutes, until the duck is cooked through.

5 Meanwhile, place the mango and stock mixture in a saucepan and add the wine vinegar and light soy sauce.

6 Bring the mixture in the saucepan to the boil and cook over a high heat, stirring, until reduced by half.

7 Heat the oil reserved in the wok and stir-fry the sliced leek and remaining mango for 1 minute. Remove from the wok, transfer to a serving dish and keep warm until required.

8 Slice the cooked duck breasts and arrange the slices on top of the leek and mango mixture. Pour the sauce over the duck slices, garnish and serve.

Duck with Pineapple

For best results, use ready-cooked duck meat, widely available from Chinese restaurants and takeaways.

NUTRITIONAL INFORMATION

Calories	187	Sugars 7g
Protein	........10g	Fat 12g
Carbohydrate	....11g	Saturates 2g

 25 MINS   10 MINS

SERVES 4

INGREDIENTS

125-175 g/4½-6 oz cooked duck meat

3 tbsp vegetable oil

1 small onion, thinly shredded

2-3 slices ginger root, thinly shredded

1 spring onion (scallion), thinly shredded

1 small carrot, thinly shredded

125 g/4½ oz canned pineapple, cut into small slices

½ tsp salt

1 tbsp red rice vinegar

2 tbsp syrup from the pineapple

1 tbsp cornflour (cornstarch) paste (see page 15)

black bean sauce, to serve (optional)

1 Using a sharp knife or metal cleaver, cut the cooked duck meat into thin even-sized strips and set aside until required.

2 Heat the oil in a preheated wok or large heavy-based frying pan (skillet).

3 Add the shredded onion and stir-fry until the shreds are opaque.

4 Add the slices of ginger root, spring onion (scallion) shreds and carrot shreds to the wok and stir-fry for about 1 minute.

5 Add the duck shreds and pineapple to the wok together with the salt, rice vinegar and the pineapple syrup. Stir until the mixture is well blended.

6 Add the cornflour (cornstarch) paste and stir for 1-2 minutes until the sauce has thickened.

7 Transfer to a serving dish and serve with black bean sauce, if desired.

COOK'S TIP

Red rice vinegar is made from fermented rice. It has a distinctive dark colour and depth of flavour. If unavailable, use red wine vinegar, which is similar in flavour.

Honey-Glazed Duck

The honey and soy glaze gives a wonderful sheen and flavour to the duck skin. Such a simple recipe, yet the result is unutterably delicious.

NUTRITIONAL INFORMATION

Calories	176	Sugars	.........8g
Protein	........22g	Fat	...........5g
Carbohydrate	...10g	Saturates	.......1g

  2¼ HOURS   30 MINS

SERVES 4

I N G R E D I E N T S

1 tsp dark soy sauce

2 tbsp clear honey

1 tsp garlic vinegar

2 garlic cloves, crushed

1 tsp ground star anise

2 tsp cornflour (cornstarch)

2 tsp water

2 large boneless duck breasts, about
   225 g/8 oz each

celery leaves, cucumber wedges and
   snipped chives, to garnish

1 Mix together the soy sauce, honey, garlic vinegar, garlic and star anise.

2 Blend the cornflour (cornstarch) with the water to form a smooth paste and stir it into the soy sauce mixture.

3 Place the duck breasts in a shallow ovenproof dish. Brush with the soy marinade, turning to coat them completely. Cover and leave to marinate in the refrigerator for at least 2 hours, or overnight if possible.

4 Remove the duck from the marinade and cook in a preheated oven, at 220°C/425°F/Gas Mark 7, for 20–25 minutes, basting frequently with the glaze.

5 Remove the duck from the oven and transfer to a preheated grill (broiler). Grill (broil) for about 3–4 minutes to caramelize the top.

6 Remove the duck from the grill (broiler) pan and cut into thin slices. Arrange the duck slices in a warm serving dish, garnish with celery leaves, cucumber wedges and snipped chives and serve immediately.

COOK'S TIP

If the duck begins to burn slightly while it is cooking in the oven, cover with foil. Check that the duck breasts are cooked through by inserting the point of a sharp knife into the thickest part of the flesh – the juices should run clear.

Turkey with Cranberry Glaze

Traditional Christmas ingredients are given a Chinese twist in this stir-fry which containing cranberries, ginger, chestnuts and soy sauce!

NUTRITIONAL INFORMATION

Calories 167	Sugars 11g	
Protein 8g	Fat 7g	
Carbohydrate ...20g	Saturates 1g	

 5 MINS   15 MINS

SERVES 4

INGREDIENTS

1 turkey breast

2 tbsp sunflower oil

15 g/½ oz/2 tbsp stem ginger

50 g/1¾ oz/½ cup fresh or frozen cranberries

100 g/3½ oz/¼ cup canned chestnuts

4 tbsp cranberry sauce

3 tbsp light soy sauce

salt and pepper

1 Remove any skin from the turkey breast. Using a sharp knife, thinly slice the turkey breast.

2 Heat the sunflower oil in a large preheated wok or heavy-based frying pan (skillet).

3 Add the turkey to the wok and stir-fry for 5 minutes, or until cooked through.

4 Using a sharp knife, finely chop the stem ginger.

5 Add the ginger and the cranberries to the wok or frying pan (skillet) and stir-fry for 2–3 minutes or until the cranberries have softened.

6 Add the chestnuts, cranberry sauce and soy sauce, season to taste with salt and pepper and allow to bubble for 2–3 minutes.

7 Transfer the turkey stir-fry to warm serving dishes and serve immediately.

COOK'S TIP

It is very important that the wok is very hot before you stir-fry. Test by by holding your hand flat about 7.5 cm/3 inches above the base of the interior – you should be able to feel the heat radiating from it.

Meat

Pork is the most popular meat in China because it is tender and suitable for all Chinese cooking methods. Lamb is popular in northern China where religious laws forbid the eating of pork. Beef, although it is used in some dishes, is less popular than pork. This is partly because of economic and religious reasons, but also because it is less versatile in

cooking. One of the favourite cooking methods in China is stir-frying because it is a simple and easy way of preparing meat, as well as being healthy and economical. Stir-frying gives a dry texture, whereas braising and steaming, which are other popular cooking methods, ensure a tender result. This is also true of double-cooking in which the meat is first tenderized by long, slow simmering in water, following by a quick crisping or stir-frying in a sauce.

Beef & Broccoli Stir-Fry

This is a great combination of ingredients in terms of colour and flavour, and it is so simple to prepare.

NUTRITIONAL INFORMATION

Calories	232	Sugars	.........1g
Protein	........12g	Fat	..........19g
Carbohydrate	....4g	Saturates	.......6g

4¼ HOURS   15 MINS

SERVES 4

INGREDIENTS

225 g/8 oz lean steak, trimmed

2 garlic cloves, crushed

dash of chilli oil

1-cm/½-inch piece fresh root ginger, grated

½ tsp Chinese five-spice powder

2 tbsp dark soy sauce

2 tbsp vegetable oil

150 g/5½ oz broccoli florets

1 tbsp light soy sauce

150 ml/¼ pint/⅔ cup beef stock

2 tsp cornflour (cornstarch)

4 tsp water

carrot strips, to garnish

1 Using a sharp knife, cut the steak into thin strips and place in a shallow glass dish.

2 Mix together the garlic, chilli oil, grated ginger, Chinese five-spice powder and dark soy sauce in a small bowl and pour over the beef, tossing to coat the strips evenly.

3 Cover the bowl and leave the meat to marinate in the refrigerator for several hours to allow the flavours to develop fully.

4 Heat 1 tablespoon of the vegetable oil in a preheated wok or large frying pan (skillet). Add the broccoli and stir-fry over a medium heat for 4–5 minutes. Remove from the wok with a slotted spoon and set aside until required.

5 Heat the remaining oil in the wok. Add the steak together with the marinade, and stir-fry for 2-3 minutes, until the steak is browned and sealed.

6 Return the broccoli to the wok and stir in the light soy sauce and stock.

7 Blend the cornflour (cornstarch) with the water to form a smooth paste and stir into the wok. Bring to the boil, stirring, until thickened and clear. Cook for 1 minute. Transfer the beef & broccoli stir-fry to a warm serving dish, arrange the carrot strips in a lattice on top and serve immediately.

Beef with Bamboo Shoots

Tender beef, marinated in a soy and tomato sauce, is stir-fried with crisp bamboo shoots and mangetout (snow peas) in this simple recipe.

NUTRITIONAL INFORMATION

Calories	275	Sugars	........3g
Protein	........21g	Fat	..........19g
Carbohydrate	....6g	Saturates	.......6g

 1¼ HOURS   10 MINS

SERVES 4

I N G R E D I E N T S

350 g/12 oz rump steak

3 tbsp dark soy sauce

1 tbsp tomato ketchup

2 cloves garlic, crushed

1 tbsp fresh lemon juice

1 tsp ground coriander

2 tbsp vegetable oil

175 g/6 oz/2¾ cups mangetout
  (snow peas)

200 g/7 oz can bamboo shoots

1 tsp sesame oil

COOK'S TIP

Leave the meat to marinate for at least 1 hour in order for the flavours to penetrate and increase the tenderness of the meat. If possible, leave for a little longer for a fuller flavour to develop.

1 Thinly slice the meat and place in a non metallic dish together with the dark soy sauce, tomato ketchup, garlic, lemon juice and ground coriander. Mix well so that all of the meat is coated in the marinade, cover and leave for at least 1 hour.

2 Heat the vegetable oil in a preheated wok. Add the meat to the wok and stir-fry for 2–4 minutes (depending on how well cooked you like your meat) or until cooked through.

3 Add the mangetout (snow peas) and bamboo shoots to the mixture in the wok and stir-fry over a high heat, tossing frequently, for a further 5 minutes.

4 Drizzle with the sesame oil and toss well to combine. Transfer to serving dishes and serve hot.

Beef & Beans

The green of the beans complements the dark colour of the beef, and is served in a rich sauce.

NUTRITIONAL INFORMATION

Calories	.381	Sugars	.3g
Protein	.25g	Fat	.27g
Carbohydrate	.10g	Saturates	.8g

 35 MINS   15 MINS

SERVES 4

I N G R E D I E N T S

450 g/1 lb rump or fillet steak, cut into
    2.5-cm/1-inch pieces

M A R I N A D E

2 tsp cornflour (cornstarch)

2 tbsp dark soy sauce

2 tsp peanut oil

S A U C E

2 tbsp vegetable oil

3 garlic cloves, crushed

1 small onion, cut into 8

225 g/8 oz thin green beans, halved

25 g/1 oz/¼ cup unsalted cashews

25 g/1 oz canned bamboo shoots, drained
    and rinsed

2 tsp dark soy sauce

2 tsp Chinese rice wine or dry sherry

125 ml/4 fl oz/½ cup beef stock

2 tsp cornflour (cornstarch)

4 tsp water

salt and pepper

1 To make the marinade, mix together the cornflour (cornstarch), soy sauce and peanut oil.

2 Place the steak in a shallow glass bowl. Pour the marinade over the steak, turn to coat thoroughly, cover and

leave to marinate in the refrigerator for at least 30 minutes.

3 To make the sauce, heat the oil in a preheated wok. Add the garlic, onion, beans, cashews and bamboo shoots and stir-fry for 2–3 minutes.

4 Remove the steak from the marinade, drain, add to the wok and stir-fry for 3–4 minutes.

5 Mix the soy sauce, Chinese rice wine or sherry and beef stock together. Blend the cornflour (cornstarch) with the water and add to the soy sauce mixture, mixing to combine.

6 Stir the mixture into the wok and bring the sauce to the boil, stirring until thickened and clear. Reduce the heat and leave to simmer for 2–3 minutes. Season to taste and serve immediately.

Spicy Beef

In this recipe, beef is marinated in a five-spice and chilli marinade for a spicy flavour.

NUTRITIONAL INFORMATION

Calories	246	Sugars	.........2g
Protein	........21g	Fat	.........13g
Carbohydrate	...10g	Saturates	.......3g

 1¼ HOURS   10 MINS

SERVES 4

I N G R E D I E N T S

225 g/8 oz fillet steak

2 garlic cloves, crushed

1 tsp powdered star anise

1 tbsp dark soy sauce

spring onion (scallion) tassels, to garnish

S A U C E

2 tbsp vegetable oil

1 bunch spring onions (scallions), halved
   lengthways

1 tbsp dark soy sauce

1 tbsp dry sherry

¼ tsp chilli sauce

150 ml/¼ pint/⅔ cup water

2 tsp cornflour (cornstarch)

4 tsp water

1 Cut the steak into thin strips and place in a shallow dish.

2 Mix together the garlic, star anise and dark soy sauce in a bowl.

3 Pour the sauce mixture over the steak strips, turning them to coat thoroughly. Cover and leave to marinate in the refrigerator for at least 1 hour.

4 To make the sauce, heat the oil in a preheated wok or large frying pan (skillet). Reduce the heat and stir-fry the spring onions (scallions) for 1-2 minutes.

5 Remove the spring onions (scallions) from the wok with a slotted spoon, drain on absorbent kitchen paper (paper towels) and set aside until required.

6 Add the beef to the wok, together with the marinade, and stir-fry for 3-4 minutes. Return the spring onions (scallions) to the wok and add the soy sauce, sherry, chilli sauce and two thirds of the water.

7 Blend the cornflour (cornstarch) with the remaining water and stir into the wok. Bring to the boil, stirring until the sauce thickens and clears.

8 Transfer to a warm serving dish, garnish and serve immediately.

Beef & Bok Choy

In this recipe, a colourful selection of vegetables is stir-fried with tender strips of steak.

NUTRITIONAL INFORMATION

Calories 369   Sugars 9g
Protein . . . . .29g   Fat 23g
Carbohydrate . . .12g   Saturates 8g

15 MINS   5 MINS

SERVES 4

INGREDIENTS

1 large head of bok choy, about
  250-275 g/9-9½ oz, torn into
  large pieces

2 tbsp vegetable oil

2 garlic cloves, crushed

500 g/1 lb 2 oz rump or fillet steak,
  cut into thin strips

150 g/5½ oz mangetout (snow peas),
  trimmed

150 g/5½ oz baby or dwarf corn

6 spring onions (scallions), chopped

2 red (bell) peppers, cored, seeded
  and thinly sliced

2 tbsp oyster sauce

1 tbsp fish sauce

1 tbsp sugar

rice or noodles, to serve

1 Steam the bok choy over boiling water until just tender. Keep warm.

2 Heat the oil in a large, heavy-based frying pan (skillet) or wok, add the garlic and steak strips and stir-fry until just browned, about 1-2 minutes.

3 Add the mangetout (snow peas), baby corn, spring onions (scallions), red (bell) pepper, oyster sauce, fish sauce and sugar to the pan, mixing well. Stir-fry for a further 2-3 minutes until the vegetables are just tender, but still crisp.

4 Arrange the bok choy leaves in the base of a heated serving dish and spoon the beef and vegetable mixture into the centre.

5 Serve the stir-fry immediately, with rice or noodles.

COOK'S TIP

Bok choy is one of the most important ingredients in this dish. If unavailable, use Chinese leaves (cabbage), kai choy (mustard leaves) or pak choy.

Beef & Black Bean Sauce

It is not necessary to use the expensive cuts of beef steak for this recipe: the meat will be tender as it is cut into small thin slices and marinated.

NUTRITIONAL INFORMATION

Calories 392	Sugars 2g	
Protein 13g	Fat 36g	
Carbohydrate 3g	Saturates 7g	

3¼ HOURS   10 MINS

SERVES 4

I N G R E D I E N T S

250-300 g/9-10½ oz beef steak (such as rump)

1 small onion

1 small green (bell) pepper, cored and seeded

about 300 ml/½ pint/1¼ cups vegetable oil

1 spring onion (scallion), cut into short sections

a few small slices of ginger root

1-2 small green or red chillies, seeded and sliced

2 tbsp crushed black bean sauce

M A R I N A D E

½ tsp bicarbonate of soda (baking soda) or baking powder

½ tsp sugar

1 tbsp light soy sauce

2 tsp rice wine or dry sherry

2 tsp cornflour (cornstarch) paste (see page 15)

2 tsp sesame oil

1 Using a sharp knife or meat cleaver, cut the beef into small, thin strips.

2 To make the marinade, mix together all the ingredients in a shallow dish. Add the beef strips, turn to coat and leave to marinate for at least 2-3 hours.

3 Cut the onion and green (bell) pepper into small cubes.

4 Heat the vegetable oil in a pre-heated wok or large frying pan (skillet). Add the beef strips and stir-fry for about 1 minute, or until the colour changes. Remove the beef strips with a slotted spoon and drain on absorbent kitchen paper (paper towels). Keep warm and set aside until required.

5 Pour off the excess oil, leaving about 1 tablespoon in the wok. Add the spring onion (scallion), ginger, chillies, onion and green (bell) pepper and stir-fry for about 1 minute.

6 Add the black bean sauce and stir until smooth. Return the beef strips to the wok, blend well and stir-fry for another minute. Transfer the stir-fry to a warm serving dish and serve hot.

Oyster Sauce Beef

Like Pork with Vegetables (see page 143), the vegetables used in this recipe can be varied as you wish.

NUTRITIONAL INFORMATION

Calories 462   Sugars 2g
Protein . . . . .16g   Fat 42g
Carbohydrate . . . .4g   Saturates 8g

4 HOURS   10 MINS

SERVES 4

I N G R E D I E N T S

300 g/10½ oz beef steak

1 tsp sugar

1 tbsp light soy sauce

1 tsp rice wine or dry sherry

1 tsp cornflour (cornstarch) paste (see page 15)

½ small carrot

60 g/2 oz mangetout (snow peas)

60 g/2 oz canned bamboo shoots

60 g/2 oz canned straw mushrooms

about 300 ml/½ pint/1¼ cups vegetable oil

1 spring onion (scallion), cut into short sections

2-3 small slices ginger root

½ tsp salt

2 tbsp oyster sauce

2-3 tbsp Chinese Stock (see page 14) or water

1 Cut the beef into small, thin slices. Place in a shallow dish with the sugar, soy sauce, wine and cornflour (cornstarch) paste and leave to marinate for 25-30 minutes.

2 Slice the carrot, mangetout (snow peas), bamboo shoots and straw mushrooms into roughly the same size pieces as each other.

3 Heat the oil in a wok and add the beef slices. Stir-fry for 1 minute, then remove and keep warm.

4 Pour off the oil, leaving about 1 tablespoon in the wok. Add the sliced vegetables with the spring onion (scallion) and ginger and stir-fry for about 2 minutes. Add the salt, beef and oyster sauce with stock or water. Blend well until heated through and serve.

VARIATION

You can use whatever vegetables are available for this dish, but it is important to get a good contrast of colour – don't use all red or all green for example.

Peppered Beef Cashew

A simple but stunning dish of tender strips of beef mixed with crunchy cashew nuts, coated in a hot sauce. Serve with rice noodles.

NUTRITIONAL INFORMATION

Calories	403	Sugars	........7g
Protein	........26g	Fat	.........29g
Carbohydrate	....11g	Saturates	.......9g

🍲 10 MINS   🕐 10 MINS

SERVES 4

INGREDIENTS

1 tbsp groundnut or sunflower oil

1 tbsp sesame oil

1 onion, sliced

1 garlic clove, crushed

1 tbsp grated ginger root

500 g/1 lb 2 oz fillet or rump steak, cut into thin strips

2 tsp palm sugar

2 tbsp light soy sauce

1 small yellow (bell) pepper, cored, seeded and sliced

1 red (bell) pepper, cored, seeded and sliced

4 spring onions (scallions), chopped

2 celery sticks, chopped

4 large open-cap mushrooms, sliced

4 tbsp roasted cashew nuts

3 tbsp stock or white wine

1 Heat the oils in a large, heavy-based frying pan (skillet) or wok. Add the onion, garlic and ginger and stir-fry for about 2 minutes until softened.

2 Add the steak strips and stir-fry for a further 2-3 minutes, until the meat has browned.

3 Add the sugar and soy sauce, stirring to mix well.

4 Add the (bell) peppers, spring onions (scallions), celery, mushrooms and cashews, mixing well.

5 Add the stock or white wine and stir-fry for 2-3 minutes until the beef is cooked through and the vegetables are tender-crisp.

6 Serve the stir-fry immediately with rice noodles.

COOK'S TIP

Palm sugar is a thick brown sugar with a slightly caramel taste. It is sold in cakes, or in small containers. If not available, use soft dark brown or demerara (brown crystal) sugar.

Red Spiced Beef

A spicy stir-fry flavoured with paprika, chilli and tomato, with a crisp bite to it from the celery strips.

NUTRITIONAL INFORMATION

Calories 431	Sugars 0g
Protein 32g	Fat 28g
Carbohydrate . . .14g	Saturates 10g

40 MINS   10 MINS

SERVES 4

I N G R E D I E N T S

625 g/1 lb 6 oz sirloin or rump steak

2 tbsp paprika

2-3 tsp mild chilli powder

½ tsp salt

6 celery sticks

4 tomatoes, peeled, seeded and sliced

6 tbsp stock or water

2 tbsp tomato purée (paste)

2 tbsp clear honey

3 tbsp wine vinegar

1 tbsp Worcestershire sauce

2 tbsp sunflower oil

4 spring onions (scallions), thinly sliced diagonally

1-2 garlic cloves, crushed

Chinese noodles, to serve

celery leaves, to garnish (optional)

1 Using a sharp knife or meat cleaver, cut the steak across the grain into narrow strips 1 cm/½ inch thick and place in a bowl.

2 Combine the paprika, chilli powder and salt, add to the beef and mix thoroughly until the meat strips are evenly coated with the spices. Leave the beef to marinate in a cool place for at least 30 minutes.

3 Cut the celery into 5 cm/2 inch lengths, then cut the lengths into strips about 5 mm/¼ inch thick.

4 Combine the stock, tomato purée (paste), honey, wine vinegar and Worcestershire sauce and set aside.

5 Heat the oil in the wok until really hot. Add the spring onion (scallions), celery and garlic and stir-fry for about 1 minute until the vegetables are beginning to soften, then add the steak strips. Stir-fry over a high heat for 3-4 minutes until the meat is well sealed.

6 Add the sauce to the wok and continue to stir-fry briskly until thoroughly coated and sizzling.

7 Serve with noodles and garnish with celery leaves, if liked.

Soy & Sesame Beef

Soy sauce and sesame seeds are classic ingredients in Chinese cookery.
Use a dark soy sauce for fuller flavour and richness.

NUTRITIONAL INFORMATION

Calories	324	Sugars	.........2g
Protein	........25g	Fat	............22g
Carbohydrate	....3g	Saturates	.......6g

 5 MINS   10 MINS

SERVES 4

I N G R E D I E N T S

25 g/1 oz/2 tbsp sesame seeds

450 g/1 lb beef fillet

2 tbsp vegetable oil

1 green (bell) pepper, deseeded and thinly sliced

4 cloves garlic, crushed

2 tbsp dry sherry

4 tbsp soy sauce

6 spring onions (scallions), sliced

noodles, to serve

1 Heat a large wok or heavy-based frying pan (skillet) until it is very hot.

2 Add the sesame seeds to the wok or frying pan (skillet) and dry fry, stirring, for 1–2 minutes or until they just begin to brown. Remove the sesame seeds from the wok and set aside until required.

3 Using a sharp knife or meat cleaver, thinly slice the beef.

4 Heat the vegetable oil in the wok or frying pan (skillet). Add the beef and stir-fry for 2–3 minutes or until sealed on all sides.

5 Add the sliced (bell) pepper and crushed garlic to the wok and continue stir-frying for 2 minutes.

6 Add the dry sherry and soy sauce to the wok together with the spring onions (scallions). Allow the mixture in the wok to bubble, stirring occasionally, for about 1 minute, but do not let the mixture burn.

7 Transfer the garlic beef stir-fry to warm serving bowls and scatter with the dry-fried sesame seeds. Serve hot with boiled noodles.

COOK'S TIP

You can spread the sesame seeds out on a baking tray (cookie sheet) and toast them under a preheated grill (broiler) until browned all over, if you prefer.

Beef with Green Peas

This recipe is the perfect example of quick stir-frying ingredients for a delicious, crisp, colourful dish.

NUTRITIONAL INFORMATION

Calories 325	Sugars 2g	
Protein 26g	Fat 22g	
Carbohydrate 8g	Saturates 7g	

5 MINS   10 MINS

SERVES 4

INGREDIENTS

450 g/1 lb rump steak

2 tbsp sunflower oil

1 onion

2 cloves garlic

150 g/5½ oz/1 cup fresh or
    frozen peas

160 g/5¾ oz jar black bean sauce

150 g/5½ oz Chinese leaves
    (cabbage), shredded

1 Using a sharp knife, trim away any fat from the beef. Cut the beef into thin slices.

2 Heat the sunflower oil in a large preheated wok.

3 Add the beef to the wok and stir-fry for 2 minutes.

4 Using a sharp knife, peel and slice the onion and crush the garlic cloves in a pestle and mortar.

5 Add the onion, garlic and peas to the wok and stir-fry for 5 minutes.

6 Add the black bean sauce and Chinese leaves (cabbage) to the wok.

7 Heat the mixture in the wok for a further 2 minutes until the Chinese leaves (cabbage) have wilted.

8 Transfer to warm serving bowls then serve immediately.

COOK'S TIP

Buy a chunky black bean sauce if you can for the best texture and flavour.

Chinese leaves (cabbage) are now widely available. They look like a pale, elongated head of lettuce with light green, tightly packed crinkly leaves.

Caramelised Beef

Palm sugar or brown sugar is used in this recipe to give the beef a slightly caramelised flavour.

NUTRITIONAL INFORMATION

Calories 335	Sugars 8g	
Protein 23g	Fat 21g	
Carbohydrate ...14g	Saturates 7g	

   1¼ HOURS   10 MINS

SERVES 4

INGREDIENTS

450 g/1 lb fillet beef

2 tbsp soy sauce

1 tsp chilli oil

1 tbsp tamarind paste

2 tbsp palm sugar or demerara (brown crystal) sugar

2 cloves garlic, crushed

2 tbsp sunflower oil

225 g/8 oz baby onions

2 tbsp chopped fresh coriander (cilantro), to garnish

1 Using a sharp knife or meat cleaver, thinly slice the beef.

2 Place the slices of beef in a large, shallow non-metallic dish.

3 Mix together the soy sauce, chilli oil, tamarind paste, palm or demerara (brown crystal) sugar and garlic in a mixing bowl.

4 Spoon the sugar mixture over the beef. Toss well to coat the beef in the mixture, cover with cling film (plastic wrap) and leave to marinate for at least 1 hour, the longer the better.

5 Heat the oil in a preheated wok or large frying pan (skillet).

6 Peel the onions and cut them in half. Add the onion pieces to the wok and stir-fry for 2–3 minutes, or until just browning.

7 Add the beef and marinade juices to the wok and stir-fry over a high heat for about 5 minutes.

8 Scatter with chopped fresh coriander (cilantro) and serve at once.

COOK'S TIP

Use the chilli oil carefully as it is very hot and could easily spoil the dish if too much is added.

Crispy Shredded Beef

A very popular Szechuan dish served in most Chinese restaurants all over the world.

NUTRITIONAL INFORMATION

Calories . . . . .341 Sugars 17g
Protein . . . . .20g Fat 17g
Carbohydrate . . .29g Saturates 4g

🐟 🐟 🐟

10 MINS   15 MINS

SERVES 4

I N G R E D I E N T S

300-350 g/10½-12 oz beef steak (such as topside or rump)

2 eggs

¼ tsp salt

4-5 tbsp plain (all-purpose) flour

vegetable oil, for deep-frying

2 medium carrots, finely shredded

2 spring onions (scallions), thinly shredded

1 garlic clove, finely chopped

2-3 small fresh green or red chillies, seeded and thinly shredded

4 tbsp sugar

3 tbsp rice vinegar

1 tbsp light soy sauce

2-3 tbsp Chinese Stock (see page 14) or water

1 tsp cornflour (cornstarch) paste (see page 15)

1 Cut the steak across the grain into thin strips. Beat the eggs in a bowl with the salt and flour, adding a little water if necessary. Add the beef strips to the batter and mix well until coated.

2 Heat the oil in a preheated wok until smoking. Add the beef strips and deep-fry for 4-5 minutes, stirring to separate the shreds. Remove with a slotted spoon and drain on absorbent kitchen paper (paper towels)

3 Add the carrots to the wok and deep-fry for about 1-1½ minutes, then remove with a slotted spoon and drain.

4 Pour off the excess oil, leaving about 1 tablespoon in the wok. Add the spring onions (scallions), garlic, chillies and carrots and stir-fry for 1 minute.

5 Add the sugar, rice vinegar, light soy sauce and Chinese stock or water to the wok, blend well and bring to the boil.

6 Stir in the cornflour (cornstarch) paste and simmer for a few minutes to thicken the sauce.

7 Return the beef to the wok and stir until the shreds of meat are well coated with the sauce. Serve hot.

Meatballs in Peanut Sauce

Choose very lean minced (ground) beef to make these meatballs – or better still, buy some lean beef and mince and grind it yourself.

NUTRITIONAL INFORMATION

Calories 553   Sugars 10g
Protein . . . . .32g   Fat 43g
Carbohydrate . . .21g   Saturates 12g

5 MINS   30 MINS

SERVES 4

I N G R E D I E N T S

500 g/1 lb 2 oz/2 cups lean minced (ground) beef

2 tsp finely grated fresh ginger root

1 small red chilli, deseeded and chopped finely

1 tbsp chopped fresh basil or coriander (cilantro)

1 tbsp sesame oil

1 tbsp vegetable oil

salt and pepper

S A U C E

2 tbsp red curry paste

300 ml/½ pint/1¼ cups coconut milk

125 g/4½ oz/1 cup ground peanuts

1 tbsp fish sauce

T O   G A R N I S H

chopped fresh basil

sprigs of fresh basil or coriander (cilantro)

1 Put the beef, ginger, chilli and basil or coriander (cilantro) into a food processor or blender. Add ¹/₂ teaspoon of salt and plenty of pepper. Process for about 10–15 seconds until finely chopped. Alternatively, chop the ingredients finely and mix together.

2 Form the beef mixture into about 12 balls. Heat the sesame oil and vegetable oil in a wok or frying pan (skillet) and fry the meatballs over a medium-high heat until well browned on all sides, about 10 minutes. Lift them out and drain on kitchen paper (paper towels).

3 To make the sauce, stir-fry the red curry paste in the wok or frying pan (skillet) for 1 minute. Add the coconut milk, peanuts and fish sauce. Heat, stirring, until just simmering.

4 Return the meatballs to the wok or frying pan (skillet) and cook gently in the sauce for 10–15 minutes. If the sauce begins to get too thick, add a little extra coconut milk or water. Season with a little salt and pepper, according to taste.

5 Serve garnished with chopped fresh basil and sprigs of fresh basil or coriander (cilantro).

VARIATION

Minced (ground) lamb makes a delicious alternative to beef. If you do use lamb, try substituting ground almonds for the peanuts and fresh mint for the basil.

Pork with Mooli

Pork and mooli (white radish) are a perfect combination, especially with the added heat of the sweet chilli sauce.

NUTRITIONAL INFORMATION

Calories 280   Sugars 1g
Protein . . . . .25g   Fat 19g
Carbohydrate . . . .2g   Saturates 4g

10 MINS   15 MINS

SERVES 4

INGREDIENTS

4 tbsp vegetable oil

450 g/1 lb pork tenderloin

1 aubergine (eggplant)

225 g/8 oz mooli (white radish)

2 cloves garlic, crushed

3 tbsp soy sauce

2 tbsp sweet chilli sauce

boiled rice or noodles, to serve

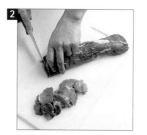

1 Heat 2 tablespoons of the vegetable oil in a large preheated wok or frying pan (skillet).

2 Using a sharp knife, thinly slice the pork into even-size pieces.

3 Add the slices of pork to the wok or frying pan (skillet) and stir-fry for about 5 minutes.

4 Using a sharp knife, trim and dice the aubergine (eggplant). Peel and slice the mooli (white radish).

5 Add the remaining vegetable oil to the wok.

6 Add the diced aubergine (eggplant) to the wok or frying pan (skillet) together with the garlic and stir-fry for 5 minutes.

7 Add the mooli (white radish) to the wok and stir-fry for about 2 minutes.

8 Stir the soy sauce and sweet chilli sauce into the mixture in the wok and cook until heated through.

9 Transfer the pork and mooli (white radish) to warm serving bowls and serve immediately with boiled rice or noodles.

COOK'S TIP

Mooli (white radish) are long white vegetables common in Chinese cooking. Usually grated, they have a milder flavour than red radish. They are generally available in most large supermarkets.

Pork with Vegetables

This is a basic 'meat and veg' recipe – the meat can be pork, chicken, beef or lamb, and the vegetables can be varied according to the season.

NUTRITIONAL INFORMATION

Calories	227	Sugars	.........4g
Protein	........15g	Fat	..........16g
Carbohydrate	....7g	Saturates	.......3g

 🍃 🍃 🍃

🍖 25 MINS   🕐 10 MINS

SERVES 4

INGREDIENTS

250 g/9 oz pork fillet

1 tsp sugar

1 tbsp light soy sauce

1 tsp rice wine or dry sherry

1 tsp cornflour (cornstarch) paste (see page 15)

1 small carrot

1 small green (bell) pepper, cored and seeded

about 175 g/6 oz Chinese leaves (cabbage)

4 tbsp vegetable oil

1 spring onion (scallion), cut into short sections

a few small slices of peeled ginger root

1 tsp salt

2-3 tbsp Chinese Stock (see page 14) or water

a few drops of sesame oil

VARIATION

This dish can be made with other meats, as mentioned in the introduction. If using chicken strips, reduce the initial cooking time in the wok.

1 Thinly slice the pork fillet into small pieces and place in a shallow dish.

2 In a small bowl, mix together half the sugar and the soy sauce, the wine or sherry and cornflour (cornstarch) paste. Pour the mixture over the pork, stir well to coat the meat and leave in the refrigerator to marinate for 10-15 minutes.

3 Cut the carrot, green (bell) pepper and Chinese leaves (cabbage) into thin slices roughly the same length and width as the pork pieces.

4 Heat the oil in a preheated wok and stir-fry the pork for about 1 minute to seal in the flavour. Remove with a slotted spoon and keep warm.

5 Add the carrot, (bell) pepper, Chinese leaves (cabbage), spring onion (scallion) and ginger and stir-fry for about 2 minutes.

6 Add the salt and remaining sugar, followed by the pork and remaining soy sauce, and the Chinese stock or water. Blend well and stir for another 1-2 minutes until hot. Sprinkle the stir-fry with the sesame oil and serve immediately.

Sweet & Sour Pork

In this classic Chinese dish, tender pork pieces are fried and served in a crunchy sauce. This dish is perfect served with plain rice.

NUTRITIONAL INFORMATION

Calories	357	Sugars	. . . . .25g
Protein	. . . . .28g	Fat	. . . . .14g
Carbohydrate	. . .30g	Saturates	. . . . . . .4g

 10 MINS   20 MINS

SERVES 4

I N G R E D I E N T S

450 g/1 lb pork tenderloin

2 tbsp sunflower oil

225 g/8 oz courgettes (zucchini)

1 red onion, cut into thin wedges

2 cloves garlic, crushed

225 g/8 oz carrots, cut into thin sticks

1 red (bell) pepper, deseeded and sliced

100 g/3½ oz/1 cup baby corn cobs

100 g/3½ oz button mushrooms, halved

175 g/6 oz/1¼ cups fresh pineapple, cubed

100 g/3½ oz/1 cup bean sprouts

150 ml/¼ pint/⅔ cup pineapple juice

1 tbsp cornflour (cornstarch)

2 tbsp soy sauce

3 tbsp tomato ketchup

1 tbsp white wine vinegar

1 tbsp clear honey

COOK'S TIP

If you prefer a crisper coating, toss the pork in a mixture of cornflour (cornstarch) and egg white and deep fry in the wok in step 2.

1 Using a sharp knife, thinly slice the pork tenderloin into even-size pieces.

2 Heat the sunflower oil in a large preheated wok. Add the pork to the wok and stir-fry for 10 minutes, or until the pork is completely cooked through and beginning to turn crispy at the edges.

3 Meanwhile, cut the courgettes (zucchini) into thin sticks.

4 Add the onion, garlic, carrots, courgettes (zucchini), (bell) pepper, corn cobs and mushrooms to the wok and stir-fry for a further 5 minutes.

5 Add the pineapple cubes and bean sprouts to the wok and stir-fry for 2 minutes.

6 Mix together the pineapple juice, cornflour (cornstarch), soy sauce, tomato ketchup, white wine vinegar and honey.

7 Pour the sweet and sour mixture into the wok and cook over a high heat, tossing frequently, until the juices thicken. Transfer the sweet and sour pork to serving bowls and serve hot.

Spicy Pork & Rice

Pork is coated in a spicy mixture before being fried until crisp in this recipe and then stirred into a delicious egg rice for a very filling meal.

NUTRITIONAL INFORMATION

Calories	599	Sugars	........11g
Protein	........30g	Fat	.........22g
Carbohydrate	...76g	Saturates	.......7g

10 MINS   35 MINS

SERVES 4

INGREDIENTS

275 g/9½ oz/1¼ cups long-grain white rice

600 ml/1 pint/2½ cups cold water

350 g/12 oz pork tenderloin

2 tsp Chinese five-spice powder

25 g/1 oz/4 tbsp cornflour (cornstarch)

3 large eggs, beaten

25 g/1 oz/2 tbsp demerara (brown crystal) sugar

2 tbsp sunflower oil

1 onion

2 cloves garlic, crushed

100 g/3½ oz carrots, diced

1 red (bell) pepper, deseeded and diced

100 g/3½ oz/¾ cup peas

15 g/½ oz/2 tbsp butter

salt and pepper

1 Rinse the rice under cold running water. Place the rice in a large saucepan, add the cold water and a pinch of salt. Bring to the boil, cover, then reduce the heat and leave to simmer for about 9 minutes, or until all of the liquid has been absorbed and the rice is tender.

2 Meanwhile, slice the pork tenderloin into very thin even-sized pieces, using a sharp knife or meat cleaver. Set the pork strips aside until required.

3 Whisk together the Chinese five-spice powder, cornflour (cornstarch), 1 egg and the demerara (brown crystal) sugar. Toss the pork in the mixture until coated.

4 Heat the sunflower oil in a large wok or frying pan (skillet). Add the pork and cook over a high heat until the pork is cooked through and crispy. Remove the pork from the wok with a slotted spoon and set aside until required.

5 Using a sharp knife, cut the onion into dice.

6 Add the onion, garlic, carrots, (bell) pepper and peas to the wok and stir-fry for 5 minutes.

7 Return the pork to the wok together with the cooked rice and stir-fry for 5 minutes.

8 Heat the butter in a frying pan (skillet). Add the remaining beaten eggs and cook until set. Turn out on to a clean board and slice thinly. Toss the strips of egg into the rice mixture and serve immediately.

Spicy Pork Balls

These small meatballs are packed with flavour and cooked in a crunchy tomato sauce for a very quick dish.

NUTRITIONAL INFORMATION

Calories 299   Sugars 3g
Protein . . . . .28g   Fat 15g
Carbohydrate . . .14g   Saturates 4g

 10 MINS   40 MINS

SERVES 4

I N G R E D I E N T S

450 g/1 lb minced (ground) pork

2 shallots, finely chopped

2 cloves garlic, crushed

1 tsp cumin seeds

½ tsp chilli powder

25 g/1 oz/½ cup wholemeal
    breadcrumbs

1 egg, beaten

2 tbsp sunflower oil

400 g/14 oz can chopped tomatoes,
    flavoured with chilli

2 tbsp soy sauce

200 g/7 oz can water chestnuts,
    drained

3 tbsp chopped fresh coriander (cilantro)

COOK'S TIP

Add a few teaspoons of chilli sauce to a tin of chopped tomatoes, if you can't find the flavoured variety.

1 Place the minced (ground) pork in a large mixing bowl. Add the shallots, garlic, cumin seeds, chilli powder, breadcrumbs and beaten egg and mix together well.

2 Form the mixture into balls between the palms of your hands.

3 Heat the oil in a large preheated wok. Add the pork balls and stir-fry, in batches, over a high heat for about 5 minutes or until sealed on all sides.

4 Add the tomatoes, soy sauce and water chestnuts and bring to the boil. Return the pork balls to the wok, reduce the heat and leave to simmer for 15 minutes.

5 Scatter with chopped fresh coriander (cilantro) and serve hot.

Pork Ribs with Plum Sauce

Pork ribs are always very popular at barbecues (grills), and you can flavour them with a number of spicy bastes.

NUTRITIONAL INFORMATION

Calories 590   Sugars 1g
Protein ....26g   Fat 51g
Carbohydrate ....3g   Saturates 17g

35 MINS   45 MINS

SERVES 4

INGREDIENTS

900 g/2 lb pork spare ribs

2 tbsp sunflower oil

1 tsp sesame oil

2 cloves garlic, crushed

2.5 cm/1 inch piece root (fresh) ginger, grated

150 ml/¼ pint/⅔ cup plum sauce

2 tbsp dry sherry

2 tbsp hoisin sauce

2 tbsp soy sauce

4–6 spring onions (scallions), to garnish (optional)

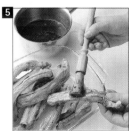

1 To prepare the garnish, trim the spring onions (scallions) to about 7.5 cm/ 3 inches long. Slice both ends into thin strips, leaving the onion intact in the centre.

2 Put the spring onions (scallions) into a bowl of iced water for at least 30 minutes until the ends start to curl up. Leave them in the water and set aside until required.

3 If you buy the spare ribs in a single piece, cut them into individual ribs. Bring a large pan of water to the boil and add the ribs. Cook for 5 minutes, then drain thoroughly.

4 Heat the oils in a pan, add the garlic and ginger and cook gently for 1–2 minutes. Stir in the plum sauce, sherry, hoisin and soy sauce and heat through.

5 Brush the sauce over the pork ribs. Barbecue (grill) over hot coals for 5–10 minutes, then move to a cooler part of the barbecue (grill) for a further 15–20 minutes, basting with the remaining sauce. Garnish and serve hot.

COOK'S TIP

Par-cooking the ribs in boiling water removes excess fat, which helps prevent the ribs from spitting during cooking. Do not be put off by the large quantity – there is only a little meat on each, but they are quite cheap to buy.

Pork Satay Stir-Fry

Satay sauce is easy to make and is one of the best known and loved sauces in Oriental cooking. It is perfect with beef, chicken or pork.

NUTRITIONAL INFORMATION

Calories 506   Sugars 11g
Protein ....31g   Fat 36g
Carbohydrate ...15g   Saturates 8g

  10 MINS   15 MINS

SERVES 4

INGREDIENTS

150 g/5½ oz carrots

2 tbsp sunflower oil

350 g/12 oz pork neck fillet, thinly sliced

1 onion, sliced

2 cloves garlic, crushed

1 yellow (bell) pepper, deseeded and sliced

150 g/5½ oz/2⅓ cups mangetout (snow peas)

75 g/2¾ oz/1½ cups fine asparagus

chopped salted peanuts, to serve

SATAY SAUCE

6 tbsp crunchy peanut butter

6 tbsp coconut milk

1 tsp chilli flakes

1 clove garlic, crushed

1 tsp tomato purée (paste)

COOK'S TIP

Cook the sauce just before serving as it tends to thicken very quickly and will not be spoonable if you cook it too far in advance.

  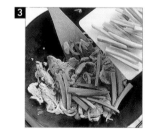

1 Using a sharp knife, slice the carrots into thin sticks.

2 Heat the oil in a large, preheated wok. Add the pork, onion and garlic and stir-fry for 5 minutes or until the lamb is cooked through.

3 Add the carrots, (bell) pepper, mangetout (snow peas) and asparagus to the wok and stir-fry for 5 minutes.

4 To make the satay sauce, place the peanut butter, coconut milk, chilli flakes, garlic and tomato purée (paste) in a small pan and heat gently, stirring, until well combined. Be careful not to let the sauce stick to the bottom of the pan.

5 Transfer the stir-fry to warm serving plates. Spoon the satay sauce over the stir-fry and scatter with chopped peanuts. Serve immediately.

Stir-Fried Pork & Cabbage

Rustle up this quick dish in a matter of moments. Assemble all your ingredients first, then everything is ready to hand as you start to stir-fry.

NUTRITIONAL INFORMATION

Calories 226   Sugars 2g
Protein ....21g   Fat 12g
Carbohydrate ....4g   Saturates 3g

5 MINS   10 MINS

SERVES 4

INGREDIENTS

375 g/13 oz pork fillet (tenderloin)

8 spring onions (scallions), trimmed

½ small white cabbage

½ cucumber

2 tsp finely grated fresh ginger root

1 tbsp fish sauce or light soy sauce

2 tbsp dry sherry

2 tbsp water

2 tsp cornflour (cornstarch)

1 tbsp chopped fresh mint or coriander (cilantro)

2 tbsp sesame oil

salt and pepper

TO GARNISH

sprigs of fresh mint or coriander (cilantro)

1 chilli flower (see Cook's Tip, right)

1 Slice the pork very thinly. Shred the spring onions (scallions) and cabbage, and cut the cucumber into matchsticks.

2 Mix together the ginger, fish sauce or soy sauce, sherry, water, cornflour (cornstarch) and chopped mint or coriander (cilantro) until blended.

3 Heat the sesame oil in a wok and add the pork. Stir-fry briskly over a high heat until browned, about 4–5 minutes.

4 Add the spring onions (scallions), cabbage and cucumber and stir-fry for a further 2 minutes. Add the cornflour (cornstarch) mixture and continue to cook for about 1 minute, until slightly thickened. Season to taste.

5 Transfer the stir-fry to a warmed dish and serve at once, garnished with sprigs of fresh mint or coriander (cilantro) and a chilli flower.

COOK'S TIP

To make chilli flowers, hold the stem of the chilli and cut down its length several times with a sharp knife. Place in a bowl of chilled water and chill so that the 'petals' turn out. Remove the chilli seeds when the 'petals' have opened.

Sweet & Sour Pork

This dish is a popular choice in Western diets, and must be one of the best known of Chinese recipes.

NUTRITIONAL INFORMATION

Calories	471	Sugars	.......47g
Protein	........16g	Fat	..........13g
Carbohydrate	...77g	Saturates	.......2g

🍲 10 MINS   🕐 20 MINS

SERVES 4

I N G R E D I E N T S

150 ml/¼ pint/⅔ cup vegetable oil, for deep-frying

225 g/8 oz pork fillet (tenderloin), cut into 1-cm/½-inch cubes

1 onion, sliced

1 green (bell) pepper, seeded and sliced

225 g/8 oz pineapple pieces

1 small carrot, cut into thin strips

25 g/1 oz canned bamboo shoots, drained, rinsed and halved

rice or noodles, to serve

B A T T E R

125 g/4½ oz/1 cup plain (all-purpose) flour

1 tbsp cornflour (cornstarch)

1½ tsp baking powder

1 tbsp vegetable oil

S A U C E

125 g/4½ oz/⅔ cup light brown sugar

2 tbsp cornflour (cornstarch)

125 ml/4 fl oz/½ cup white wine vinegar

2 garlic cloves, crushed

4 tbsp tomato purée (paste)

6 tbsp pineapple juice

1 To make the batter, sift the plain (all-purpose) flour into a mixing bowl, together with the cornflour (cornstarch) and baking powder. Add the vegetable oil and stir in enough water to make a thick, smooth batter (about 175 ml/6 fl oz/ ¾ cup).

2 Pour the vegetable oil into a preheated wok and heat until almost smoking.

3 Dip the cubes of pork into the batter, and cook in the hot oil, in batches, until the pork is cooked through. Remove the pork from the wok with a slotted spoon and drain on absorbent kitchen paper (paper towels). Set aside and keep warm until required.

4 Drain all but 1 tablespoon of oil from the wok and return it to the heat. Add the onion, (bell) pepper, pineapple pieces, carrot and bamboo shoots and stir-fry for 1-2 minutes. Remove from the wok with a slotted spoon and set aside.

5 Mix all of the sauce ingredients together and pour into the wok. Bring to the boil, stirring until thickened and clear. Cook for 1 minute, then return the pork and vegetables to the wok. Cook for a further 1–2 minutes, then transfer to a serving plate and serve with rice or noodles.

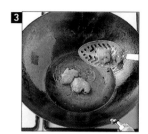

Roast Red Pork

Pork fillet (tenderloin) is given a marvellous flavour and distinctive red colour in this excellent recipe.

NUTRITIONAL INFORMATION

Calories 305	Sugars 4g	
Protein 40g	Fat 13g	
Carbohydrate 5g	Saturates 5g	

12¼ HOURS   40 MINS

SERVES 4

INGREDIENTS

750 g/1 lb 10 oz pork fillet (tenderloin)

1 tsp red food colouring

4 garlic cloves, crushed

1 tsp Chinese five-spice powder

1 tbsp light soy sauce

1 tbsp fish sauce

1 tbsp dry sherry

1 tbsp dark muscovado sugar

1 tbsp sesame oil

1 tbsp finely grated fresh ginger root

TO GARNISH

lettuce

spring onions (scallions), finely sliced

1 Rinse the pork and trim off any fat. Place in a large, clear plastic food bag or freezer bag and add the red food colouring. Roll the pork around in the bag to coat it in the colouring.

2 Mix all the remaining ingredients together and add the mixture to the pork in the plastic bag. Secure the opening and chill overnight, or for at least 12 hours, turning the bag over occasionally.

3 Place the pork on a rack over a roasting tin (pan). Cook in a preheated oven at 220°C/425°F/Gas Mark 7 for 15 minutes. Remove from the oven and baste with the remaining marinade.

4 Reduce the oven temperature to 180°C/350°F/Gas Mark 4 and roast the pork for a further 25 minutes, basting with any remaining marinade. Leave to cool for at least 10 minutes before slicing.

5 Slice thinly, arrange on a serving platter, garnish and serve.

COOK'S TIP

Putting the pork in a plastic bag helps to prevent your hands from turning red from the food colouring.

Lamb with Garlic Sauce

This dish contains Szechuan pepper, which is quite hot and may be replaced with black pepper, if preferred.

NUTRITIONAL INFORMATION

Calories	320	Sugars	.........2g
Protein	........25g	Fat	..........21g
Carbohydrate	....4g	Saturates	.......6g

 35 MINS   10 MINS

SERVES 4

I N G R E D I E N T S

450 g/1 lb lamb fillet or loin

2 tbsp dark soy sauce

2 tsp sesame oil

2 tbsp Chinese rice wine or dry sherry

½ tsp Szechuan pepper

4 tbsp vegetable oil

4 garlic cloves, crushed

60 g/2 oz water chestnuts, quartered

1 green (bell) pepper, seeded and sliced

1 tbsp wine vinegar

1 tbsp sesame oil

rice or noodles, to serve

1 Cut the lamb into 2.5-cm/1-inch pieces and place in a shallow dish.

2 Mix together 1 tablespoon of the soy sauce, the sesame oil, Chinese rice wine or sherry and Szechuan pepper. Pour the mixture over the lamb, turning to coat, and leave to marinate for 30 minutes.

3 Heat the vegetable oil in a preheated wok. Remove the lamb from the marinade and add to the wok, together with the garlic. Stir-fry for 2–3 minutes.

4 Add the water chestnuts and (bell) pepper to the wok and stir-fry for 1 minute.

5 Add the remaining soy sauce and the wine vinegar, mixing together well.

6 Add the sesame oil and cook, stirring constantly, for 1–2 minutes, or until the lamb is cooked through.

7 Transfer the lamb and garlic sauce to a warm serving dish and serve immediately with rice or noodles.

COOK'S TIP

Chinese chives, also known as garlic chives, would make an appropriate garnish for this dish.

Sesame oil is used as a flavouring, rather than for frying, as it burns readily, hence it is added at the end of cooking.

Hot Lamb

This is quite a spicy dish, using 2 chillies in the sauce. Halve the number of chillies to reduce the heat or seed the chillies before using if desired.

NUTRITIONAL INFORMATION

Calories	323	Sugars	. . . . .4g
Protein	. . . . .26g	Fat	. . . . .22g
Carbohydrate	. . . .5g	Saturates	. . . . . . .7g

25 MINS   15 MINS

SERVES 4

I N G R E D I E N T S

450 g/1 lb lean, boneless lamb

2 tbsp hoisin sauce

1 tbsp dark soy sauce

1 garlic clove, crushed

2 tsp grated fresh root ginger

2 tbsp vegetable oil

2 onions, sliced

1 fennel bulb, sliced

4 tbsp water

S A U C E

1 large fresh red chilli, cut into thin strips

1 fresh green chilli, cut into thin strips

2 tbsp rice wine vinegar

2 tsp light brown sugar

2 tbsp peanut oil

1 tsp sesame oil

VARIATION

Use beef, pork or duck instead of the lamb and vary the vegetables, using leeks or celery instead of the onion and fennel.

  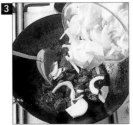 

1 Cut the lamb into 2.5-cm/1-inch cubes and place in a glass dish.

2 Mix together the hoisin sauce, soy sauce, garlic and ginger and pour over the lamb, turning to coat well. Leave to marinate for 20 minutes.

3 Heat the oil in a preheated wok and stir-fry the lamb for 1–2 minutes. Add the onions and fennel and cook for a further 2 minutes, or until they are just beginning to brown. Stir in the water, cover and cook for 2–3 minutes.

4 To make the sauce, place all the ingredients in a pan and cook over a low heat for 3-4 minutes, stirring.

5 Transfer the lamb and onions to a serving dish, toss lightly in the sauce and serve immediately.

Lamb with Satay Sauce

This recipe demonstrates the classic serving of lamb satay – lamb marinated in chilli and coconut and threaded on to wooden skewers.

NUTRITIONAL INFORMATION

Calories 501	Sugars 6g
Protein 34g	Fat 37g
Carbohydrate 9g	Saturates 10g

 35 MINS 25 MINS

SERVES 4

I N G R E D I E N T S

450 g/1 lb lamb loin fillet

1 tbsp mild curry paste

150 ml/5 fl oz/⅔ cup coconut milk

2 cloves garlic, crushed

½ tsp chilli powder

½ tsp cumin

S A T A Y   S A U C E

1 tbsp corn oil

1 onion, diced

6 tbsp crunchy peanut butter

1 tsp tomato purée (paste)

1 tsp fresh lime juice

100 ml/3½ fl oz/1⅓ cup cold water

1 Using a sharp knife, thinly slice the lamb and place in a large dish.

2 Mix together the curry paste, coconut milk, garlic, chilli powder and cumin in a bowl. Pour over the lamb, toss well, cover and marinate for 30 minutes.

3 To make the satay sauce. Heat the oil in a large wok and stir-fry the onion for 5 minutes, then reduce the heat and cook for 5 minutes.

4 Stir in the peanut butter, tomato purée (paste), lime juice and water.

5 Thread the lamb on to wooden skewers, reserving the marinade.

6 Grill (broil) the lamb skewers under a hot grill (broiler) for 6–8 minutes, turning once.

7 Add the reserved marinade to the wok, bring to the boil and cook for 5 minutes. Serve the lamb skewers with the satay sauce.

COOK'S TIP

Soak the wooden skewers in cold water for 30 minutes before grilling (broiling) to prevent the skewers from burning.

Sesame Lamb Stir-Fry

This is a very simple, but delicious, dish in which lean pieces of lamb are cooked in sugar and soy sauce and then sprinkled with sesame seeds.

NUTRITIONAL INFORMATION

Calories	276	Sugars	.........4g
Protein	........25g	Fat	..........18g
Carbohydrate	....5g	Saturates	.......6g

5 MINS   10 MINS

SERVES 4

INGREDIENTS

450 g/1 lb boneless lean lamb

2 tbsp peanut oil

2 leeks, sliced

1 carrot, cut into matchsticks

2 garlic cloves, crushed

85 ml/3 fl oz/⅓ cup lamb or vegetable stock

2 tsp light brown sugar

1 tbsp dark soy sauce

4½ tsp sesame seeds

1 Using a sharp knife, cut the lamb into thin strips.

2 Heat the peanut oil in a preheated wok or large frying pan (skillet) until it is really hot.

3 Add the lamb and stir-fry for 2–3 minutes. Remove the lamb from the wok with a slotted spoon and set aside until required.

4 Add the leeks, carrot and garlic to the wok or frying pan (skillet) and stir-fry in the remaining oil for 1–2 minutes.

5 Remove the vegetables from the wok with a slotted spoon and set aside.

6 Drain any remaining oil from the wok. Place the lamb or vegetable stock,

light brown sugar and dark soy sauce in the wok and add the lamb. Cook, stirring constantly to coat the lamb, for 2–3 minutes.

7 Sprinkle the sesame seeds over the top, turning the lamb to coat.

8 Spoon the leek, carrot and garlic mixture on to a warm serving dish and top with the lamb. Serve immediately.

COOK'S TIP

Be careful not to burn the sugar in the wok when heating and coating the meat, otherwise the flavour of the dish will be spoiled.

Spare Ribs with Chilli

For best results, chop the spare ribs into small bite-size pieces after cooking, so they are easy to eat.

NUTRITIONAL INFORMATION

Calories	497	Sugars	.........3g
Protein	........13g	Fat	.........47g
Carbohydrate	....4g	Saturates	......11g

🥔 60 MINS   🕐 20 MINS

SERVES 4

INGREDIENTS

500 g/1 lb 2 oz pork spare ribs

1 tsp sugar

1 tbsp light soy sauce

1 tsp rice wine or dry sherry

1 tsp cornflour (cornstarch)

about 600 ml/1 pint/2½ cups vegetable oil

1 garlic clove, finely chopped

1 spring onion (scallion), cut into short sections

1 small hot chilli pepper (green or red), thinly sliced

2 tbsp black bean sauce

about 150 ml/¼ pint/⅔ cup Chinese Stock (see page 14) or water

1 small onion, diced

1 medium green (bell) pepper, cored, seeded and diced

COOK'S TIP

Be very careful when handling and cutting chilli peppers as their juice can cause irritation of the skin. Be sure to wash your hands after handling, and keep well away from face and eyes. The seeds of the chilli are the hottest part – remove seeds if you want a milder dish.

1 Trim any excess fat from the ribs. Using a sharp knife or meat cleaver, chop each rib into 3-4 bite-sized piecess and place in a shallow dish.

2 Mix together the sugar, soy sauce, wine and cornflour (cornstarch) and pour the mixture over the pork ribs. Leave to marinate for 35-45 minutes.

3 Heat the vegetable oil in a large preheated wok or frying pan (skillet).

4 Add the spare ribs to the wok and deep-fry for 2-3 minutes until light brown. Remove with a slotted spoon and drain on absorbent kitchen paper (paper towels).

5 Pour off the oil, leaving about 1 tablespoon in the wok. Add the garlic, spring onion (scallion), chilli pepper and black bean sauce and stir-fry for 30-40 seconds.

6 Add the spare ribs, blend well, then add the stock or water. Bring to the boil, then reduce the heat, cover and braise for 8-10 minutes, stirring once or twice.

7 Add the onion and green (bell) pepper, increase the heat to high, and stir uncovered for about 2 minutes to reduce the sauce a little. Serve hot.

Five-Spice Lamb

Chinese five-spice powder is a blend of cinnamon, fennel, star anise, ginger and cloves, all finely ground together.

NUTRITIONAL INFORMATION

Calories	361	Sugars	.........3g
Protein	........35g	Fat	.........22g
Carbohydrate	....5g	Saturates	.......8g

1¼ HOURS   10 MINS

SERVES 4

INGREDIENTS

625 g/1 lb 6 oz lean boneless lamb (leg or fillet)

2 tsp Chinese five-spice powder

3 tbsp sunflower oil

1 red (bell) pepper, cored, seeded and thinly sliced

1 green (bell) pepper, cored, seeded and thinly sliced

1 yellow or orange (bell) pepper, cored, seeded and thinly sliced

4-6 spring onions (scallions), thinly sliced diagonally

175 g/6 oz French (green) or fine beans, cut into 4 cm/1½ inch lengths

2 tbsp soy sauce

4 tbsp sherry

salt and pepper

Chinese noodles, to serve

TO GARNISH

strips of red and yellow (bell) pepper

fresh coriander (cilantro) leaves

1 Cut the lamb into narrow strips, about 4 cm/1½ inches long, across the grain. Place in a bowl, add the five-spice powder and ¼ teaspoon salt, mix well and leave to marinate, covered, in a cool place for at least an hour and up to 24 hours.

2 Heat half the oil in the wok, swirling it around until really hot. Add the lamb and stir-fry briskly for 3-4 minutes until almost cooked through. Remove from the pan and set aside.

3 Add the remaining oil to the wok and when hot add the (bell) peppers and spring onions (scallions). Stir-fry for 2-3 minutes, then add the beans and stir for a minute or so.

4 Add the soy sauce and sherry to the wok and when hot return the lamb and any juices to the wok. Stir-fry for 1-2 minutes until the lamb is really hot again and thoroughly coated in the sauce. Season to taste.

5 Serve the five-spice lamb with Chinese noodles, garnished with strips of red and green (bell) pepper and fresh coriander (cilantro).

Fish & Seafood

China's many miles of coastline, rivers and lakes offer an enormous variety of fresh and salt-water fish and seafood. Among the most popular are carp, bass, bream, clams, crab,

crawfish and prawns (shrimp). Dishes which include shark's fins, abalone, squid and edible seaweed are also common. When buying fish and seafood for Chinese cooking, freshness is imperative to flavour, so be sure to buy it and use it as soon as possible, preferably the same day. Chinese chefs buy fish which are kept alive until just before cooking. Favourite cooking methods for fish are steaming and quick poaching in boiling water or broth.

Shrimp Fu-Yong

The classic ingredients of this popular dish are eggs, carrots and shrimps. Add extra ingredients such as peas or crabmeat, if desired.

NUTRITIONAL INFORMATION

Calories 240	Sugars 1g
Protein 22g	Fat 16g
Carbohydrate 1g	Saturates 3g

 5 MINS   10 MINS

SERVES 4

INGREDIENTS

2 tbsp vegetable oil

1 carrot, grated

5 eggs, beaten

225 g/8 oz raw (small) shrimp, peeled

1 tbsp light soy sauce

pinch of Chinese five-spice powder

2 spring onions (scallions), chopped

2 tsp sesame seeds

1 tsp sesame oil

COOK'S TIP

If only cooked prawns (shrimp) are available, add them just before the end of cooking, but make sure they are fully incorporated into the fu yong. They require only heating through. Overcooking will make them chewy and tasteless.

1 Heat the vegetable oil in a preheated wok or frying pan (skillet), swirling it around until the oil is really hot.

2 Add the grated carrot and stir-fry for 1–2 minutes.

3 Push the carrot to one side of the wok or frying pan (skillet) and add the beaten eggs. Cook, stirring gently, for 1–2 minutes.

4 Stir the (small) shrimp, light soy sauce and five-spice powder into the mixture in the wok. Stir-fry the mixture for 2–3 minutes, or until the (small) shrimps change colour and the mixture is almost dry.

5 Turn the (small) shrimp fu yong out on to a warm plate and sprinkle the spring onions (scallions), sesame seeds and sesame oil on top. Serve immediately.

Chilli Prawns (Shrimp)

Large prawns (shrimp) are marinated in a chilli mixture then stir-fried with cashews. Serve with a fluffy rice and braised vegetables.

NUTRITIONAL INFORMATION

Calories 435	Sugars 2g	
Protein 4.2g	Fat 23	
Carbohydrate . . .10g	Saturates 4g	

2¼ HOURS   5 MINS

SERVES 4

I N G R E D I E N T S

5 tbsp soy sauce

5 tbsp dry sherry

3 dried red chillies, seeded and
    chopped

2 garlic cloves, crushed

2 tsp grated ginger root

5 tbsp water

625 g/1 lb 6 oz shelled tiger prawns
    (jumbo shrimp)

1 large bunch spring onions (scallions),
    chopped

90 g/3 oz/⅔ cup salted cashew nuts

3 tbsp vegetable oil

2 tsp cornflour (cornstarch)

1 Mix the soy sauce, sherry, chillies, garlic, ginger and water in a bowl.

2 Add the tiger prawns (jumbo shrimp), spring onions (scallions) and cashews and mix well. Cover tightly and leave to marinate for at least 2 hours, stirring occasionally.

3 Heat the oil in a large wok. Remove the prawns (shrimp), spring onions (scallions) and cashews from the marinade with a slotted spoon and add to the wok, reserving the marinade. Stir-fry over a high heat for 1-2 minutes.

4 Mix the reserved marinade with the cornflour (cornstarch), add to the wok and stir-fry for about 30 seconds, until the marinade forms a slightly thickened shiny glaze over the prawn (shrimp) mixture. Serve immediately.

COOK'S TIP

For an attractive presentation serve this dish on mixed wild rice and basmati rice. Start cooking the wild rice in boiling water. After 10 minutes, add the basmati rice or other rice and continue boiling until all grains are tender. Drain well and adjust the seasoning.

Fried Prawns with Cashews

Cashew nuts are delicious as part of a stir-fry with almost any other ingredient. Use the unsalted variety in cooking.

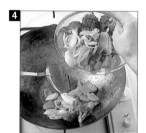

NUTRITIONAL INFORMATION

Calories	406	Sugar	.........3g
Protein	........31g	Fat	..........25g
Carbohydrate	...13g	Saturates	.......4g

5 MINS   5 MINS

SERVES 4

INGREDIENTS

2 garlic cloves, crushed

1 tbsp cornflour (cornstarch)

pinch of caster (superfine) sugar

450 g/1 lb raw tiger prawns
  (jumbo shrimp)

4 tbsp vegetable oil

1 leek, sliced

125 g/4½ oz broccoli florets

1 orange (bell) pepper, seeded
  and diced

75 g/2¾ oz/¾ cup unsalted
  cashew nuts

SAUCE

175 ml/6 fl oz/¾ cup fish stock

1 tbsp cornflour (cornstarch)

dash of chilli sauce

2 tsp sesame oil

1 tbsp Chinese rice wine

1 Mix together the garlic, cornflour (cornstarch) and sugar in a bowl.

2 Peel and devein the prawns (shrimp). Stir the prawns (shrimp) into the mixture to coat thoroughly.

3 Heat the vegetable oil in a preheated wok and add the prawn (shrimp) mixture. Stir-fry over a high heat for 20–30 seconds until the prawns (shrimp) turn pink. Remove the prawns (shrimp) from the wok with a slotted spoon, drain on absorbent kitchen paper (paper towels) and set aside until required.

4 Add the leek, broccoli and (bell) pepper to the wok and stir-fry for 2 minutes.

5 To make the sauce, place the fish stock, cornflour (cornstarch), chilli sauce to taste, the sesame oil and Chinese rice wine in a small bowl. Mix until thoroughly.

6 Add the sauce to the wok, together with the cashew nuts. Return the prawns (shrimp) to the wok and cook for 1 minute to heat through.

7 Transfer the prawn (shrimp) stir-fry to a warm serving dish and serve immediately.

Seared Scallops

Scallops have a terrific, subtle flavour which is complemented in this dish by the buttery sauce.

NUTRITIONAL INFORMATION

Calories	272	Sugars	.........0g
Protein	........28g	Fat	..........17g
Carbohydrate	....2g	Saturates	.......8g

 5 MINS   10 MINS

SERVES 4

I N G R E D I E N T S

450 g/1 lb fresh scallops, without roe, or the same amount of frozen scallops, defrosted thoroughly

6 spring onions (scallions)

2 tbsp vegetable oil

1 green chilli, deseeded and sliced

3 tbsp sweet soy sauce

50 g/1¾ oz/1½ tbsp butter, cubed

1 Rinse the scallops thoroughly under cold running water, drain and pat the scallops dry with absorbent kitchen paper (paper towels).

2 Using a sharp knife, slice each scallop in half horizontally.

COOK'S TIP

If you buy scallops on the shell, slide a knife underneath the membrane to loosen it and cut off the tough muscle that holds the scallop to the shell. Discard the black stomach sac and intestinal vein.

3 Using a sharp knife, trim and slice the spring onions (scallions).

4 Heat the vegetable oil in a large preheated wok or heavy-based frying pan (skillet), swirling the oil around the base of the wok until it is really hot.

5 Add the sliced green chilli, spring onions (scallions) and scallops to the wok and stir-fry over a high heat for

4–5 minutes, or until the scallops are just cooked through. If using frozen scallops, be sure not to overcook them as they will easily disintegrate.

6 Add the soy sauce and butter to the scallop stir-fry and heat through until the butter melts.

7 Transfer to warm serving bowls and serve hot.

Scallop Pancakes

Scallops, like most shellfish, require very little cooking, and this original dish is a perfect example of how to use shellfish to its full potential.

NUTRITIONAL INFORMATION

Calories 240	Sugars 1g
Protein 29g	Fat 9g
Carbohydrate 11g	Saturates 1g

 5 MINS   30 MINS

SERVES 4

I N G R E D I E N T S

100 g/3½ oz fine green beans

1 red chilli

450 g/1 lb scallops, without roe

1 egg

3 spring onions (scallions), sliced

50 g/1¾ oz/½ cup rice flour

1 tbsp fish sauce

oil, for frying

salt

sweet chilli dip, to serve

1 Using a sharp knife, trim the green beans and slice them very thinly.

2 Using a sharp knife, deseed and very finely chop the red chilli.

3 Bring a small saucepan of lightly salted water to the boil. Add the green beans to the pan and cook for 3–4 minutes or until just softened.

4 Roughly chop the scallops and place them in a large bowl. Add the cooked beans to the scallops.

5 Mix the egg with the spring onions (scallions), rice flour, fish sauce and chilli until well combined. Add to the scallops and mix well.

6 Heat about 2.5 cm/1 inch of oil in a large preheated wok. Add a ladleful of the mixture to the wok and cook for 5 minutes until golden and set.

7 Remove the pancake from the wok and leave to drain on absorbent kitchen paper (paper towels). Keep warm while cooking the remaining pancake mixture. Serve the pancakes hot with a sweet chilli dip.

VARIATION

You could use prawns (shrimp) or shelled clams instead of the scallops, if you prefer.

Scallops in Ginger Sauce

Scallops are both attractive and delicious. Cooked with ginger and orange, this dish is perfect served with plain rice.

NUTRITIONAL INFORMATION

Calories 216   Sugars 4g
Protein . . . . .30g   Fat 8g
Carbohydrate . . . .8g   Saturates 1g

5 MINS   10 MINS

SERVES 4

INGREDIENTS

2 tbsp vegetable oil

450 g/1 lb scallops, cleaned and halved

2.5-cm/1-inch piece fresh root ginger, finely chopped

3 garlic cloves, crushed

2 leeks, shredded

75 g/2¾ oz/¾ cup shelled peas

125 g/4½ oz canned bamboo shoots, drained and rinsed

2 tbsp light soy sauce

2 tbsp unsweetened orange juice

1 tsp caster (superfine) sugar

orange zest, to garnish

1 Heat the vegetable oil in a preheated wok or large frying pan (skillet). Add the scallops and stir-fry for 1–2 minutes. Remove the scallops from the wok with a slotted spoon, keep warm and set aside until required.

2 Add the ginger and garlic to the wok and stir-fry for 30 seconds. Stir in the leeks and peas and cook, stirring, for a further 2 minutes.

3 Add the bamboo shoots and return the scallops to the wok. Stir gently to mix without breaking up the scallops.

4 Stir in the soy sauce, orange juice and caster (superfine) sugar and cook for 1–2 minutes.

5 Transfer the stir-fry to a serving dish, garnish with the orange zest and serve immediately.

COOK'S TIP

The edible parts of a scallop are the round white muscle and the orange and white coral or roe. The frilly skirt surrounding the muscle – the gills and mantle – may be used for making shellfish stock. All other parts should be discarded.

Cantonese Prawns (Shrimp)

This prawn (shrimp) dish is very simple and is ideal for supper or lunch when time is short.

NUTRITIONAL INFORMATION

Calories	460	Sugar	.........3g
Protein	........53g	Fat	24
Carbohydrate	....6g	Saturates	.......5g

10 MINS   20 MINS

SERVES 4

INGREDIENTS

5 tbsp vegetable oil

4 garlic cloves, crushed

675 g/1½ lb raw prawns (shrimp), shelled and deveined

5-cm/2-inch piece fresh root ginger, chopped

175 g/6 oz lean pork, diced

1 leek, sliced

3 eggs, beaten

shredded leek and red (bell) pepper matchsticks, to garnish

rice, to serve

SAUCE

2 tbsp Chinese rice wine or dry sherry

2 tbsp light soy sauce

2 tsp caster (superfine) sugar

150 ml/¼ pint/⅔ cup fish stock

4½ tsp cornflour (cornstarch)

3 tbsp water

1 Heat 2 tablespoons of the vegetable oil in a preheated wok.

2 Add the garlic to the wok and stir-fry for 30 seconds.

3 Add the prawns (shrimp) to the wok and stir-fry for 5 minutes, or until

they change colour. Remove the prawns (shrimp) from the wok or frying pan (skillet) with a slotted spoon, set aside and keep warm.

4 Add the remaining oil to the wok and heat, swirling the oil around the base of the wok until it is really hot.

5 Add the ginger, diced pork and leek to the wok and stir-fry over a medium heat for 4-5 minutes, or until the pork is lightly coloured and sealed.

6 To make the sauce, add the rice wine or sherry, soy sauce, caster (superfine) sugar and fish stock to the wok and stir to blend.

7 In a small bowl, blend the cornflour (cornstarch) with the water to form a smooth paste and stir it into the wok. Cook, stirring, until the sauce thickens and clears.

8 Return the prawns (shrimp) to the wok and add the beaten eggs. Cook for 5-6 minutes, gently stirring occasionally, until the eggs set.

9 Transfer to a warm serving dish, garnish with shredded leek and (bell) pepper matchsticks and serve immediately with rice.

Mussels with Lemon Grass

Give fresh mussels a Far-Eastern flavour by using some Kaffir lime leaves, garlic and lemon grass in the stock used for steaming them.

NUTRITIONAL INFORMATION

Calories 194   Sugar 0g
Protein ....33g   Fat 7g
Carbohydrate ....1g   Saturates 1g

10 MINS   10 MINS

SERVES 4

I N G R E D I E N T S

750 g/1 lb 10 oz live mussels

1 tbsp sesame oil

3 shallots, chopped finely

2 garlic cloves, chopped finely

1 stalk lemon grass

2 Kaffir lime leaves

2 tbsp chopped fresh coriander (cilantro)

finely grated rind of 1 lime

2 tbsp lime juice

300 ml/½ pint/1¼ cups hot vegetable stock

crusty bread, to serve

fresh coriander (cilantro), to garnish

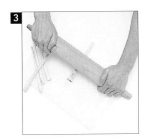

1 Using a small sharp knife, scrape the beards off the mussels under cold running water. Scrub them well, discarding any that are damaged or remain open when tapped. Keep rinsing until there is no trace of sand.

2 Heat the sesame oil in a large saucepan and fry the shallots and garlic gently until softened, about 2 minutes.

3 Bruise the lemon grass, using a meat mallet or rolling pin, and add to the pan with the Kaffir lime leaves, coriander (cilantro), lime rind and juice, mussels and stock. Put the lid on the saucepan and cook over a moderate heat for 3–5 minutes. Shake the pan from time to time.

4 Lift the mussels out into 4 warmed soup plates, discarding any that remain shut. Boil the remaining liquid rapidly to reduce slightly. Remove the lemon grass and lime leaves, then pour the liquid over the mussels.

5 Garnish with coriander (cilantro) and lime wedges, and serve at once.

COOK'S TIP

Mussels are now farmed, so they should be available from good fishmongers throughout the year.

Mussels in Black Bean Sauce

This dish looks so impressive, the combination of colours making it look almost too good to eat!

NUTRITIONAL INFORMATION

Calories ....174 Sugars 4g
Protein ....19g Fat 8g
Carbohydrate ....6g Saturates 1g

5 MINS   10 MINS

SERVES 4

I N G R E D I E N T S

350 g/12 oz leeks

350 g/12 oz cooked green-lipped mussels (shelled)

1 tsp cumin seeds

2 tbsp vegetable oil

2 cloves garlic, crushed

1 red (bell) pepper, deseeded and sliced

50 g/1¾ oz/¾ cup canned bamboo shoots, drained

175 g/6 oz baby spinach

160 g/5¾ oz jar black bean sauce

1 Using a sharp knife, trim the leeks and shred them.

2 Place the cooked green-lipped mussels in a large bowl, sprinkle with the cumin seeds and toss well to coat all over. Set aside until required.

COOK'S TIP

If the green-lipped mussels are not available they can be bought shelled in cans and jars from most large supermarkets.

3 Heat the vegetable oil in a preheated wok, swirling the oil around the base of the wok until it is really hot.

4 Add the shredded leeks, garlic and sliced red (bell) pepper to the wok and stir-fry for 5 minutes, or until the vegetables are tender.

5 Add the bamboo shoots, baby spinach leaves and cooked green-lipped mussels to the wok and stir-fry for about 2 minutes.

6 Pour the black bean sauce over the ingredients in the wok, toss well to coat all the ingredients in the sauce and leave to simmer for a few seconds, stirring occasionally.

7 Transfer the stir-fry to warm serving bowls and serve immediately.

Crab with Chinese Leaves

The delicate flavour of Chinese leaves (cabbage) and crab meat are enhanced by the coconut milk in this recipe.

NUTRITIONAL INFORMATION

Calories 109   Sugars 1g
Protein . . . . .11g   Fat 6g
Carbohydrate . . . .2g   Saturates 1g

 5 MINS   10 MINS

SERVES 4

INGREDIENTS

225 g/8 oz shiitake mushrooms

2 tbsp vegetable oil

2 cloves garlic, crushed

6 spring onions (scallions), sliced

1 head Chinese leaves (cabbage),
   shredded

1 tbsp mild curry paste

6 tbsp coconut milk

200 g/7 oz can white crab meat,
   drained

1 tsp chilli flakes

1 Using a sharp knife, cut the mushrooms into slices.

2 Heat the vegetable oil in a large preheated wok or heavy-based frying pan (skillet).

3 Add the mushrooms and garlic to the wok or frying pan (skillet) and stir-fry for 3 minutes or until the mushrooms have softened.

4 Add the spring onions (scallions) and shredded Chinese leaves (cabbage) to the wok and stir-fry until the leaves have wilted.

5 Mix together the mild curry paste and coconut milk in a small bowl.

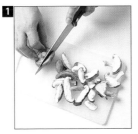

6 Add the curry paste and coconut milk mixture to the wok, together with the crab meat and chilli flakes. Mix together until well combined.

7 Heat the mixture in the wok until the juices start to bubble.

8 Transfer the crab and vegetable stir-fry to warm serving bowls and serve immediately.

COOK'S TIP

Shiitake mushrooms are now readily available in the fresh vegetable section of most large supermarkets.

Crab Claws with Chilli

Crab claws are frequently used in Chinese cooking, and look sensational. They are perfect with this delicious chilli sauce.

NUTRITIONAL INFORMATION

Calories ....154 Sugar 3g
Protein ....16g Fat 7g
Carbohydrate ....8g Saturates 1g

     5 MINS 🕐 10 MINS

SERVES 4

INGREDIENTS

700 g/1 lb 9 oz crab claws

1 tbsp corn oil

2 cloves garlic, crushed

1 tbsp grated fresh root ginger

3 red chillies, deseeded and finely chopped

2 tbsp sweet chilli sauce

3 tbsp tomato ketchup

300 ml/½ pint/1¼ cups cooled fish stock

1 tbsp cornflour (cornstarch)

salt and pepper

1 tbsp fresh chives, snipped

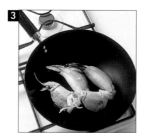

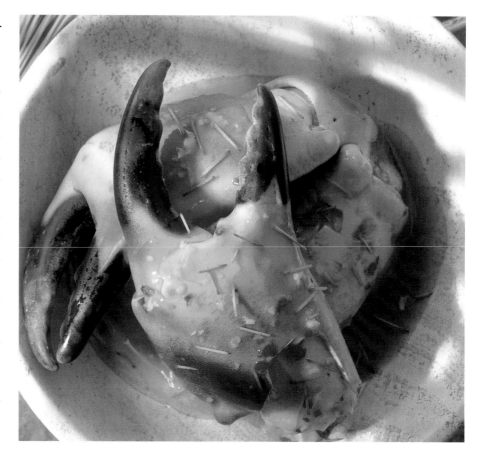

1 Gently crack the crab claws with a nut cracker. This process will allow the flavours of the chilli, garlic and ginger to fully penetrate the crab meat.

2 Heat the corn oil in a large preheated wok.

3 Add the crab claws to the wok and stir-fry for about 5 minutes.

4 Add the garlic, ginger and chillies to the wok and stir-fry for 1 minute, tossing the crab claws to coat all over.

5 Mix together the sweet chilli sauce, tomato ketchup, fish stock and cornflour (cornstarch) in a small bowl. Add this mixture to the wok and cook, stirring occasionally, until the sauce starts to thicken.

6 Season the mixture in the wok with salt and pepper to taste.

7 Transfer the crab claws and chilli sauce to warm serving dishes, garnish with snipped fresh chives and serve.

COOK'S TIP

If crab claws are not easily available, use a whole crab, cut into eight pieces, instead.

Crab Meat Cakes

Make these tasty crab-meat cakes to serve as a snack or starter, or as an accompaniment to a main meal.

NUTRITIONAL INFORMATION

Calories 262   Sugars 4g
Protein ....13g   Fat 17g
Carbohydrate ...14g   Saturates 3g

20 MINS   55 MINS

SERVES 4

INGREDIENTS

90 g/3 oz/generous 1 cup long-grain rice

1 tbsp sesame oil

1 small onion, chopped finely

1 large garlic clove, crushed

2 tbsp chopped fresh coriander (cilantro)

200 g/7 oz can of crab meat, drained

1 tbsp fish sauce or light soy sauce

250 ml/9 fl oz/1 cup coconut milk

2 eggs

4 tbsp vegetable oil

salt and pepper

sliced spring onions (scallions), to garnish

1 Cook the rice in plenty of boiling, lightly salted water until just tender, about 12 minutes. Rinse with cold water and drain well.

2 Heat the sesame oil in a small frying pan (skillet) and fry the onion and garlic gently for about 5 minutes, until softened and golden brown.

3 Combine the rice, onion, garlic, coriander (cilantro), crab meat, fish sauce or soy sauce and coconut milk. Season. Beat the eggs and add to the mixture. Divide the mixture between 8 greased ramekin dishes or teacups and place them in a baking dish or roasting tin (pan) with enough warm water to come halfway up their sides. Place in a preheated oven at 180°C/ 350°F/Gas Mark 4 for 25 minutes, until set. Leave to cool.

4 Turn the crab cakes out of the ramekin dishes . Heat the oil in a wok or frying pan (skillet) and fry the crab cakes in the oil until golden brown. Drain on kitchen paper (paper towels), garnish and serve.

COOK'S TIP

If you want, you can prepare these crab cakes up to the point where they have been baked. Cool them, then cover and chill, ready for frying when needed.

Baked Crab with Ginger

In Chinese restaurants, only live crabs are used, but ready-cooked ones can be used at home quite successfully.

NUTRITIONAL INFORMATION

Calories 261   Sugars 0.5g
Protein . . . . .18g   Fat 17g
Carbohydrate . . . .5g   Saturates 2g

25 MINS   10 MINS

SERVES 4

I N G R E D I E N T S

1 large or 2 medium crabs, weighing about 750 g/1 lb 10 oz in total

2 tbsp Chinese rice wine or dry sherry

1 egg, lightly beaten

1 tbsp cornflour (cornstarch)

3-4 tbsp vegetable oil

1 tbsp finely chopped ginger root

3-4 spring onions (scallions), cut into sections

2 tbsp light soy sauce

1 tsp sugar

about 75 ml/5 tbsp/⅓ cup Chinese Stock (see page 14) or water

½ tsp sesame oil

coriander (cilantro) leaves, to garnish

1 Cut the crab in half from the under-belly. Break off the claws and crack them with the back of a cleaver or a large kitchen knife.

2 Discard the legs and crack the shell, breaking it into several pieces. Discard the feathery gills and the stomach sac. Place the crab meat in a bowl.

3 Mix together the wine or sherry, egg and cornflour (cornstarch). Pour the mixture over the crab and leave to marinate for 10-15 minutes.

4 Heat the vegetable oil in a preheated wok and stir-fry the crab with the chopped ginger and spring onions (scallions) for 2-3 minutes.

5 Add the soy sauce, sugar and Chinese stock or water, blend well and bring to the boil. Cover and cook for 3-4 minutes, then remove the lid, sprinkle with sesame oil and serve, garnished with fresh coriander (cilantro) leaves.

COOK'S TIP

Crabs are almost always sold ready-cooked. The crab should feel heavy for its size, and when it is shaken, there should be no sound of water inside. A good medium-sized crab should yield about 500 g/1 lb 2 oz meat, enough for 3-4 people.

Fried Squid Flowers

The addition of green (bell) pepper and black bean sauce to the squid makes a colourful and delicious dish from the Cantonese school.

NUTRITIONAL INFORMATION

Calories 172   Sugars 1g
Protein . . . . .13g   Fat 13g
Carbohydrate . . . .2g   Saturates 1g

10 MINS   5 MINS

SERVES 4

I N G R E D I E N T S

350-400 g/12-14 oz prepared and cleaned squid (see Cook's Tip, below)

1 medium green (bell) pepper, cored and seeded

3-4 tbsp vegetable oil

1 garlic clove, finely chopped

¼ tsp finely chopped ginger root

2 tsp finely chopped spring onions (scallions)

½ tsp salt

2 tbsp crushed black bean sauce

1 tsp Chinese rice wine or dry sherry

a few drops sesame oil

boiled rice, to serve

1 If ready-prepared squid is not available, prepare as instructed in the Cook's Tip, below.

2 Open up the squid and, using a meat cleaver or sharp knife, score the inside of the flesh in a criss-cross pattern.

3 Cut the squid into pieces about the size of an oblong postage stamp.

4 Blanch the squid pieces in a bowl of boiling water for a few seconds. Remove and drain; dry well on absorbent kitchen paper (paper towels).

5 Cut the (bell) pepper into small triangular pieces. Heat the oil in a preheated wok or large frying pan (skillet) and stir-fry the (bell) pepper for about 1 minute.

6 Add the garlic, ginger, spring onion (scallion), salt and squid. Continue stirring for another minute.

7 Finally add the black bean sauce and Chinese rice wine or dry sherry, and blend well.

8 Transfer the squid flowers to a serving dish, sprinkle with sesame oil and serve with boiled rice.

COOK'S TIP

Clean the squid by first cutting off the head. Cut off the tentacles and reserve. Remove the small soft bone at the base of the tentacles and the transparent backbone, as well as the ink bag. Peel off the thin skin, then wash and dry well.

Squid with Black Bean Sauce

Squid really is wonderful if quickly cooked as in this recipe, and contrary to popular belief, it is not tough and rubbery unless it is overcooked.

NUTRITIONAL INFORMATION

Calories	180	Sugars	.........2g
Protein	........19g	Fat	...........7g
Carbohydrate	...10g	Saturates	.......1g

5 MINS   20 MINS

SERVES 4

INGREDIENTS

450 g/1 lb squid rings

2 tbsp plain (all-purpose) flour

½ tsp salt

1 green (bell) pepper

2 tbsp groundnut oil

1 red onion, sliced

160 g/5¾ oz jar black bean sauce

1 Rinse the squid rings under cold running water and pat dry thoroughly with absorbent kitchen paper (paper towels).

2 Place the plain (all-purpose) flour and salt in a bowl and mix together. Add the squid rings and toss until they are evenly coated.

3 Using a sharp knife, deseed the (bell) pepper. Slice the (bell) pepper into thin strips.

4 Heat the groundnut oil in a large preheated wok or heavy-based frying pan (skillet), swirling the oil around the base of the wok until it is really hot.

5 Add the (bell) pepper slices and red onion to the wok or frying pan (skillet) and stir-fry for about 2 minutes, or until the vegetables are just softening.

6 Add the squid rings to the wok or frying pan (skillet) and cook for a further 5 minutes, or until the squid is cooked through. Be careful not to overcook the squid.

7 Add the black bean sauce to the wok and heat through until the juices are bubbling. Transfer the squid stir-fry to warm serving bowls and serve immediately.

COOK'S TIP

Serve this recipe with fried rice or noodles tossed in soy sauce, if you wish.

Octopus & Squid with Chilli

Try to buy cleaned squid tubes for this dish; if they are not available, see page 173 for instructions on preparing squid.

NUTRITIONAL INFORMATION

Calories 319	Sugars 2g
Protein 40g	Fat 13g
Carbohydrate 4g	Saturates 1g

8½ HOURS   10 MINS

SERVES 6

INGREDIENTS

150 ml/¼ pint/⅔ cup rice vinegar

50 ml/2 fl oz/¼ cup dry sherry

2 red chillies, chopped

1 tsp sugar

4 tbsp oil

12 baby octopus

12 small squid tubes, cleaned

2 spring onions (scallions), sliced

1 garlic clove, crushed

2.5 cm/1 inch piece ginger, grated

4 tbsp sweet chilli sauce

salt

1 Combine the vinegar, dry sherry, red chillies, sugar, 2 tbsp of the oil and a pinch of salt in a large bowl.

2 Wash each octopus under cold running water and drain. Lay each on its side on a chopping board. Find the 'neck' and cut through. The 'beak' of the octopus should be left in the head; if it is not, make a cut nearer the tentacles and check again. Discard the head and beak, and put the tentacles, which should all be in one piece, into the vinegar mixture.

3 Put the squid tubes into the vinegar mixture and turn to coat well. Cover and chill for 8 hours or overnight.

4 Heat the remaining oil in a wok and stir-fry the spring onions (scallions), garlic and ginger for 1 minute over a very hot barbecue. Remove from the heat and add the chilli sauce. Set aside.

5 Drain the fish from the marinade. Cut the pointed bottom end off each squid tube, so the tubes are of even width. Open out the squid so that it is flat. Score the squid to create a lattice pattern.

6 Cook the octopus and squid over the hottest part of the barbecue for 4–5 minutes, turning them constantly. The octopus tentacles will curl up, and are cooked when the flesh is no longer translucent. The squid tubes will curl back on themselves, revealing the lattice cuts.

7 When cooked, toss them into the pan with the chilli sauce to coat completely and serve immediately.

Seafood Medley

Use any combination of fish and seafood in this delicious dish of coated fish served in a wine sauce.

NUTRITIONAL INFORMATION

Calories	168	Sugars	.........2g
Protein	........29g	Fat	...........3g
Carbohydrate	....4g	Saturates	.......1g

5 MINS   15 MINS

SERVES 4

INGREDIENTS

2 tbsp dry white wine

1 egg white, lightly beaten

½ tsp Chinese five-spice powder

1 tsp cornflour (cornstarch)

300 g/10½ oz raw prawns (shrimp), peeled and deveined

125 g/4½ oz prepared squid, cut into rings

125 g/4½ oz white fish fillets, cut into strips

vegetable oil, for deep-frying

1 green (bell) pepper, seeded and cut into thin strips

1 carrot, cut into thin strips

4 baby corn cobs, halved lengthways

1 Mix the wine, egg white, five-spice powder and cornflour (cornstarch) in a large bowl. Add the prawns (shrimp), squid rings and fish fillets and stir to coat evenly. Remove the fish and seafood with a slotted spoon, reserving any leftover cornflour (cornstarch) mixture.

2 Heat the oil in a preheated wok and deep-fry the prawns (shrimp), squid and fish for 2–3 minutes. Remove the

seafood mixture from the wok with a slotted spoon and set aside.

3 Pour off all but 1 tablespoon of oil from the wok and return to the heat. Add the (bell) pepper, carrot and corn cobs and stir-fry for 4–5 minutes.

4 Return the seafood to the wok with any remaining cornflour (cornstarch) mixture. Heat through, stirring, and serve.

COOK'S TIP

Open up the squid rings and using a sharp knife, score a lattice pattern on the flesh to make them look attractive.

Gingered Monkfish

This dish is a real treat and is perfect for special occasions. Monkfish has a tender flavour which is ideal with asparagus, chilli and ginger.

NUTRITIONAL INFORMATION

Calories 133	Sugars 0g	
Protein 21g	Fat 5g	
Carbohydrate 1g	Saturates 1g	

 5 MINS 10 MINS

SERVES 4

INGREDIENTS

450 g/1 lb monkfish

1 tbsp freshly grated root ginger

2 tbsp sweet chilli sauce

1 tbsp corn oil

100 g/3½ oz/1 cup fine asparagus

3 spring onions (scallions), sliced

1 tsp sesame oil

1 Using a sharp knife, slice the monkfish into thin flat rounds. Set aside until required.

2 Mix together the freshly grated root ginger and the sweet chilli sauce in a small bowl until thoroughly blended. Brush the ginger and chilli sauce mixture over the monkfish pieces, using a pastry brush.

COOK'S TIP

Monkfish is quite expensive, but it is well worth using as it has a wonderful flavour and texture. At a push you could use cubes of chunky cod fillet instead.

  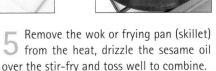

3 Heat the corn oil in a large preheated wok or heavy-based frying pan (skillet).

4 Add the monkfish pieces, asparagus and chopped spring onions (scallions) to the wok or frying pan (skillet) and cook for about 5 minutes, stirring gently so the fish pieces do not break up.

5 Remove the wok or frying pan (skillet) from the heat, drizzle the sesame oil over the stir-fry and toss well to combine.

6 Transfer the stir-fried gingered monkfish to warm serving plates and serve immediately.

Szechuan White Fish

Szechuan pepper is quite hot and should be used sparingly to avoid making the dish unbearably spicy.

NUTRITIONAL INFORMATION

Calories .... 225 Sugars 3g
Protein .... 20g Fat 8g
Carbohydrate ... 17g Saturates 1g

5 MINS   20 MINS

SERVES 4

INGREDIENTS

350 g/12 oz white fish fillets

1 small egg, beaten

3 tbsp plain (all-purpose) flour

4 tbsp dry white wine

3 tbsp light soy sauce

vegetable oil, for frying

1 garlic clove, cut into slivers

1-cm/½-inch piece fresh root ginger, finely chopped

1 onion, finely chopped

1 celery stick, chopped

1 fresh red chilli, chopped

3 spring onions (scallions), chopped

1 tsp rice wine vinegar

½ tsp ground Szechuan pepper

175 ml/6 fl oz/¾ cup fish stock

1 tsp caster (superfine) sugar

1 tsp cornflour (cornstarch)

2 tsp water

1 Cut the fish into 4-cm/1½-inch cubes. Beat together the egg, flour, wine and 1 tablespoon of soy sauce to make a batter. Dip the cubes of fish into the batter to coat well.

2 Heat the oil in a wok, reduce the heat slightly and cook the fish, in batches, for 2–3 minutes, until golden brown. Remove with a slotted spoon, drain on kitchen paper (paper towels), set aside and keep warm.

3 Pour all but 1 tablespoon of oil from the wok and return to the heat. Add the garlic, ginger, onion, celery, chilli and spring onions (scallions) and stir-fry for 1–2 minutes. Stir in the remaining soy sauce and the vinegar.

4 Add the Szechuan pepper, fish stock and caster (superfine) sugar to the wok. Mix the cornflour (cornstarch) with the water to form a smooth paste and stir it into the stock. Bring to the boil and cook, stirring, for 1 minute, until the sauce thickens and clears.

5 Return the fish cubes to the wok and cook for 1–2 minutes. Serve immediately.

Salmon with Pineapple

Presentation plays a major part in Chinese cooking and this dish demonstrates this perfectly with the wonderful combination of colours.

NUTRITIONAL INFORMATION

Calories 347	Sugars 12g
Protein 24g	Fat 20g
Carbohydrate . . .16g	Saturates 3g

 10 MINS   15 MINS

SERVES 4

INGREDIENTS

2 tbsp sunflower oil

1 red onion, sliced

1 orange (bell) pepper, deseeded and sliced

1 green (bell) pepper, deseeded and sliced

100 g/3½ oz/1 cup baby corn cobs

450 g/1 lb salmon fillet, skin removed

1 tbsp paprika

225 g/8 oz can cubed pineapple, drained

100 g/3½ oz/1 cup bean sprouts

2 tbsp tomato ketchup

2 tbsp soy sauce

2 tbsp medium sherry

1 tsp cornflour (cornstarch)

1 Cut each baby corn in half. Heat the oil in a large preheated wok. Add the onion, (bell) peppers and baby corn cobs to the wok and stir-fry for 5 minutes.

2 Rinse the salmon fillet under cold running water and pat dry with absorbent kitchen paper (paper towels).

3 Cut the salmon flesh into thin strips and place in a large bowl. Sprinkle with the paprika and toss well to coat.

4 Add the salmon to the wok together with the pineapple and stir-fry for a

further 2–3 minutes or until the fish is tender.

5 Add the bean sprouts to the wok and toss well.

6 Mix together the tomato ketchup, soy sauce, sherry and cornflour (cornstarch). Add to the wok and cook until the juices start to thicken. Transfer to warm serving plates and serve immediately.

VARIATION

You can use trout fillets instead of the salmon as an alternative, if you prefer.

Sesame Salmon with Cream

Salmon fillet holds its shape when tossed in sesame seeds and stir-fried. It is served in a creamy sauce of diced courgettes (zucchini).

NUTRITIONAL INFORMATION

Calories 550   Sugars 1g
Protein . . . . .35g   Fat 45g
Carbohydrate . . . .2g   Saturates 12g

5 MINS   10 MINS

SERVES 4

INGREDIENTS

625-750 g/1 lb 6 oz-1 lb 10 oz
  salmon or pink trout fillets

2 tbsp light soy sauce

3 tbsp sesame seeds

3 tbsp sunflower oil

4 spring onions (scallions), thinly
  sliced diagonally

2 large courgettes (zucchini),
  diced, or 2.5-cm/5-inch piece
  cucumber, diced

grated rind of ½ lemon

1 tbsp lemon juice

½ tsp turmeric

6 tbsp fish stock or water

3 tbsp double (heavy) cream or fromage
  frais

salt and pepper

curly endive, to garnish

1 Skin the fish and cut into strips about 4 x 2 cm/1½ x ¾ inches. Pat dry on kitchen paper (paper towels). Season lightly, then brush with soy sauce and sprinkle all over with sesame seeds.

2 Heat 2 tablespoons of oil in the wok. Add the pieces of fish and stir-fry for 3-4 minutes until lightly browned all over. Remove with a fish slice, drain on kitchen paper (paper towels) and keep warm.

3 Heat the remaining oil in the wok and add the spring onions (scallions) and courgettes (zucchini) or cucumber and stir-fry for 1-2 minutes. Add the lemon rind and juice, turmeric, stock and seasoning and bring to the boil for 1 minute. Stir in the cream or fromage frais.

4 Return the fish pieces to the wok and toss gently in the sauce until they are really hot. Garnish and serve.

COOK'S TIP

Lay the fillet skin-side down. Insert a sharp, flexible knife at one end between the flesh and the skin. Hold the skin tightly at the end and push the knife along, keeping the knife blade as flat as possible against the skin.

Stir-Fried Salmon with Leeks

Salmon is marinated in a deliciously rich, sweet sauce, stir-fried and served on a bed of crispy leeks.

NUTRITIONAL INFORMATION

Calories	360	Sugars	.........9g
Protein	........24g	Fat	25
Carbohydrate	....11g	Saturates	.......4g

35 MINS   15 MINS

SERVES 4

I N G R E D I E N T S

450 g/1 lb salmon fillet, skinned

2 tbsp sweet soy sauce

2 tbsp tomato ketchup

1 tsp rice wine vinegar

1 tbsp demerara (brown crystal)
   sugar

1 clove garlic, crushed

4 tbsp corn oil

450 g/1 lb leeks, thinly shredded

finely chopped red chillies,
   to garnish

1 Using a sharp knife, cut the salmon into slices. Place the slices of salmon in a shallow non-metallic dish.

2 Mix together the soy sauce, tomato ketchup, rice wine vinegar, sugar and garlic.

3 Pour the mixture over the salmon, toss well and leave to marinate for about 30 minutes.

4 Meanwhile, heat 3 tablespoons of the corn oil in a large preheated wok.

5 Add the leeks to the wok and stir-fry over a medium-high heat for about 10 minutes, or until the leeks become crispy and tender.

6 Using a slotted spoon, carefully remove the leeks from the wok and transfer to warmed serving plates.

7 Add the remaining oil to the wok. Add the salmon and the marinade to the wok and cook for 2 minutes.

8 Remove the salmon from the wok and spoon over the leeks, garnish with finely chopped red chillies and serve immediately.

VARIATION

You can use a fillet of beef instead of the salmon, if you prefer.

Fish with Saffron Sauce

White fish cooked in a bamboo steamer over the wok and served with a light creamy saffron sauce with a real bite to it.

NUTRITIONAL INFORMATION

Calories 254	Sugars 0.5g
Protein 30g	Fat 14g
Carbohydrate 2g	Saturates 5g

5 MINS   30 MINS

SERVES 4

INGREDIENTS

625-750 g/1 lb 6 oz-1 lb 10 oz white fish fillets (cod, haddock, whiting etc)

pinch of Chinese five-spice powder

4 sprigs fresh thyme

large pinch saffron threads

250 ml/9 fl oz/1 cup boiling fish or vegetable stock

2 tbsp sunflower oil

125 g/4½ oz button mushrooms, thinly sliced

grated rind of ½ lemon

1 tbsp lemon juice

½ tsp freshly chopped thyme or ¼ tsp dried thyme

½ bunch watercress, chopped

1½ tsp cornflour (cornstarch)

3 tbsp single or double (heavy) cream

salt and pepper

1 Skin the fish and cut into 4 even-sized portions. Season with salt and pepper and five-spice powder. Arrange the fish on a plate and place in the bottom of a bamboo steamer, laying a sprig of thyme on each piece of fish.

2 Stand a low metal trivet in a wok and add water to come almost to the top of it. Bring to the boil, stand the bamboo steamer on the trivet and cover with the bamboo lid and then the lid of the wok or a piece of foil. Simmer for 20 minutes until the fish is tender, adding more boiling water to the wok if necessary. Meanwhile, soak the saffron threads in the boiling stock.

3 When the fish is tender, remove and keep warm. Empty the wok and wipe dry. Heat the oil in the wok and stir-fry the mushrooms for about 2 minutes. Add the saffron stock, lemon rind and juice and chopped thyme and bring to the boil. Add the watercress and simmer for 1-2 minutes.

4 Blend the cornflour (cornstarch) with the cream, add a little of the sauce from the wok, then return to the wok and heat gently until thickened. Serve the fish surrounded by the sauce.

Braised Fish Fillets

Any white fish, such as lemon sole or plaice, is ideal for this delicious dish.

NUTRITIONAL INFORMATION

Calories	107	Sugars	. . . . .2g
Protein	. . . . .17g	Fat	. . . . .2g
Carbohydrate	. . . .6g	Saturates	. . . . .0.3g

45 MINS   10 MINS

SERVES 4

INGREDIENTS

3-4 small Chinese dried mushrooms

300-350 g/10½-12 oz fish fillets

1 tsp salt

½ egg white, lightly beaten

1 tsp cornflour (cornstarch) paste
(see page 15)

600 ml/1 pint/2½ cups vegetable oil

1 tsp finely chopped ginger root

2 spring onions (scallions),
finely chopped

1 garlic clove, finely chopped

½ small green (bell) pepper, deseeded
and cut into small cubes

½ small carrot, thinly sliced

60 g/2 oz/½ cup canned sliced bamboo
shoots, rinsed and drained

½ tsp sugar

1 tbsp light soy sauce

1 tsp rice wine or dry sherry

1 tbsp chilli bean sauce

2-3 tbsp Chinese Stock (see page 14)
or water

a few drops of sesame oil

1 Soak the dried mushrooms in a bowl of warm water for 30 minutes. Drain thoroughly on kitchen paper (paper towels), reserving the soaking water for stock or soup. Squeeze the mushrooms to extract all of the moisture, cut off and discard any hard stems and slice thinly.

2 Cut the fish into bite-sized pieces, then place in a shallow dish and mix with a pinch of salt, the egg white and cornflour (cornstarch) paste, turning the fish to coat well.

3 Heat the oil in a preheated wok. Add the fish pieces to the wok and deep-fry for about 1 minute. Remove the fish pieces with a slotted spoon and leave to drain on kitchen paper (paper towels).

4 Pour off the excess oil, leaving about 1 tablespoon in the wok. Add the ginger, spring onions (scallions) and garlic to flavour the oil for a few seconds, then add the (bell) pepper, carrots and bamboo shoots and stir-fry for about 1 minute.

5 Add the sugar, soy sauce, wine, chilli bean sauce, stock or water, and the remaining salt and bring to the boil. Add the fish pieces, stirring to coat with the sauce, and braise for 1 minute. Sprinkle with sesame oil and serve.

Fish with Coconut & Basil

Fish curries are sensational and this is no exception. Red curry and coconut are fantastic flavours with the fried fish.

NUTRITIONAL INFORMATION

Calories 209   Sugars 10g
Protein . . . . .21g   Fat 8g
Carbohydrate . . .15g   Saturates 1g

  5 MINS   15 MINS

SERVES 4

I N G R E D I E N T S

2 tbsp vegetable oil

450 g/1 lb skinless cod fillet

25 g/1 oz/¼ cup seasoned flour

1 clove garlic, crushed

2 tbsp red curry paste

1 tbsp fish sauce

300 ml/½ pint/1¼ cups coconut milk

175 g/6 oz cherry tomatoes, halved

20 fresh basil leaves

fragrant rice, to serve

1 Heat the vegetable oil in a large preheated wok.

2 Using a sharp knife, cut the fish into large cubes, removing any bones with a pair of clean tweezers.

3 Place the seasoned flour in a bowl. Add the cubes of fish and mix until well coated.

4 Add the coated fish to the wok and stir-fry over a high heat for 3–4 minutes, or until the fish just begins to brown at the edges.

5 In a small bowl, mix together the garlic, curry paste, fish sauce and coconut milk. Pour the mixture over the fish and bring to the boil.

6 Add the tomatoes to the mixture in the wok and leave to simmer for 5 minutes.

7 Roughly chop or tear the fresh basil leaves. Add the basil to the wok, stir carefully to combine, taking care not to break up the cubes of fish.

8 Transfer to serving plates and serve hot with fragrant rice.

COOK'S TIP

Take care not to overcook the dish once the tomatoes are added, otherwise they will break down and the skins will come away.

Fish & Ginger Stir-Fry

This delicious and spicy recipe is a really quick fish dish, ideal for midweek family meals or light lunches at weekends.

NUTRITIONAL INFORMATION

Calories 280	Sugars 2g	
Protein 31g	Fat 10g	
Carbohydrate ...17g	Saturates 2g	

  5 MINS   15 MINS

SERVES 4

I N G R E D I E N T S

4 tbsp cornflour (cornstarch)

½ tsp ground ginger

675 g/1½ lb firm white fish fillets, skinned and cubed

3 tbsp peanut oil

2.5-cm/1-inch fresh ginger root, grated

1 leek, thinly sliced

1 tbsp white wine vinegar

2 tbsp Chinese rice wine or dry sherry

3 tbsp dark soy sauce

1 tsp caster (superfine) sugar

2 tbsp lemon juice

finely shredded leek, to garnish

1 Mix the cornflour (cornstarch) and ground ginger in a bowl.

2 Add the cubes of fish, in batches, to the cornflour (cornstarch) mixture, turning to coat the fish thoroughly in the mixture.

3 Heat the peanut oil in a preheated wok or large, heavy-based frying pan (skillet), swirling the oil around the base of the wok until it is really hot.

4 Add the grated fresh ginger and sliced leek to the wok or frying pan (skillet) and stir-fry for 1 minute.

5 Add the coated fish to the wok and cook for a further 5 minutes, until browned, stirring to prevent the fish from sticking to the base of the wok.

6 Add the remaining ingredients and cook over a low heat for 3–4 minutes, until the fish is cooked through.

7 Transfer the fish and ginger stir-fry to a serving dish and serve immediately.

VARIATION

Use any firm white fish which will hold its shape, such as cod, haddock or monkfish.

Steamed Stuffed Snapper

Red mullet may be used instead of the snapper, although they are a little more difficult to stuff because of their size. Use one mullet per person.

NUTRITIONAL INFORMATION

Calories 406   Sugar 4g
Protein ....68g   Fat 9g
Carbohydrate ....9g   Saturates 0g

20 MINS   10 MINS

SERVES 4

INGREDIENTS

1.4 kg/3 lb whole snapper, cleaned and scaled

175 g/6 oz spinach

orange slices and shredded spring onion (scallion), to garnish

STUFFING

60 g/2 oz/2 cups cooked long-grain rice

1 tsp grated fresh root ginger

2 spring onions (scallions), finely chopped

2 tsp light soy sauce

1 tsp sesame oil

½ tsp ground star anise

1 orange, segmented and chopped

1 Rinse the fish inside and out under cold running water and pat dry with kitchen paper (paper towels).

2 Blanch the spinach for 40 seconds, rinse in cold water and drain well, pressing out as much moisture as possible.

3 Arrange the spinach on a heatproof plate and place the fish on top.

4 To make the stuffing, mix together the cooked rice, grated ginger, spring onions (scallions), soy sauce, sesame oil, star anise and orange in a bowl.

5 Spoon the stuffing into the body cavity of the fish, pressing it in well with a spoon.

6 Cover the plate and cook in a steamer for 10 minutes, or until the fish is cooked through.

7 Transfer the fish to a warmed serving dish, garnish with orange slices and shredded spring onion (scallion) and serve.

COOK'S TIP

The name snapper covers a family of tropical and subtropical fish that vary in colour. They may be red, orange, pink, grey or blue-green. Some are striped or spotted and they range in size from about 15 cm/ 6 inches to 90 cm/3 ft.

Tuna & Vegetable Stir-Fry

Fresh tuna is a dark, meaty fish and is now widely available at fresh fish counters. It lends itself perfectly to the rich flavours in this recipe.

NUTRITIONAL INFORMATION

Calories 245	Sugars 11g	
Protein 30g	Fat 7g	
Carbohydrate ...14g	Saturates 1g	

10 MINS   10 MINS

SERVES 4

I N G R E D I E N T S

225 g/8 oz carrots

1 onion

175 g/6 oz/1¾ cups baby corn cobs

2 tbsp corn oil

175 g/6 oz/2½ cups mangetout (snow peas)

450 g/1 lb fresh tuna

2 tbsp fish sauce

15 g/½ oz/1 tbsp palm sugar

finely grated zest and juice of 1 orange

2 tbsp sherry

1 tsp cornflour (cornstarch)

rice or noodles, to serve

1 Using a sharp knife, cut the carrots into thin sticks, slice the onion and halve the baby corn cobs.

2 Heat the corn oil in a large preheated wok or frying pan (skillet).

3 Add the onion, carrots, mangetout (snow peas) and baby corn cobs to the wok or frying pan (skillet) and stir-fry for 5 minutes.

4 Using a sharp knife, thinly slice the fresh tuna.

5 Add the tuna slices to the wok or frying pan (skillet) and stir-fry for about 2–3 minutes, or until the tuna turns opaque.

6 Mix together the fish sauce, palm sugar, orange zest and juice, sherry and cornflour (cornstarch).

7 Pour the mixture over the tuna and vegetables and cook for 2 minutes, or until the juices thicken. Serve the stir-fry with rice or noodles.

VARIATION

Try using swordfish steaks instead of the tuna. Swordfish steaks are now widely available and are similar in texture to tuna.

Mullet with Ginger

Ginger is used widely in Chinese cooking for its strong, pungent flavour. Although fresh ginger is best, ground ginger may be used instead.

NUTRITIONAL INFORMATION

Calories 195   Sugars 6g
Protein . . . . .31g   Fat 3g
Carbohydrate . . . .9g   Saturates 0g

 10 MINS   15 MINS

SERVES 4

INGREDIENTS

1 whole mullet, cleaned and scaled

2 spring onions (scallions), chopped

1 tsp grated fresh root ginger

125 ml/4 fl oz/½ cup garlic wine
    vinegar

125 ml/4 fl oz/½ cup light soy sauce

3 tsp caster (superfine) sugar

dash of chilli sauce

125 ml/4 fl oz/½ cup fish stock

1 green (bell) pepper, seeded and
    thinly sliced

1 large tomato, skinned, seeded and
    cut into thin strips

salt and pepper

sliced tomato, to garnish

1 Rinse the fish inside and out and pat dry with kitchen paper (paper towels).

2 Make 3 diagonal slits in the flesh on each side of the fish. Season the fish with salt and pepper inside and out, according to taste.

3 Place the fish on a heatproof plate and scatter the chopped spring onions (scallions) and grated ginger over the top. Cover and steam for 10 minutes, or until the fish is cooked through.

4 Meanwhile, place the garlic wine vinegar, light soy sauce, caster (superfine) sugar, chilli sauce, fish stock, (bell) pepper and tomato in a saucepan and bring to the boil, stirring occasionally.

5 Cook the sauce over a high heat until the sauce has slightly reduced and thickened.

6 Remove the fish from the steamer and transfer to a warm serving dish. Pour the sauce over the fish, garnish with tomato slices and serve immediately.

VARIATION

Use fillets of fish for this recipe if preferred, and reduce the cooking time to 5–7 minutes.

Trout with Pineapple

Pineapple is widely used in Chinese cooking. The tartness of fresh pineapple complements fish particularly well.

NUTRITIONAL INFORMATION

Calories 243	Sugars 4g	
Protein 30g	Fat 11g	
Carbohydrate 6g	Saturates 2g	

5 MINS

15 MINS

SERVES 4

INGREDIENTS

4 trout fillets, skinned

2 tbsp vegetable oil

2 garlic cloves, cut into slivers

4 slices fresh pineapple, peeled and diced

1 celery stick, sliced

1 tbsp light soy sauce

50 ml/2 fl oz/¼ cup fresh or unsweetened pineapple juice

150 ml/¼ pint/⅔ cup fish stock

1 tsp cornflour (cornstarch)

2 tsp water

shredded celery leaves and fresh red chilli slices, to garnish

1 Cut the trout fillets into strips. Heat 1 tablespoon of the vegetable oil in a preheated wok until almost smoking. Reduce the heat slightly, add the fish and sauté for 2 minutes. Remove from the wok and set aside.

2 Add the remaining oil to the wok, reduce the heat and add the garlic, diced pineapple and celery. Stir-fry for 1–2 minutes.

3 Add the soy sauce, pineapple juice and fish stock to the wok. Bring to the boil and cook, stirring, for 2–3 minutes, or until the sauce has reduced.

4 Blend the cornflour (cornstarch) with the water to form a paste and stir it into the wok. Bring the sauce to the boil and cook, stirring constantly, until the sauce thickens and clears.

5 Return the fish to the wok, and cook, stirring gently, until heated through. Transfer to a warmed serving dish and serve, garnished with shredded celery leaves and red chilli slices.

VARIATION

Use canned pineapple instead of fresh pineapple if you wish, choosing slices in unsweetened, natural juice in preference to a syrup.

Noodles

Noodles are a symbol of longevity in China and are always served at birthday and New Year celebrations. It is considered bad luck to cut noodles into shorter lengths because the Chinese believe the longer they are the longer and happier your life will be. Noodles are available in several varieties, both fresh and dried, made from wheat,

buckwheat or rice flours, or you can even make your own if you have time! They come in fine threads, strings or flat ribbons and can be bought from large supermarkets or oriental food shops. Like rice, noodles are very versatile and can be boiled, fried, added to soups, or served plain. Noodles are precooked as part of the manufacturing process so most only need soaking in hot water to rehydrate them.

Fried Noodles (Chow Mein)

This is a basic recipe for Chow Mein. Additional ingredients such as chicken or pork can be added if liked.

NUTRITIONAL INFORMATION

Calories	716	Sugars	. . . . .2g
Protein	. . . . .4g	Fat	. . . . .12g
Carbohydrate	. . .14g	Saturates	. . . . . . .1g

  5 MINS   15 MINS

SERVES 4

I N G R E D I E N T S

275 g/9½ oz egg noodles

3-4 tbsp vegetable oil

1 small onion, finely shredded

125 g/4½ oz fresh bean sprouts

1 spring onion (scallion),
   finely shredded

2 tbsp light soy sauce

a few drops of sesame oil

salt

1 Bring a wok or saucepan of salted water to the boil.

2 Add the egg noodles to the saucepan or wok and cook according to the instructions on the packet (usually no more than 4-5 minutes).

COOK'S TIP

Noodles, a symbol of longevity, are made from wheat or rice flour, water and egg. Handmade noodles are made by an elaborate process of kneading, pulling and twisting the dough, and it takes years to learn the art.

3 Drain the noodles well and rinse in cold water; drain thoroughly again, then transfer to a large mixing bowl and toss with a little vegetable oil.

4 Heat the remaining vegetable oil in a preheated wok or large frying pan (skillet) until really hot.

5 Add the shredded onion to the wok and stir-fry for about 30-40 seconds.

6 Add the bean sprouts and drained noodles to the wok, stir and toss for 1 more minute.

7 Add the shredded spring onion (scallion) and light soy sauce and blend well.

8 Transfer the noodles to a warm serving dish, sprinkle with the sesame oil and serve immediately.

Curried Prawn Noodles

Athough these noodles are almost a meal in themselves, if served as an accompaniment, they are ideal with plain vegetable or fish dishes.

NUTRITIONAL INFORMATION

Calories 246   Sugars 1g
Protein . . . . .17g   Fat 14g
Carbohydrate . . .14g   Saturates 2g

5 MINS   15 MINS

SERVES 4

INGREDIENTS

225 g/8 oz rice noodles

4 tbsp vegetable oil

1 onion, sliced

2 ham slices, shredded

2 tbsp Chinese curry powder

150 ml/¼ pint/⅔ cups fish stock

225 g/8 oz peeled, raw prawns (shrimp)

2 garlic cloves, crushed

6 spring onions (scallions), chopped

1 tbsp light soy sauce

2 tbsp hoisin sauce

1 tbsp dry sherry

2 tsp lime juice

fresh snipped chives, to garnish

COOK'S TIP

Hoisin sauce is made from soy beans, sugar, flour, vinegar, salt, garlic, chilli and sesame seed oil. Sold in cans or jars, it will keep in the refrigerator for several months.

1 Cook the noodles in a pan of boiling water for 3-4 minutes. Drain well, rinse under cold water and drain again.

2 Heat 2 tablespoons of the oil in a wok. Add the onion and ham and stir-fry for 1 minute. Add the curry powder and stir-fry for a further 30 seconds.

3 Stir the noodles and fish stock into the wok and cook for 2-3 minutes.

Remove the noodles from the wok and keep warm.

4 Heat the remaining oil in the wok. Add the prawns (shrimp), garlic and spring onions (scallions) and stir-fry for about 1 minute.

5 Stir in the remaining ingredients. Pour the mixture over the noodles, toss to mix and garnish with fresh chives.

Chilli Pork Noodles

This is quite a spicy dish, with a delicious peanut flavour. Increase or reduce the amount of chilli to your liking.

NUTRITIONAL INFORMATION

Calories 421   Sugars 3g
Protein . . . . .27g   Fat 26g
Carbohydrate . . .20g   Saturates 6g

 35 MINS   10 MINS

SERVES 4

I N G R E D I E N T S

350 g/12 oz minced (ground) pork

1 tbsp light soy sauce

1 tbsp dry sherry

350 g/12 oz egg noodles

2 tsp sesame oil

2 tbsp vegetable oil

2 garlic cloves, crushed

2 tsp grated fresh root ginger

2 fresh red chillies, sliced

1 red (bell) pepper, seeded and finely sliced

25 g/1 oz/¼ cup unsalted peanuts

3 tbsp peanut butter

3 tbsp dark soy sauce

dash of chilli oil

300 ml/½ pint/1¼ cups pork stock

1 Mix together the pork, light soy sauce and dry sherry in a large bowl. Cover and leave to marinate for 30 minutes.

2 Meanwhile, cook the noodles in a saucepan of boiling water for 4 minutes. Drain well, rinse in cold water and drain again. Toss the noodles in the sesame oil.

3 Heat the vegetable oil in a preheated wok and stir-fry the garlic, ginger, chillies and (bell) pepper for 30 seconds.

4 Add the pork to the mixture in the wok, together with the marinade. Continue cooking for about 1 minute, until the pork is sealed.

5 Add the peanuts, peanut butter, soy sauce, chilli oil and stock and cook for 2-3 minutes.

6 Toss the noodles in the mixture and serve at once.

VARIATION

Minced (ground) chicken or lamb would also be excellent in this recipe instead of the pork.

Chicken on Crispy Noodles

Blanched noodles are fried in the wok until crisp and brown, and then topped with a shredded chicken sauce for a delightfully tasty dish.

NUTRITIONAL INFORMATION

Calories	376	Sugars	.........2g
Protein	........15g	Fat	..........27g
Carbohydrate	...17g	Saturates	.......4g

  35 MINS 25 MINS

SERVES 4

I N G R E D I E N T S

225 g/8 oz skinless, boneless chicken breasts, shredded

1 egg white

5 tsp cornflour (cornstarch)

225 g/8 oz thin egg noodles

300 ml/½ pint/1¾ cups vegetable oil

600 ml/1 pint/2½ cups chicken stock

2 tbsp dry sherry

2 tbsp oyster sauce

1 tbsp light soy sauce

1 tbsp hoisin sauce

1 red (bell) pepper, seeded and very thinly sliced

2 tbsp water

3 spring onions (scallions), chopped

1 Mix together the chicken, egg white and 2 teaspoons of the cornflour (cornstarch) in a bowl. Leave to stand for at least 30 minutes.

2 Blanch the noodles in boiling water for 2 minutes, then drain thoroughly.

3 Heat the vegetable oil in a preheated wok. Add the noodles, spreading them to cover the base of the wok. Cook over a low heat for about 5 minutes, until the noodles are browned on the underside.

Flip the noodles over and brown on the other side. Remove from the wok when crisp and browned, place on a serving plate and keep warm. Drain the oil from the wok.

4 Add 300 ml/½ pint/1¼ cups of the chicken stock to the wok. Remove from the heat and add the chicken, stirring well so that it does not stick. Return to the heat and cook for 2 minutes. Drain, discarding the stock.

5 Wipe the wok with kitchen paper (paper towels) and return to the heat. Add the sherry, sauces, (bell) pepper and the remaining stock and bring to the boil. Blend the remaining cornflour (cornstarch) with the water and stir it into the mixture.

6 Return the chicken to the wok and cook over a low heat for 2 minutes. Place the chicken on top of the noodles and sprinkle with spring onions (scallions).

Hot & Crispy Noodles

These crispy noodles will add a delicious crunch to your Chinese meal.
They can be served as a side dish or as an appetizer for people to share.

NUTRITIONAL INFORMATION

Calories 104   Sugars 0.3g
Protein . . . . .2g   Fat 6g
Carbohydrate . . . .11g   Saturates 1g

 5 MINS   15 MINS

SERVES 4

INGREDIENTS

250 g/9 oz rice noodles

oil, for deep-frying

2 garlic cloves, chopped finely

8 spring onions (scallions), trimmed and
chopped finely

1 small red or green chilli, deseeded and
chopped finely

2 tbsp fish sauce

2 tbsp light soy sauce

2 tbsp lime or lemon juice

2 tbsp molasses sugar

TO GARNISH

spring onions (scallions), shredded

cucumber, sliced thinly

fresh chillies

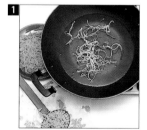

1 Break the noodles into smaller pieces with your hands. Heat the oil for deep-frying in a wok or large frying pan (skillet) and fry small batches of the noodles until pale golden brown and puffed up. Lift the noodles out with a perforated spoon and leave to drain on kitchen paper (paper towels).

2 When all of the noodles are cooked, pour off the oil, leaving 3 tbsp in the wok. Add the garlic, spring onions (scallions) and chilli, and stir-fry for 2 minutes.

3 Mix together the fish sauce, soy sauce, lime or lemon juice and sugar. Add to the wok or frying pan (skillet) and cook for 2 minutes, until the sugar has dissolved. Tip all the noodles back into the wok and toss lightly to coat with the sauce mixture.

4 Serve the noodles garnished with shredded spring onions (scallions), thinly sliced cucumber and chillies.

VARIATION

Stir-fry some uncooked peeled prawns (shrimp) or chopped raw chicken with the spring onions (scallions) and garlic in step 2. Cook for an extra 3–4 minutes to make sure they are thoroughly cooked.

Curried Rice Noodles

Rice noodles or vermicelli are also known as rice sticks. The ideal meat to use in this dish is pork.

NUTRITIONAL INFORMATION

Calories 223	Sugars 2g	
Protein 15g	Fat 13g	
Carbohydrate 11g	Saturates 2g	

15 MINS   15 MINS

SERVES 4

I N G R E D I E N T S

200 g/7 oz rice vermicelli

125 g/4½ oz cooked chicken or pork

60 g/2 oz peeled prawns (shrimp),
   defrosted if frozen

4 tbsp vegetable oil

1 medium onion, thinly shredded

125 g/4¼ oz fresh bean sprouts

1 tsp salt

1 tbsp mild curry powder

2 tbsp light soy sauce

2 spring onions (scallions),
   thinly shredded

1-2 small fresh green or red chilli peppers,
   seeded and thinly shredded

1 Soak the rice vermicelli in boiling water for about 8-10 minutes, then rinse in cold water and drain well. Set aside until required.

2 Using a sharp knife or meat cleaver, thinly slice the cooked meat.

3 Dry the prawns (shrimp) on absorbent kitchen paper (paper towels).

4 Heat the vegetable oil in a preheated wok or large frying pan (skillet).

5 Add the shredded onion to the wok or pan and stir-fry until opaque. Add the bean sprouts and stir-fry for 1 minute.

6 Add the drained noodles with the meat and prawns (shrimp), and continue stirring for another minute.

7 Mix together the salt, curry powder and soy sauce in a little bowl.

8 Blend the sauce mixture into the wok, followed by the spring onions (scallions) and chilli peppers. Stir-fry for one more minute, then serve immediately.

COOK'S TIP

Rice noodles are very delicate noodles made from rice flour. They become soft and pliable after being soaked for about 15 minutes. If you wish to store them after they have been soaked, toss them in sesame oil then place them in a container in the refrigerator.

Satay Noodles

Rice noodles and vegetables are tossed in a crunchy peanut and chilli sauce for a quick satay-flavoured recipe.

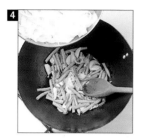

NUTRITIONAL INFORMATION

Calories 281	Sugars 7g
Protein 9g	Fat 20g
Carbohydrate . . .18g	Saturates 4g

 5 MINS   20 MINS

SERVES 4

I N G R E D I E N T S

275 g/9½ oz rice sticks (wide, flat rice noodles)

3 tbsp groundnut oil

2 cloves garlic, crushed

2 shallots, sliced

225 g/8 oz green beans, sliced

100 g/3¾ oz cherry tomatoes, halved

1 tsp chilli flakes

4 tbsp crunchy peanut butter

150 ml/¼ pint/⅔ cup coconut milk

1 tbsp tomato purée (paste)

sliced spring onions (scallions), to garnish

1 Place the rice sticks (wide, flat rice noodles) in a large bowl and pour over enough boiling water to cover. Leave to stand for 10 minutes.

2 Heat the groundnut oil in a large preheated wok or heavy-based frying pan (skillet).

3 Add the crushed garlic and sliced shallots to the wok or frying pan (skillet) and stir-fry for 1 minute.

4 Drain the rice sticks (wide, flat rice noodles) thoroughly. Add the green beans and drained noodles to the wok or frying pan (skillet) and stir-fry for about 5 minutes.

5 Add the cherry tomatoes to the wok and mix well.

6 Mix together the chilli flakes, peanut butter, coconut milk and tomato purée (paste).

7 Pour the chilli mixture over the noodles, toss well until all the ingredients are thoroughly combined and heat through.

8 Transfer the satay noodles to warm serving dishes and garnish with spring onion (scallion) slices and serve immediately.

Oyster Sauce Noodles

Chicken and noodles are cooked and then tossed in an oyster sauce and egg mixture in this delicious recipe.

NUTRITIONAL INFORMATION

Calories	278	Sugars	.........2g
Protein	........30g	Fat	..........12g
Carbohydrate	...13g	Saturates	.......3g

5 MINS   25 MINS

SERVES 4

INGREDIENTS

250 g/9 oz egg noodles

450 g/1 lb chicken thighs

2 tbsp groundnut oil

100 g/3½ oz carrots, sliced

3 tbsp oyster sauce

2 eggs

3 tbsp cold water

1 Place the egg noodles in a large bowl or dish. Pour enough boiling water over the noodles to cover and leave to stand for 10 minutes.

2 Meanwhile, remove the skin from the chicken thighs. Cut the chicken flesh into small pieces, using a sharp knife.

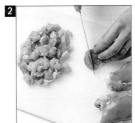

3 Heat the groundnut oil in a large preheated wok or frying pan (skillet), swirling the oil around the base of the wok until it is really hot.

4 Add the pieces of chicken and the carrot slices to the wok and stir-fry for about 5 minutes.

5 Drain the noodles thoroughly. Add the noodles to the wok and stir-fry for a further 2–3 minutes or until the noodles are heated through.

6 Beat together the oyster sauce, eggs and 3 tablespoons of cold water. Drizzle the mixture over the noodles and stir-fry for a further 2–3 minutes or until the eggs set.

7 Transfer the mixture in the wok to warm serving bowls and serve hot.

VARIATION

Flavour the eggs with soy sauce or hoisin sauce as an alternative to the oyster sauce, if you prefer.

Quick Chicken Noodles

Chicken and fresh vegetables are flavoured with ginger and Chinese five-spice powder in this speedy stir-fry.

NUTRITIONAL INFORMATION

Calories	266	Sugars	........4g
Protein	........25g	Fat	..........13g
Carbohydrate	...12g	Saturates	.......2g

 10 MINS   15 MINS

SERVES 4

I N G R E D I E N T S

175 g/6 oz Chinese thread egg noodles

2 tbsp sesame or vegetable oil

25 g/1 oz/¼ cup peanuts

1 bunch spring onions (scallions), sliced

1 green (bell) pepper, deseeded and cut into thin strips

1 large carrot, cut into matchsticks

125 g/4½ oz cauliflower, broken into small florets

350 g/12 oz skinless, boneless chicken, cut into strips

250 g/9 oz mushrooms, sliced

1 tsp finely grated ginger root

1 tsp Chinese five-spice powder

1 tbsp chopped fresh coriander (cilantro)

1 tbsp light soy sauce

salt and pepper

fresh chives, to garnish

1 Put the noodles in a large bowl and cover with boiling water. Leave to soak for 6 minutes.

2 Heat the oil in a wok and stir-fry the peanuts for 1 minute until browned. Remove from the wok and leave to drain.

3 Add the spring onions (scallions), (bell) pepper, carrot, cauliflower and chicken to the pan. Stir-fry over a high heat for 4–5 minutes.

4 Drain the noodles thoroughly and add to the wok. Add the mushrooms and stir-fry for 2 minutes. Add the ginger, five-spice and coriander (cilantro); stir-fry for 1 minute.

5 Season with soy sauce and salt and pepper. Sprinkle with the peanuts, garnish and serve.

VARIATION

Instead of ginger root, ½ teaspoon ground ginger can be used.

Vary the vegetables according to what is in season. Make the most of bargains bought from your greengrocer or market.

Twice-Cooked Lamb

Here lamb is first boiled and then fried with soy sauce, oyster sauce and spinach and finally tossed with noodles for a richly flavoured dish.

NUTRITIONAL INFORMATION

Calories 315	Sugars 5g
Protein 27g	Fat 16g
Carbohydrate . . .16g	Saturates 6g

5 MINS   30 MINS

SERVES 4

I N G R E D I E N T S

250 g/9 oz packet egg noodles

450 g/1 lb lamb loin fillet,
    thinly sliced

2 tbsp soy sauce

2 tbsp sunflower oil

2 cloves garlic, crushed

1 tbsp caster (superfine) sugar

2 tbsp oyster sauce

175 g/6 oz baby spinach

1 Place the egg noodles in a large bowl and cover with boiling water. Leave to soak for about 10 minutes.

2 Bring a large saucepan of water to the boil. Add the lamb and cook for 5 minutes. Drain thoroughly.

3 Place the slices of lamb in a bowl and mix with the soy sauce and 1 tablespoon of the sunflower oil.

4 Heat the remaining sunflower oil in a large preheated wok, swirling the oil around until it is really hot.

5 Add the marinated lamb and crushed garlic to the wok and stir-fry for about 5 minutes or until the meat is just beginning to brown.

6 Add the caster (superfine) sugar and oyster sauce to the wok and stir well to combine.

7 Drain the noodles thoroughly. Add the noodles to the wok and stir-fry for a further 5 minutes.

8 Add the spinach to the wok and cook for 1 minute or until the leaves just wilt. Transfer the lamb and noodles to serving bowls and serve hot.

COOK'S TIP

If using dried noodles, follow the instructions on the packet as they require less soaking.

Crispy Noodles & Tofu

This dish requires a certain amount of care and attention to get the crispy noodles properly cooked, but it is well worth the effort.

NUTRITIONAL INFORMATION

Calories 242   Sugars 2g
Protein . . . . .13g   Fat 17g
Carbohydrate . . .10g   Saturates 3g

 35 MINS   🕐 25 MINS

SERVES 4

I N G R E D I E N T S

175 g/6 oz thread egg noodles

600 ml/1 pint/2½ cups sunflower oil, for
    deep-frying

2 tsp grated lemon peel

1 tbsp light soy sauce

1 tbsp rice vinegar

1 tbsp lemon juice

1½ tbsp sugar

250 g/9 oz/1 cup marinated tofu (bean
    curd), diced

2 garlic cloves, crushed

1 red chilli, sliced finely

1 red (bell) pepper, diced

4 eggs, beaten

red chilli flower, to
    garnish

1 Blanch the egg noodles briefly in hot
water, to which a little of the oil has
been added. Drain the noodles and spread
out to dry for at least 30 minutes. Cut into
threads about 7 cm/3 inches long.

2 Combine the lemon peel, light soy
sauce, rice vinegar, lemon juice and
sugar in a small bowl. Set the mixture
aside until required.

3 Heat the sunflower oil in a wok or
large, heavy frying pan (skillet), and

test the temperature with a few strands of noodles. They
should swell to many times their size, but if they do not,
wait until the oil is hot enough; otherwise they will be
tough and stringy, not puffy and light.

4 Cook the noodles in batches. As soon as they turn a
pale gold colour, scoop them out and drain on plenty
of absorbent kitchen paper (paper towels). Leave to cool.

5 Reserve 2 tablespoons of the oil and drain off the rest.
Heat the reserved oil in the wok or pan (skillet).

6 Add the marinated tofu (bean curd) to the wok or
frying pan (skillet) and cook quickly over a high heat
to seal.

7 Add the crushed garlic cloves, sliced red chilli and
diced red (bell) pepper to the wok. Stir-fry for
1–2 minutes.

8 Add the reserved vinegar mixture to the wok, stir to
mix well and add the beaten eggs, stirring until they
are set.

9 Serve the tofu (bean curd) mixture with the crispy fried
noodles, garnished with a red chilli flower.

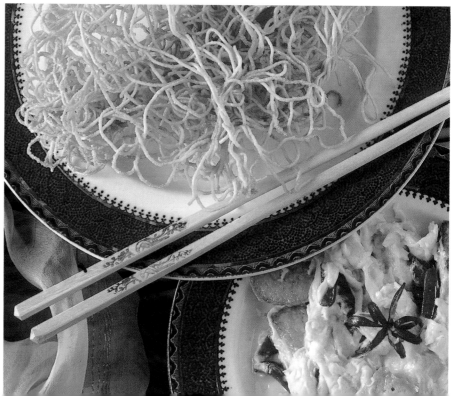

Yellow Bean Noodles

Cellophane or thread noodles are excellent re-heated, unlike other noodles which must be served as soon as they are ready.

NUTRITIONAL INFORMATION

Calories 212	Sugars 0.5g
Protein 28g	Fat 7g
Carbohydrate . . .10g	Saturates 2g

5 MINS   30 MINS

SERVES 4

I N G R E D I E N T S

175 g/6 oz cellophane noodles

1 tbsp peanut oil

1 leek, sliced

2 garlic cloves, crushed

450 g/1 lb minced (ground) chicken

425 ml/¾ pint/1 cup chicken stock

1 tsp chilli sauce

2 tbsp yellow bean sauce

4 tbsp light soy sauce

1 tsp sesame oil

chopped chives, to garnish

1 Place the cellophane noodles in a bowl, pour over boiling water and soak for 15 minutes.

COOK'S TIP

Cellophane noodles are available from many supermarkets and all Chinese supermarkets.

2 Drain the noodles thoroughly and cut into short lengths with a pair of kitchen scissors.

3 Heat the oil in a wok or frying pan (skillet) and stir-fry the leek and garlic for 30 seconds.

4 Add the chicken to the wok and stir-fry for 4-5 minutes, until the chicken is completely cooked through.

5 Add the chicken stock, chilli sauce, yellow bean sauce and soy sauce to the wok and cook for 3-4 minutes.

6 Add the drained noodles and sesame oil to the wok and cook, tossing to mix well, for 4-5 minutes.

7 Spoon the mixture into warm serving bowls, sprinkle with chopped chives and serve immediately.

Garlic Pork & Noodles

This is a wonderful one-pot dish of stir-fried pork fillet with (small) shrimps and noodles that is made in minutes.

NUTRITIONAL INFORMATION

Calories 424   Sugars 1g
Protein ....33g   Fat 27g
Carbohydrate ...13g   Saturates 5g

5 MINS   15 MINS

SERVES 4

INGREDIENTS

250 g/9 oz packet medium egg noodles

3 tbsp vegetable oil

2 garlic cloves, crushed

350 g/12 oz pork fillet, cut into strips

4 tbsp/⅓ cup dried (small) shrimps, or
   125 g/4½ oz peeled prawns (shrimp)

1 bunch spring onions (scallions), finely
   chopped

90 g/3 oz/¾ cup chopped roasted and
   shelled unsalted peanuts

3 tbsp fish sauce

1½ tsp palm or demerara (brown crystal)
   sugar

1-2 small red chillies, seeded and finely
   chopped (to taste)

3 tbsp lime juice

3 tbsp chopped fresh coriander (cilantro)

1 Place the noodles in a large pan of boiling water, then immediately remove from the heat. Cover and leave to stand for 6 minutes, stirring once halfway through the time. After 6 minutes the noodles will be perfectly cooked. Alternatively, follow the instructions on the packet. Drain and keep warm.

2 Heat the oil in a wok, add the garlic and pork and stir-fry until the pork strips are browned, about 2-3 minutes.

3 Add the dried (small) shrimps or shelled prawns (shrimp), spring onions (scallions), peanuts, fish sauce, palm or demerara (brown crystal) sugar, chillies to taste and lime juice. Stir-fry for a further 1 minute.

4 Add the cooked noodles and chopped fresh coriander (cilantro) and stir-fry until heated through, about 1 minute. Serve the stir-fry immediately.

COOK'S TIP

Fish sauce is made from pressed, salted fish and is widely available in supermarkets and oriental stores. It is very salty, so no extra salt should be added.

Chicken Chow Mein

This classic dish requires no introduction as it is already a favourite amongst most Chinese food-eaters.

NUTRITIONAL INFORMATION

Calories 230   Sugars 2g
Protein ....19g   Fat 11g
Carbohydrate ...14g   Saturates 2g

5 MINS   20 MINS

SERVES 4

INGREDIENTS

250 g/9 oz packet medium egg noodles

2 tbsp sunflower oil

275 g/9½ oz cooked chicken breasts, shredded

1 clove garlic, finely chopped

1 red (bell) pepper, deseeded and thinly sliced

100 g/3½ oz shiitake mushrooms, sliced

6 spring onions (scallions), sliced

100 g/3½ oz/1 cup bean sprouts

3 tbsp soy sauce

1 tbsp sesame oil

VARIATION

You can make the chow mein with a selection of vegetables for a vegetarian dish, if you prefer.

1 Place the egg noodles in a large bowl or dish and break them up slightly. Pour over enough boiling water to cover the noodles and leave to stand.

2 Heat the sunflower oil in a large preheated wok. Add the shredded chicken, finely chopped garlic, (bell) pepper slices, mushrooms, spring onions (scallions) and bean sprouts to the wok and stir-fry for about 5 minutes.

3 Drain the noodles thoroughly. Add the noodles to the wok, toss well and stir-fry for a further 5 minutes.

4 Drizzle the soy sauce and sesame oil over the chow mein and toss until well combined.

5 Transfer the chicken chow mein to warm serving bowls and serve immediately.

Speedy Peanut Pan-Fry

Thread egg noodles are the ideal accompaniment to this quick dish because they can be cooked quickly and easily while the stir-fry sizzles.

NUTRITIONAL INFORMATION

Calories	563	Sugars	.........7g
Protein	........45g	Fat	..........33g
Carbohydrate	...22g	Saturates	.......7g

 5 MINS   15 MINS

SERVES 4

I N G R E D I E N T S

300 g/10½ oz/2 cups courgettes (zucchini)

250 g/9 oz/1⅓ cups baby corn (corn-on-the-cob)

250 g/9 oz thread egg noodles

2 tbsp corn oil

1 tbsp sesame oil

8 boneless chicken thighs or 4 breasts, sliced thinly

300 g/10½ oz/3¾ cups button mushrooms

350 g/12 oz/1½ cups bean sprouts

4 tbsp smooth peanut butter

2 tbsp soy sauce

2 tbsp lime or lemon juice

60 g/2 oz/½ cup roasted peanuts

salt and pepper

coriander (cilantro), to garnish

 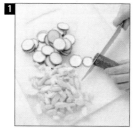 

1 Using a sharp knife, trim and thinly slice the courgettes (zucchini) and baby corn (corn-on-the-cob). Set the vegetables aside until required.

2 Cook the noodles in lightly salted boiling water for 3–4 minutes.

3 Meanwhile, heat the corn oil and sesame oil in a large wok or frying pan (skillet) and fry the chicken over a fairly high heat for 1 minute.

4 Add the courgettes (zucchini), corn and mushrooms and stir-fry for 5 minutes.

5 Add the bean sprouts, peanut butter, soy sauce, lime or lemon juice and pepper, then cook for a further 2 minutes.

6 Drain the noodles thoroughly. Scatter with the roasted peanuts and serve with the courgette (zucchini) and mushroom mixture. Garnish and serve.

COOK'S TIP

Try serving this stir-fry with rice sticks. These are broad, pale, translucent ribbon noodles made from ground rice.

Noodles in Soup

Noodles in soup are far more popular than fried noodles in China. You can use different ingredients for the dressing according to taste.

NUTRITIONAL INFORMATION

Calories	231	Sugars	.........1g
Protein	........18g	Fat	...........11g
Carbohydrate	...16g	Saturates	.......2g

    10 MINS   15 MINS

SERVES 4

INGREDIENTS

250 g/9 oz chicken fillet, pork fillet, or any other ready-cooked meat

3-4 Chinese dried mushrooms, soaked

125 g/4½ oz canned sliced bamboo shoots, rinsed and drained

125 g/4½ oz spinach leaves, lettuce hearts, or Chinese leaves (cabbage), shredded

2 spring onions (scallions), finely shredded

250 g/9 oz egg noodles

about 600 ml/1 pint/2½ cups Chinese Stock (see page 14)

2 tbsp light soy sauce

2 tbsp vegetable oil

1 tsp salt

½ tsp sugar

2 tsp Chinese rice wine or dry sherry

a few drops sesame oil

1 tsp red chilli oil (optional)

1 Using a sharp knife or meat cleaver, cut the meat into thin shreds.

2 Squeeze dry the soaked Chinese mushrooms and discard the hard stalk.

3 Thinly shred the mushrooms, bamboo shoots, spinach leaves and spring onions (scallions).

4 Cook the noodles in boiling water according to the instructions on the packet, then drain and rinse under cold water. Place the noodles in a bowl.

5 Bring the Chinese stock to the boil, add about 1 tablespoon soy sauce and pour over the noodles. Keep warm.

6 Heat the vegetable oil in a preheated wok, add about half of the spring onions (scallions), the meat and the vegetables (mushrooms, bamboo shoots and greens). Stir-fry for about 2-3 minutes. Add all the seasonings and stir until well combined.

7 Pour the mixture in the wok over the noodles, garnish with the remaining spring onions (scallions) and serve immediately.

COOK'S TIP

Noodle soup is wonderfully satisfying and is ideal to serve on cold winter days.

Chicken Noodles

Rice noodles are used in this recipe. They are available in large supermarkets or specialist Chinese supermarkets.

NUTRITIONAL INFORMATION

Calories	169	Sugars	.........2g
Protein	........14g	Fat	...........7g
Carbohydrate	...12g	Saturates	.......2g

 5 MINS   15 MINS

SERVES 4

I N G R E D I E N T S

225 g/8 oz rice noodles

2 tbsp peanut oil

225 g/8 oz skinless, boneless chicken breast, sliced

2 garlic cloves, crushed

1 tsp grated fresh root ginger

1 tsp Chinese curry powder

1 red (bell) pepper, seeded and thinly sliced

75 g/2¾ oz mangetout (snow peas), shredded

1 tbsp light soy sauce

2 tsp Chinese rice wine

2 tbsp chicken stock

1 tsp sesame oil

1 tbsp chopped fresh coriander (cilantro)

1 Soak the rice noodles for 4 minutes in warm water. Drain thoroughly and set aside until required.

2 Heat the peanut oil in a preheated wok or large heavy-based frying pan (skillet) and stir-fry the chicken slices for 2–3 minutes.

3 Add the garlic, ginger and Chinese curry powder and stir-fry for a further 30 seconds. Add the red (bell) pepper and mangetout (snow peas) to the mixture in the wok and stir-fry for 2–3 minutes.

4 Add the noodles, soy sauce, Chinese rice wine and chicken stock to the wok and mix well, stirring occasionally, for 1 minute.

5 Sprinkle the sesame oil and chopped coriander (cilantro) over the noodles. Transfer to serving plates and serve.

VARIATION

You can use pork or duck in this recipe instead of the chicken, if you prefer.

Noodles with Cod & Mango

Fish and fruit are tossed with a trio of (bell) peppers in this spicy dish served with noodles for a quick, healthy meal.

NUTRITIONAL INFORMATION

Calories 274   Sugars 11g
Protein ....25g   Fat 8g
Carbohydrate ...26g   Saturates 1g

10 MINS   25 MINS

SERVES 4

I N G R E D I E N T S

250 g/9 oz packet egg noodles

450 g/1 lb skinless cod fillet

1 tbsp paprika

2 tbsp sunflower oil

1 red onion, sliced

1 orange (bell) pepper, deseeded and sliced

1 green (bell) pepper, deseeded and sliced

100 g/3½ oz baby corn cobs, halved

1 mango, sliced

100 g/3½ oz/1 cup bean sprouts

2 tbsp tomato ketchup

2 tbsp soy sauce

2 tbsp medium sherry

1 tsp cornflour (cornstarch)

1 Place the egg noodles in a large bowl and cover with boiling water. Leave to stand for about 10 minutes.

2 Rinse the cod fillet and pat dry with absorbent kitchen paper (paper towels). Cut the cod flesh into thin strips.

3 Place the cod strips in a large bowl. Add the paprika and toss well to coat the fish.

4 Heat the sunflower oil in a large preheated wok.

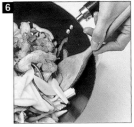

5 Add the onion, (bell) peppers and baby corn cobs to the wok and stir-fry for about 5 minutes.

6 Add the cod to the wok together with the sliced mango and stir-fry for a further 2–3 minutes or until the fish is tender.

7 Add the bean sprouts to the wok and toss well to combine.

8 Mix together the tomato ketchup, soy sauce , sherry and cornflour (cornstarch). Add the mixture to the wok and cook, stirring occasionally, until the juices thicken.

9 Drain the noodles thoroughly and transfer to warm serving bowls. Transfer the cod and mango stir-fry to separate serving bowls and serve immediately.

Chilli (Small) Shrimp Noodles

Cellophane or 'glass' noodles are made from mung beans. They are sold dried, so they need soaking before use.

NUTRITIONAL INFORMATION

Calories 152   Sugars 2g
Protein ....11g   Fat 8g
Carbohydrate ...10g   Saturates 1g

 25 MINS   10 MINS

SERVES 4

I N G R E D I E N T S

2 tbsp light soy sauce

1 tbsp lime or lemon juice

1 tbsp fish sauce

125 g/4½ oz firm tofu (bean curd), cut into chunks

125 g/4½ oz cellophane noodles

2 tbsp sesame oil

4 shallots, sliced finely

2 garlic cloves, crushed

1 small red chilli, deseeded and chopped finely

2 celery sticks, sliced finely

2 carrots, sliced finely

125 g/4½ oz/⅔ cup cooked, peeled (small) shrimps

60 g/2 oz/1 cup bean sprouts

TO GARNISH

celery leaves

fresh chillies

1 Mix together the light soy sauce, lime or lemon juice and fish sauce in a small bowl. Add the tofu (bean curd) cubes and toss them until coated in the mixture. Cover and set aside for 15 minutes.

2 Put the noodles into a large bowl and cover with warm water. Leave them to soak for about 5 minutes, and then drain them well.

3 Heat the sesame oil in a wok or large frying pan (skillet). Add the shallots, garlic and red chilli, and stir-fry for 1 minute.

4 Add the sliced celery and carrots to the wok or pan and stir-fry for a further 2–3 minutes.

5 Tip the drained noodles into the wok or frying pan (skillet) and cook, stirring, for 2 minutes, then add the (small) shrimps, bean sprouts and tofu (bean curd), with the soy sauce mixture. Cook over a medium high heat for 2–3 minutes until heated through.

6 Transfer the mixture in the wok to a serving dish and garnish with celery leaves and chillies.

Egg Noodles with Beef

Quick and easy, this mouth-watering Chinese-style noodle dish can be cooked in minutes.

NUTRITIONAL INFORMATION

Calories 329	Sugars 3g	
Protein 23g	Fat 16g	
Carbohydrate . . .20g	Saturates 4g	

 10 MINS   15 MINS

SERVES 4

INGREDIENTS

285 g/10 oz egg noodles

3 tbsp walnut oil

2.5 cm/1 inch piece fresh root ginger, cut into thin strips

5 spring onions (scallions), finely shredded

2 garlic cloves, finely chopped

1 red (bell) pepper, cored, seeded and thinly sliced

100 g/3½ oz button mushrooms, thinly sliced

350 g/12 oz fillet steak, cut into thin strips

1 tbsp cornflour (cornstarch)

5 tbsp dry sherry

3 tbsp soy sauce

1 tsp soft brown sugar

225 g/8 oz/1 cup bean sprouts

1 tbsp sesame oil

salt and pepper

spring onion (scallion) strips, to garnish

1 Bring a large saucepan of water to the boil. Add the egg noodles and cook according to the instructions on the packet. Drain the noodles, rinse under cold running water, drain thoroughly again and set aside.

2 Heat the walnut oil in a preheated wok until it is really hot.

3 Add the grated fresh root ginger, shredded spring onions (scallions) and chopped garlic and stir-fry for 45 seconds.

4 Add the red (bell) pepper, button mushrooms and steak and stir-fry for 4 minutes. Season to taste with salt and pepper.

5 Mix together the cornflour (cornstarch), dry sherry and soy sauce in a small jug to form a paste, and pour into the wok. Sprinkle over the brown sugar and stir-fry all of the ingredients for a further 2 minutes.

6 Add the bean sprouts, drained noodles and sesame oil to the wok, stir and toss together for 1 minute.

7 Transfer the stir-fry to warm serving dishes, garnish with strips of spring onion (scallion) and serve.

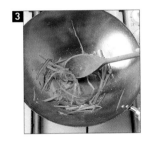

Beef with Crispy Noodles

Crispy noodles are terrific and may also be served on their own as a side dish, sprinkled with sugar and salt.

NUTRITIONAL INFORMATION

Calories 244	Sugars 9g
Protein 20g	Fat 10g
Carbohydrate ...19g	Saturates 2g

5 MINS   30 MINS

SERVES 4

INGREDIENTS

225 g/8 oz medium egg noodles

350 g/12 oz beef fillet

2 tbsp sunflower oil

1 tsp ground ginger

1 clove garlic, crushed

1 red chilli, deseeded and very finely chopped

100 g/3½ oz carrots, cut into thin sticks

6 spring onions (scallions), sliced

2 tbsp lime marmalade

2 tbsp soy sauce

oil, for frying

1 Place the noodles in a large dish or bowl. Pour over enough boiling water to cover the noodles and leave to stand for about 10 minutes while you stir-fry the rest of the ingredients.

2 Using a sharp knife, thinly slice the beef fillet.

3 Heat the sunflower oil in a large preheated wok or frying pan (skillet).

4 Add the beef and ground ginger to the wok or frying pan (skillet) and stir-fry for about 5 minutes.

5 Add the crushed garlic, chopped chilli, carrots and spring onions (scallions) to the wok and stir-fry for a further 2–3 minutes.

6 Add the lime marmalade and soy sauce to the wok and allow to bubble for 2 minutes. Remove the chilli beef and ginger mixture, set aside and keep warm until required.

7 Heat the oil for frying in the wok or frying pan (skillet).

8 Drain the noodles thoroughly and pat dry with absorbent kitchen paper (paper towels). Carefully lower the noodles into the hot oil and cook for 2–3 minutes or until crispy. Drain the noodles on absorbent kitchen paper (paper towels).

9 Divide the noodles between 4 warm serving plates and top with the chilli beef and ginger mixture. Serve immediately.

Mushroom & Pork Noodles

This dish benefits from the use of coloured oyster mushrooms. If these are unavailable, plain grey mushrooms will suffice.

NUTRITIONAL INFORMATION

Calories 286   Sugars 3g
Protein . . . . .23g   Fat 13g
Carbohydrate . . .21g   Saturates 3g

10 MINS   20 MINS

SERVES 4

INGREDIENTS

450 g/1 lb thin egg noodles

2 tbsp peanut oil

350 g/12 oz pork fillet (tenderloin), sliced

2 garlic cloves, crushed

1 onion, cut into 8 pieces

225 g/8 oz oyster mushrooms

4 tomatoes, skinned, seeded and thinly sliced

2 tbsp light soy sauce

50 ml/2 fl oz/¼ cup pork stock

1 tbsp chopped fresh coriander (cilantro)

1 Cook the noodles in a saucepan of boiling water for 2-3 minutes. Drain well, rinse under cold running water and drain thoroughly again.

2 Heat 1 tablespoon of the oil in a preheated wok or frying pan (skillet).

3 Add the noodles to the wok or frying pan (skillet) and stir-fry for about 2 minutes.

4 Using a slotted spoon, remove the noodles from the wok, drain well and set aside until required.

5 Heat the remaining peanut oil in the wok. Add the pork slices and stir-fry for 4-5 minutes.

6 Stir in the crushed garlic and chopped onion and stir-fry for a further 2-3 minutes.

7 Add the oyster mushrooms, tomatoes, light soy sauce, pork stock and drained noodles. Stir well and cook for 1-2 minutes.

8 Sprinkle with chopped coriander (cilantro) and serve immediately.

COOK'S TIP

For crisper noodles, add 2 tablespoons of oil to the wok and fry the noodles for 5-6 minutes, spreading them thinly in the wok and turning half-way through cooking.

Sesame Hot Noodles

Plain egg noodles are tossed in a dressing made with sesame oil, soy sauce, peanut butter, coriander (cilantro), lime, chilli and sesame seeds.

NUTRITIONAL INFORMATION

Calories	300	Sugars	.........1g
Protein	.........7g	Fat	..........21g
Carbohydrate	...21g	Saturates	.......3g

5 MINS   10 MINS

SERVES 4

INGREDIENTS

2 x 250 g/9 oz packets medium egg noodles

3 tbsp sunflower oil

2 tbsp sesame oil

1 garlic clove, crushed

1 tbsp smooth peanut butter

1 small green chilli, seeded and very finely chopped

3 tbsp toasted sesame seeds

4 tbsp light soy sauce

½ tbsp lime juice

salt and pepper

4 tbsp chopped fresh coriander (cilantro)

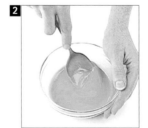

1 Place the noodles in a large pan of boiling water, then immediately remove from the heat. Cover and leave to stand for 6 minutes, stirring once halfway through the time. At the end of 6 minutes the noodles will be perfectly cooked. Alternatively, cook the noodles following the packet instructions.

2 Meanwhile, make the dressing. Mix together the sunflower oil, sesame oil, crushed garlic and peanut butter in a mixing bowl until smooth.

3 Add the chopped green chilli, sesame seeds and light soy sauce to the other dressing ingredients. Add the lime juice, according to taste, and mix well. Season with salt and pepper.

4 Drain the noodles thoroughly then place in a heated serving bowl.

5 Add the dressing and chopped fresh coriander (cilantro) to the noodles and toss well to mix. Serve hot as a main meal accompaniment.

COOK'S TIP

If you are cooking the noodles ahead of time, toss the cooked, drained noodles in 2 teaspoons of sesame oil, then turn into a bowl. Cover and keep warm until required.

Seafood Chow Mein

Use whatever seafood is available for this delicious noodle dish – mussels or crab would also be suitable.

NUTRITIONAL INFORMATION

Calories 281	Sugars 1g	
Protein 15g	Fat 18g	
Carbohydrate . . .16g	Saturates 2g	

 15 MINS   15 MINS

SERVES 4

I N G R E D I E N T S

90 g/3 oz squid, cleaned

3-4 fresh scallops

90 g/3 oz raw prawns (shrimp), shelled

½ egg white, lightly beaten

1 tbsp cornflour (cornstarch) paste (see page 15)

275 g/9½ oz egg noodles

5-6 tbsp vegetable oil

2 tbsp light soy sauce

60 g/2 oz mangetout (snow peas)

½ tsp salt

½ tsp sugar

1 tsp Chinese rice wine

2 spring onions (scallions), finely shredded

a few drops of sesame oil

COOK'S TIP

Chinese rice wine, made from glutinous rice, is also known as 'Yellow wine' because of its golden amber colour. If it is unavailable, a good dry or medium sherry is an acceptable substitute.

1 Open up the squid and score the inside in a criss-cross pattern, then cut into pieces about the size of a postage stamp. Soak the squid in a bowl of boiling water until all the pieces curl up. Rinse in cold water and drain.

2 Cut each scallop into 3-4 slices. Cut the prawns (shrimp) in half lengthways if large. Mix the scallops and prawns (shrimp) with the egg white and cornflour (cornstarch) paste.

3 Cook the noodles in boiling water according to the packet instructions, then drain and rinse under cold water. Drain well, then toss with about 1 tablespoon of oil.

4 Heat 3 tablespoons of oil in a preheated wok. Add the noodles and 1 tablespoon of the soy sauce and stir-fry for 2-3 minutes. Remove to a large serving dish.

5 Heat the remaining oil in the wok and add the mangetout (snow peas) and seafood. Stir-fry for about 2 minutes, then add the salt, sugar, wine, remaining soy sauce and about half the spring onions (scallions). Blend well and add a little stock or water if necessary. Pour the seafood mixture on top of the noodles and sprinkle with sesame oil. Garnish with the remaining spring onions (scallions) and serve.

Special Noodles

This dish combines meat, vegetables, prawns (shrimp) and noodles in a curried coconut sauce. Serve as a main meal or as an accompaniment.

NUTRITIONAL INFORMATION

Calories 409   Sugars 12g
Protein . . . . .24g   Fat 23g
Carbohydrate . . .28g   Saturates 8g

 5 MINS   25 MINS

SERVES 4

I N G R E D I E N T S

250 g/9 oz thin rice noodles

4 tbsp groundnut oil

2 cloves garlic, crushed

2 red chillies, deseeded and very finely chopped

1 tsp grated fresh ginger

2 tbsp Madras curry paste

2 tbsp rice wine vinegar

1 tbsp caster (superfine) sugar

225 g/8 oz cooked ham, finely shredded

100 g/3½ oz/1¼ cups canned water chestnuts, sliced

100 g/3½ oz mushrooms, sliced

100 g/3½ oz/¾ cup peas

1 red (bell) pepper, deseeded and thinly sliced

100 g/3½ oz peeled prawns (shrimp)

2 large eggs

4 tbsp coconut milk

25 g/1 oz/¼ cup desiccated (shredded) coconut

2 tbsp chopped fresh coriander (cilantro)

1 Place the rice noodles in a large bowl, cover with boiling water and leave to soak for about 10 minutes. Drain the noodles thoroughly, then toss with 2 tablespoons of groundnut oil.

2 Heat the remaining groundnut oil in a large preheated wok until the oil is really hot.

3 Add the garlic, chillies, ginger, curry paste, rice wine vinegar and caster (superfine) sugar to the wok and stir-fry for 1 minute.

4 Add the ham, water chestnuts, mushrooms, peas and red (bell) pepper to the wok and stir-fry for 5 minutes.

5 Add the noodles and prawns (shrimps) to the wok and stir-fry for 2 minutes.

6 In a small bowl, beat together the eggs and coconut milk. Drizzle over the mixture in the wok and stir-fry until the egg sets.

7 Add the desiccated (shredded) coconut and chopped fresh coriander (cilantro) to the wok and toss to combine. Transfer the noodles to warm serving dishes and serve immediately.

Homemade Noodles

These noodles are simple to make; you do not need a pasta-making machine as they are rolled out by hand.

NUTRITIONAL INFORMATION

Calories	294	Sugars	.........3g
Protein	.........7g	Fat	..........15g
Carbohydrate	...35g	Saturates	.......2g

20 MINS　　15 MINS

SERVES 2–4

INGREDIENTS

NOODLES

125 g/4½ oz/1 cup plain (all-purpose) flour

2 tbsp cornflour (cornstarch)

½ tsp salt

125 ml/4 fl oz/½ cup boiling water

5 tbsp vegetable oil

STIR-FRY

1 courgette (zucchini), cut into thin sticks

1 celery stick, cut into thin sticks

1 carrot, cut into thin sticks

125 g/4½ oz open-cup mushrooms, sliced

125 g/4½ oz broccoli florets and stalks, peeled and thinly sliced

1 leek, sliced

125 g/4½ oz/2 cups bean sprouts

1 tbsp soy sauce

2 tsp rice wine vinegar

½ tsp sugar

  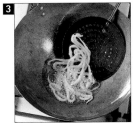

1 To prepare the noodles, sift the flour, cornflour (cornstarch) and salt into a bowl. Make a well in the centre and pour in the boiling water and 1 teaspoon of oil. Mix quickly to make a soft dough. Cover and leave for 5–6 minutes.

2 Make the noodles by breaking off small pieces of dough and rolling into balls. Roll each ball across a very lightly oiled work surface (counter) with the palm of your hand to form thin noodles. Do not worry if some of the noodles break into shorter lengths. Set the noodles aside.

3 Heat 3 tablespoons of oil in a wok. Add the noodles in batches and fry over a high heat for 1 minute. Reduce the heat and cook for a further 2 minutes. Remove and drain on kitchen paper (paper towels). Set aside.

4 Heat the remaining oil in the pan. Add the courgette (zucchini), celery and carrot, and stir-fry for 1 minute. Add the mushrooms, broccoli and leek, and stir-fry for a further minute. Stir in the remaining ingredients and mix well until thoroughly heated.

5 Add the noodles and cook over a high heat, tossing to mix the ingredients. Serve immediately.

Noodles with Prawns (Shrimp)

This is a simple dish using egg noodles and large prawns (shrimp), which give the dish a wonderful flavour, texture and colour.

NUTRITIONAL INFORMATION

Calories 142   Sugars 0.4g
Protein ....11g   Fat 7g
Carbohydrate ....11g Saturates 1g

 5 MINS   10 MINS

SERVES 4

I N G R E D I E N T S

225 g/8 oz thin egg noodles

2 tbsp peanut oil

1 garlic clove, crushed

½ tsp ground star anise

1 bunch spring onions (scallions), cut into 5-cm/2-inch pieces

24 raw tiger prawns (jumbo shrimp), peeled with tails intact

2 tbsp light soy sauce

2 tsp lime juice

lime wedges, to garnish

1 Blanch the noodles in a saucepan of boiling water for about 2 minutes.

2 Drain the noodles well, rinse under cold water and drain thoroughly again. Keep warm and set aside until required.

3 Heat the peanut oil in a preheated wok or large frying pan (skillet) until almost smoking.

4 Add the crushed garlic and ground star anise to the wok and stir-fry for 30 seconds.

5 Add the spring onions (scallions) and tiger prawns (jumbo shrimp) to the wok and stir-fry for 2-3 minutes.

6 Stir in the light soy sauce, lime juice and noodles and mix well.

7 Cook the mixture in the wok for about 1 minute until thoroughly heated through and all the ingredients are thoroughly incorporated.

8 Spoon the noodle and prawn mixture into a warm serving dish. Transfer to serving bowls, garnish with lime wedges and serve immediately.

COOK'S TIP

If fresh egg noodles are available, these require very little cooking: simply place in boiling water for about 3 minutes, then drain and toss in oil. Noodles can be boiled and eaten plain, or stir-fried with meat and vegetables for a light meal or snack.

Chilled Noodles & Peppers

This is a convenient dish to serve when you are arriving home just before family or friends. Quick to prepare and assemble, it is ready in minutes.

NUTRITIONAL INFORMATION

Calories	260	Sugars	........4g
Protein	.........4g	Fat	..........21g
Carbohydrate	...15g	Saturates	.......4g

 5 MINS   15 MINS

SERVES 4–6

I N G R E D I E N T S

250 g/9 oz ribbon noodles, or Chinese egg noodles

1 tbsp sesame oil

1 red (bell) pepper

1 yellow (bell) pepper

1 green (bell) pepper

6 spring onions (scallions), cut into matchstick strips

salt

D R E S S I N G

5 tbsp sesame oil

2 tbsp light soy sauce

1 tbsp tahini (sesame seed paste)

4-5 drops hot pepper sauce

1 Preheat the grill (broiler) to medium. Cook the noodles in a large pan of boiling, salted water until they are almost tender. Drain them in a colander, run cold water through them and drain thoroughly. Tip the noodles into a bowl, stir in the sesame oil, cover and chill.

2 Cook the (bell) peppers under the grill (broiler), turning them frequently, until they are blackened on all sides. Plunge into cold water, then skin them. Cut in half, remove the core and seeds and cut the flesh into thick strips. Set aside in a covered container.

3 To make the dressing, mix together the sesame oil, light soy sauce, tahini (sesame seed paste) and hot pepper sauce until well combined.

4 Pour the dressing on the noodles, reserving 1 tablespoon, and toss well. Turn the noodles into a serving dish, arrange the grilled (bell) peppers over the noodles and spoon on the reserved dressing. Scatter on the spring onion (scallion) strips.

COOK'S TIP

If you have time, another way of skinning (bell) peppers is to first grill (broil) them, then place in a plastic bag, seal and leave for about 20 minutes. The skin will then peel off easily.

Pork Chow Mein

This is a basic recipe – the meat and/or vegetables can be varied as much as you like.

NUTRITIONAL INFORMATION

Calories . . . . . . .239 Sugars 1g
Protein . . . . .17g Fat 14g
Carbohydrate . . .12g Saturates 2g

15 MINS   15 MINS

SERVES 4

INGREDIENTS

250 g/9 oz egg noodles

4-5 tbsp vegetable oil

250 g/9 oz pork fillet, cooked

125 g/4½ oz French (green) beans

2 tbsp light soy sauce

1 tsp salt

½ tsp sugar

1 tbsp Chinese rice wine or dry sherry

2 spring onions (scallions), finely shredded

a few drops sesame oil

chilli sauce, to serve (optional)

1 Cook the noodles in boiling water according to the instructions on the packet, then drain and rinse under cold water. Drain again then toss with 1 tablespoon of the oil.

2 Slice the pork into thin shreds and top and tail the beans.

3 Heat 3 tablespoons of oil in a preheated wok until hot. Add the noodles and stir-fry for 2-3 minutes with 1 tablespoon soy sauce, then remove to a serving dish. Keep warm.

4 Heat the remaining oil and stir-fry the beans and meat for 2 minutes. Add the salt, sugar, wine or sherry, the remaining soy sauce and about half the spring onions (scallions) to the wok.

5 Stir the mixture in the wok, adding a little stock if necessary, then pour on top of the noodles, and sprinkle with sesame oil and the remaining spring onions (scallions).

6 Serve the chow mein hot or cold with chilli sauce, if desired.

COOK'S TIP

Chow Mein literally means 'stir-fried noodles' and is highly popular in the West as well as in China. Almost any ingredient can be added, such as fish, meat, poultry or vegetables. It is very popular for lunch and makes a tasty salad served cold.

Fried Vegetable Noodles

In this recipe, noodles are first boiled and then deep-fried for a crisply textured dish, and tossed with fried vegetables.

NUTRITIONAL INFORMATION

Calories . . . . . . .229 Sugars 4g
Protein . . . . .5g Fat 15g
Carbohydrate . . .20g Saturates 2g

5 MINS   25 MINS

SERVES 4

I N G R E D I E N T S

350 g/12 oz/3 cups dried egg noodles

2 tbsp peanut oil

2 garlic cloves, crushed

½ tsp ground star anise

1 carrot, cut into matchsticks

1 green (bell) pepper, cut into matchsticks

1 onion, quartered and sliced

125 g/4½ oz broccoli florets

75 g/2¾ oz bamboo shoots

1 celery stick, sliced

1 tbsp light soy sauce

150 ml/¼ pint/⅔ cup vegetable stock

oil, for deep-frying

1 tsp cornflour (cornstarch)

2 tsp water

1 Cook the noodles in a saucepan of boiling water for 1–2 minutes. Drain well and rinse under cold running water. Leave the noodles to drain thoroughly in a colander until required.

2 Heat the peanut oil in a preheated wok until smoking. Reduce the heat, add the crushed garlic and ground star anise and stir-fry for 30 seconds. Add the remaining vegetables and stir-fry for 1–2 minutes.

3 Add the soy sauce and vegetable stock to the wok and cook over a low heat for 5 minutes.

4 Heat the oil for deep-frying in a separate wok to 180°C/350°F, or until a cube of bread browns in 30 seconds.

5 Using a fork, twist the drained noodles and form them into rounds. Deep-fry them in batches until crisp, turning once. Leave to drain on kitchen paper (paper towels).

6 Blend the cornflour (cornstarch) with the water to form a paste and stir into the vegetables. Bring to the boil, stirring until the sauce is thickened and clear.

7 Arrange the noodles on a warm serving plate, spoon the vegetables on top and serve immediately.

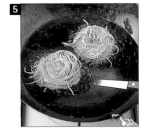

Lamb with Noodles

Lamb is quick fried, coated in a soy sauce and served on a bed of transparent noodles for a richly flavoured dish.

NUTRITIONAL INFORMATION

Calories ....285 Sugars 1g
Protein ....27g Fat 16g
Carbohydrate ...10g Saturates 6g

 5 MINS   15 MINS

SERVES 4

I N G R E D I E N T S

150 g/5½ oz cellophane noodles

2 tbsp peanut oil

450 g/1 lb lean lamb, thinly sliced

2 garlic cloves, crushed

2 leeks, sliced

3 tbsp dark soy sauce

250 ml/9 fl oz/1 cup lamb stock

dash of chilli sauce

red chilli strips, to garnish

1 Bring a large saucepan of water to the boil. Add the cellophane noodles and cook for 1 minute. Drain the noodles well, place in a sieve, rinse under cold running water and drain thoroughly again. Set aside until required.

2 Heat the peanut oil in a preheated wok or frying pan (skillet), swirling the oil around until it is really hot.

3 Add the lamb to the wok or frying pan (skillet) and stir-fry for about 2 minutes.

4 Add the crushed garlic and sliced leeks to the wok and stir-fry for a further 2 minutes.

5 Stir in the dark soy sauce, lamb stock and chilli sauce and cook for 3-4

minutes, stirring frequently, until the meat is cooked through.

6 Add the drained cellophane noodles to the wok or frying pan (skillet) and cook for about 1 minute, stirring, until heated through.

7 Transfer the lamb and cellophane noodles to serving plates, garnish with red chilli strips and serve.

COOK'S TIP

Transparent noodles are available in Chinese supermarkets. Use egg noodles instead if transparent noodles are unavailable, and cook them according to the instructions on the packet.

Chicken & Noodle One-Pot

Flavoursome chicken and vegetables cooked with Chinese egg noodles in a coconut sauce. Serve in deep soup bowls.

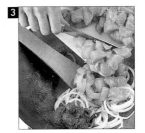

NUTRITIONAL INFORMATION

Calories	256	Sugars 7g
Protein	........30g	Fat 8g
Carbohydrate	...18g	Saturates 2g

 5 MINS   20 MINS

SERVES 4

INGREDIENTS

1 tbsp sunflower oil

1 onion, sliced

1 garlic clove, crushed

2.5 cm/1 inch root ginger, peeled and grated

1 bunch spring onions (scallions), sliced diagonally

500 g/1 lb 2 oz chicken breast fillet, skinned and cut into bite-sized pieces

2 tbsp mild curry paste

450 ml/16 fl oz/2 cups coconut milk

300 ml/½ pint/1¼ cups chicken stock

250 g/9 oz Chinese egg noodles

2 tsp lime juice

salt and pepper

basil sprigs, to garnish

1 Heat the sunflower oil in a wok or large, heavy-based frying pan (skillet).

2 Add the onion, garlic, ginger and spring onions (scallions) to the wok and stir-fry for 2 minutes until softened.

3 Add the chicken and curry paste and stir-fry for 4 minutes, or until the vegetables and chicken are golden brown. Stir in the coconut milk, stock and salt and pepper to taste, and mix well.

4 Bring to the boil, break the noodles into large pieces, if necessary, add to the pan, cover and simmer for about 6-8 minutes until the noodles are just tender, stirring occasionally.

5 Add the lime juice and adjust the seasoning, if necessary.

6 Serve the chicken and noodle one-pot at once in deep soup bowls, garnished with basil sprigs.

COOK'S TIP

If you enjoy hot flavours, substitute the mild curry paste in the above recipe with hot curry paste (found in most supermarkets) but reduce the quantity to 1 tablespoon.

Noodles with Chilli & Prawn

This is a simple dish to prepare and is packed with flavour, making it an ideal choice for special occasions.

NUTRITIONAL INFORMATION

Calories 259   Sugars 9g
Protein ....28g   Fat 8g
Carbohydrate ...20g   Saturates 1g

10 MINS   5 MINS

SERVES 4

INGREDIENTS

250 g/9 oz thin glass noodles

2 tbsp sunflower oil

1 onion, sliced

2 red chillies, deseeded and very finely chopped

4 lime leaves, thinly shredded

1 tbsp fresh coriander (cilantro)

2 tbsp palm or caster (superfine) sugar

2 tbsp fish sauce

450 g/1 lb raw tiger prawns (jumbo shrimp), peeled

1 Place the noodles in a large bowl. Pour over enough boiling water to cover the noodles and leave to stand for 5 minutes. Drain thoroughly and set aside until required.

COOK'S TIP

If you cannot buy raw tiger prawns (jumbo shrimp), use cooked prawns (shrimp) instead and cook them with the noodles for 1 minute only, just to heat through.

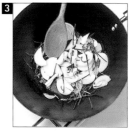  

2 Heat the sunflower oil in a large preheated wok or frying pan (skillet) until it is really hot.

3 Add the onion, red chillies and lime leaves to the wok and stir-fry for 1 minute.

4 Add the coriander (cilantro), palm or caster (superfine) sugar, fish sauce and prawns (shrimp) to the wok or frying pan (skillet) and stir-fry for a further 2 minutes or until the prawns (shrimp) turn pink.

5 Add the drained noodles to the wok, toss to mix well, and stir-fry for 1–2 minutes or until heated through.

6 Transfer the noodles and prawns (shrimp) to warm serving bowls and serve immediately.

Sweet & Sour Noodles

This delicious dish combines sweet and sour flavours with the addition of egg, rice noodles, king prawns (shrimp) and vegetables for a real treat.

NUTRITIONAL INFORMATION

Calories 352   Sugars 14g
Protein ....23g   Fat 17g
Carbohydrate ...29g   Saturates 3g

10 MINS   10 MINS

SERVES 4

INGREDIENTS

3 tbsp fish sauce

2 tbsp distilled white vinegar

2 tbsp caster (superfine) or palm sugar

2 tbsp tomato purée (paste)

2 tbsp sunflower oil

3 cloves garlic, crushed

350 g/12 oz rice noodles, soaked in boiling water for 5 minutes

8 spring onions (scallions), sliced

175 g/6 oz carrot, grated

150 g/5½ oz/1¼ cups bean sprouts

2 eggs, beaten

225 g/8 oz peeled king prawns (shrimp)

50 g/1¾ oz/½ cup chopped peanuts

1 tsp chilli flakes, to garnish

1 Mix together the fish sauce, vinegar, sugar and tomato purée (paste).

2 Heat the sunflower oil in a large preheated wok.

3 Add the garlic to the wok and stir-fry for 30 seconds.

4 Drain the noodles thoroughly and add them to the wok together with the fish sauce and tomato purée (paste) mixture. Mix well to combine.

5 Add the spring onions (scallions), carrot and bean sprouts to the wok and stir-fry for 2–3 minutes.

6 Move the contents of the wok to one side, add the beaten eggs to the empty part of the wok and cook until the egg sets. Add the noodles, prawns (shrimp) and peanuts to the wok and mix well. Transfer to warm serving dishes and garnish with chilli flakes. Serve hot.

COOK'S TIP

Chilli flakes may be found in the spice section of large supermarkets.

Rice

Together with noodles, rice forms the central part of a Chinese meal, particularly in southern China. In the north, the staple foods tend to be more wheat-based. For an everyday meal, plain rice is served with one or two dishes and a soup. Rice can be boiled and then steamed or it can be fried with other ingredients such as eggs, prawns

(shrimp), meat and vegetables and then flavoured with soy sauce. The most common type of rice used in Chinese cooking is short-grain or glutinous rice, which become slightly sticky when cooked and is therefore ideal for eating with chopsticks. This chapter includes some delicious rice dishes which can be eaten on their own or as an accompaniment. Fried rice is a particular favourite in Western restaurants so several variations are included here.

Egg Fried Rice

In this classic Chinese dish, boiled rice is fried with peas, spring onions (scallions) and egg and flavoured with soy sauce.

NUTRITIONAL INFORMATION

Calories 203   Sugars 1g
Protein . . . . .9g   Fat 11g
Carbohydrate . . .19g   Saturates 2g

20 MINS   10 MINS

SERVES 4

INGREDIENTS

150 g/5½ oz/⅔ cup long-grain rice

3 eggs, beaten

2 tbsp vegetable oil

2 garlic cloves, crushed

4 spring onions (scallions), chopped

125 g/4½oz/1 cup cooked peas

1 tbsp light soy sauce

pinch of salt

shredded spring onion (scallion),
   to garnish

1 Cook the rice in a pan of boiling water for 10-12 minutes, until almost cooked, but not soft. Drain well, rinse under cold water and drain again.

2 Place the beaten eggs in a saucepan and cook over a gentle heat, stirring until softly scrambled.

3 Heat the vegetable oil in a preheated wok or large frying pan (skillet), swirling the oil around the base of the wok until it is really hot.

4 Add the crushed garlic, spring onions (scallions) and peas and sauté, stirring occasionally, for 1-2 minutes. Stir the rice into the wok, mixing to combine.

5 Add the eggs, light soy sauce and a pinch of salt to the wok or frying pan (skillet) and stir to mix the egg in thoroughly.

6 Transfer the egg fried rice to serving dishes and serve garnished with the shredded spring onion (scallion).

COOK'S TIP

The rice is rinsed under cold water to wash out the starch and prevent it from sticking together.

Chilli Fried Rice

Not so much a side dish as a meal in itself, this delicious fried rice can be served on its own or as an accompaniment to many Chinese dishes.

NUTRITIONAL INFORMATION

Calories 290   Sugars 2g
Protein ....11g   Fat 14g
Carbohydrate ...26g   Saturates 2g

20 MINS   15 MINS

SERVES 4

I N G R E D I E N T S

250 g/9 oz/generous 1 cup long-grain rice

4 tbsp vegetable oil

2 garlic cloves, chopped finely

1 small red chilli, deseeded and chopped finely

8 spring onions (scallions), trimmed and sliced finely

1 tbsp red curry paste or 2 tsp chilli sauce

1 red (bell) pepper, cored, deseeded and chopped

90 g/3 oz/¾ cup dwarf green beans, chopped

250 g/9 oz/1½ cups cooked peeled prawns (shrimp) or chopped cooked chicken

2 tbsp fish sauce

T O   G A R N I S H

cucumber slices

shredded spring onion (scallion)

COOK'S TIP

Cook the rice the day before if you can remember – it will give an even better result. Alternatively, use rice left over from another dish to make this recipe.

1 Cook the rice in plenty of boiling, lightly salted water until tender, about 12 minutes. Drain, rinse with cold water and drain thoroughly.

2 Heat the vegetable oil in a wok or large frying pan (skillet) until the oil is really hot.

3 Add the garlic to the wok and fry gently for 2 minutes until golden.

4 Add the chilli and spring onions (scallions) and cook, stirring, for 3–4 minutes.

5 Add the red curry paste or chilli sauce to the wok or frying pan (skillet) and fry for 1 minute, then add the red (bell) pepper and dwarf green beans. Stir-fry briskly for 2 minutes.

6 Tip the cooked rice into the wok or frying pan (skillet) and add the prawns (shrimp) or chicken and the fish sauce. Stir-fry over a medium-high heat for about 4–5 minutes, until the rice is hot.

7 Transfer the chilli fried rice to warm serving dishes, garnish with cucumber slices and shredded spring onion (scallion) and serve.

Fragrant Coconut Rice

This fragrant, sweet rice is delicious served with meat, vegetable or fish dishes as part of a Chinese menu.

NUTRITIONAL INFORMATION

Calories 306   Sugars 2g
Protein . . . . .5g   Fat 6g
Carbohydrate . . .61g   Saturates 4g

🕐 5 MINS   🕐 15 MINS

SERVES 4

INGREDIENTS

275 g/9½ oz long-grain white rice

600 ml/1 pint/2½ cups water

½ tsp salt

100 ml/3½ fl oz/⅓ cup coconut milk

25 g/1 oz/¼ cup desiccated (shredded) coconut

1 Rinse the rice thoroughly under cold running water until the water runs completely clear.

2 Drain the rice thoroughly in a sieve set over a large bowl. This is to remove some of the starch and to prevent the grains from sticking together.

3 Place the rice in a wok with 600 ml/ 1 pint/2½ cups water.

4 Add the salt and coconut milk to the wok and bring to the boil.

5 Cover the wok with a lid or a lid made of foil, curved into a domed shape and resting on the sides of the wok. Reduce the heat and leave to simmer for 10 minutes.

6 Remove the lid from the wok and fluff up the rice with a fork – all of the liquid should be absorbed and the rice grains should be tender. If not, add more water and continue to simmer for a few more minutes until all the liquid has been absorbed.

7 Spoon the rice into a warm serving bowl and scatter with the desiccated (shredded) coconut. Serve immediately.

COOK'S TIP

Coconut milk is not the liquid found inside coconuts – that is called coconut water. Coconut milk is made from the white coconut flesh soaked in water and milk and then squeezed to extract all of the flavour. You can make your own or buy it in cans.

Sweet Chilli Pork Fried Rice

This is a variation of egg fried rice which may be served as an accompaniment to a main meal dish.

NUTRITIONAL INFORMATION

Calories .... .366   Sugars 5g
Protein ....29g   Fat 16g
Carbohydrate ...28g   Saturates 4g

25 MINS   20 MINS

SERVES 4

INGREDIENTS

450 g/1 lb pork tenderloin

2 tbsp sunflower oil

2 tbsp sweet chilli sauce, plus extra
to serve

1 onion, sliced

175 g/6 oz carrots, cut into thin sticks

175 g/6 oz courgettes (zucchini),
cut into sticks

100 g/3½ oz/1 cup canned bamboo shoots,
drained

275 g/9½ oz/4¾ cups cooked long-grain
rice

1 egg, beaten

1 tbsp chopped fresh parsley

1 Using a sharp knife, cut the pork tenderloin into thin slices.

2 Heat the sunflower oil in a large preheated wok or frying pan (skillet).

3 Add the pork to the wok and stir-fry for 5 minutes.

4 Add the chilli sauce to the wok and allow to bubble, stirring, for 2–3 minutes or until syrupy.

5 Add the onion, carrots, courgettes (zucchini) and bamboo shoots to the wok and stir-fry for a further 3 minutes.

6 Add the cooked rice and stir-fry for 2–3 minutes, or until the rice is heated through.

7 Drizzle the beaten egg over the top of the fried rice and cook, tossing the ingredients in the wok with two spoons, until the egg sets.

8 Scatter with chopped fresh parsley and serve immediately, with extra sweet chilli sauce, if desired.

COOK'S TIP

For a really quick dish,
add frozen mixed vegetables
to the rice instead of the freshly
prepared vegetables.

Special Fried Rice

This dish is a popular choice in Chinese restaurants. Ham and prawns (shrimp) are mixed with vegetables in a soy-flavoured rice.

NUTRITIONAL INFORMATION

Calories 301   Sugars 1g
Protein . . . . .26g   Fat 13g
Carbohydrate . . .21g   Saturates 3g

5 MINS   30 MINS

SERVES 4

INGREDIENTS

150 g/5½ oz/⅔ cup long-grain rice

2 tbsp vegetable oil

2 eggs, beaten

2 garlic cloves, crushed

1 tsp grated fresh root ginger

3 spring onions (scallions), sliced

75 g/2¾ oz/¾ cup cooked peas

150 g/5½ oz/⅔ cup bean sprouts

225 g/8 oz/1⅓ cups shredded ham

150 g/5½ oz peeled, cooked prawns (shrimp)

2 tbsp light soy sauce

1 Cook the rice in a saucepan of boiling water for about 15 minutes. Drain well, rinse under cold water and drain thoroughly again.

2 Heat 1 tablespoon of the vegetable oil in a preheated wok.

3 Add the beaten eggs and a further 1 teaspoon of oil. Tilt the wok so that the egg covers the base to make a thin pancake.

4 Cook until lightly browned on the underside, then flip the pancake over and cook on the other side for 1 minute. Remove from the wok and leave to cool.

5 Heat the remaining oil in the wok and stir-fry the garlic and ginger for 30 seconds. Add the spring onions (scallions), peas, bean sprouts, ham and prawns (shrimp). Stir-fry for 2 minutes.

6 Stir in the soy sauce and rice and cook for a further 2 minutes. Transfer the rice to serving dishes. Roll up the pancake, slice it very thinly and use to garnish the rice. Serve immediately.

COOK'S TIP

As this recipe contains meat and fish, it is ideal served with simpler vegetable dishes.

Chicken & Rice Casserole

This is a quick-cooking, spicy casserole of rice, chicken, vegetables and chilli in a soy and ginger flavoured liquor.

NUTRITIONAL INFORMATION

Calories 502   Sugars 2g
Protein . . . . .55g   Fat 9g
Carbohydrate . . .52g   Saturates 3g

35 MINS   50 MINS

SERVES 4

I N G R E D I E N T S

150 g/5½ oz/⅔ cup long-grain rice

1 tbsp dry sherry

2 tbsp light soy sauce

2 tbsp dark soy sauce

2 tsp dark brown sugar

1 tsp salt

1 tsp sesame oil

900 g/2 lb skinless, boneless chicken meat, diced

850 ml/1½ pints/3¾ cups chicken stock

2 open-cap mushrooms, sliced

60 g/2 oz water chestnuts, halved

75 g/2¾ oz broccoli florets

1 yellow (bell) pepper, sliced

4 tsp grated fresh root ginger

whole chives, to garnish

VARIATION

This dish would work equally well with beef or pork. Chinese dried mushrooms may be used instead of the open-cap mushrooms, if rehydrated before adding to the dish.

1 Cook the rice in a saucepan of boiling water for about 15 minutes. Drain well, rinse under cold water and drain again thoroughly.

2 Mix together the sherry, soy sauces, sugar, salt and sesame oil.

3 Stir the chicken into the soy mixture, turning to coat the chicken well. Leave to marinate for about 30 minutes.

4 Bring the stock to the boil in a saucepan or preheated wok. Add the chicken with the marinade, mushrooms, water chestnuts, broccoli, (bell) pepper and ginger.

5 Stir in the rice, reduce the heat, cover and cook for 25-30 minutes, until the chicken and vegetables are cooked through. Transfer to serving plates, garnish with chives and serve.

Fried Rice with Prawns

Use either large peeled prawns (shrimp) or tiger prawns (jumbo shrimp) for this rice dish.

NUTRITIONAL INFORMATION

Calories	599	Sugars	.........0g
Protein	........26g	Fat	..........16g
Carbohydrate	...94g	Saturates	.......3g

5 MINS 35 MINS

SERVES 4

INGREDIENTS

300 g/10½ oz/1½ cups long-grain rice

2 eggs

4 tsp cold water

salt and pepper

3 tbsp sunflower oil

4 spring onions (scallions), thinly sliced diagonally

1 garlic clove, crushed

125 g/4½ oz closed-cup or button mushrooms, thinly sliced

2 tbsp oyster or anchovy sauce

1 x 200 g/7 oz can water chestnuts, drained and sliced

250 g/9 oz peeled prawns (shrimp), defrosted if frozen

½ bunch watercress, roughly chopped

watercress sprigs, to garnish (optional)

1 Cook the rice in a saucepan of boiling salted water for 15 minutes. Drain well, rinse under cold running water and drain again thoroughly.

2 Beat each egg separately with 2 teaspoons of cold water and salt and pepper.

3 Heat 2 teaspoons of sunflower oil in a wok or large frying pan (skillet),

swirling it around until really hot. Pour in the first egg, swirl it around and leave to cook undisturbed until set. Remove to a plate or board and repeat with the second egg. Cut the omelettes into 2.5 cm/1 inch squares.

4 Heat the remaining oil in the wok and when really hot add the spring onions (scallions) and garlic and stir-fry for 1 minute. Add the mushrooms and continue to cook for a further 2 minutes.

5 Stir in the oyster or anchovy sauce and seasoning and add the water chestnuts and prawns (shrimp); stir-fry for 2 minutes.

6 Stir in the cooked rice and stir-fry for 1 minute, then add the watercress and omelette squares and stir-fry for a further 1-2 minutes until piping hot. Serve at once garnished with sprigs of watercress, if liked.

Coconut Rice with Lentils

Rice and green lentils are cooked with coconut, lemon grass and curry leaves. It will serve 2 people as a main course or 4 as a side dish.

NUTRITIONAL INFORMATION

Calories 511	Sugars 3g	
Protein 12g	Fat 24g	
Carbohydrate ...67g	Saturates 15g	

5 MINS   50 MINS

SERVES 4

INGREDIENTS

90 g/3 oz/⅓ cup green lentils

250 g/9 oz/generous 1 cup long-grain rice

2 tbsp vegetable oil

1 onion, sliced

2 garlic cloves, crushed

3 curry leaves

1 stalk lemon grass, chopped (if unavailable, use grated rind of ½ lemon)

1 green chilli, deseeded and chopped

½ tsp cumin seeds

1½ tsp salt

90 g/3 oz/⅓ cup creamed coconut

600 ml/1 pint/2½ cups hot water

2 tbsp chopped fresh coriander (cilantro)

TO GARNISH

shredded radishes

shredded cucumber

1 Wash the lentils and place in a saucepan. Cover with cold water, bring to the boil and boil rapidly for 10 minutes.

2 Wash the rice thoroughly and drain well. Set aside until required.

3 Heat the vegetable oil in a large saucepan which has a tight-fitting lid and fry the onion for 3–4 minutes. Add the garlic, curry leaves, lemon grass, chilli, cumin seeds and salt, and stir well.

4 Drain the lentils and rinse. Add to the onion and spices with the rice and mix well.

5 Add the creamed coconut to the hot water and stir until dissolved. Stir the coconut liquid into the rice mixture and bring to the boil. Turn down the heat to low, put the lid on tightly and leave to cook undisturbed for 15 minutes.

6 Without removing the lid, remove the pan from the heat and leave to rest for 10 minutes to allow the rice and lentils to finish cooking in their own steam.

7 Stir in the coriander (cilantro) and remove the curry leaves. Serve garnished with the radishes and cucumber.

Vegetable Fried Rice

This dish can be served as part of a substantial meal for a number of people or as a vegetarian meal in itself for four.

NUTRITIONAL INFORMATION

Calories 175   Sugars 3g
Protein . . . . .3g   Fat 10g
Carbohydrate . . .20g   Saturates 2g

10 MINS   20 MINS

SERVES 4

I N G R E D I E N T S

125 g/4½ oz/⅔ cup long-grain white rice

3 tbsp peanut oil

2 garlic cloves, crushed

½ tsp Chinese five-spice powder

60 g/2 oz/⅓ cup green beans

1 green (bell) pepper, seeded and chopped

4 baby corn cobs, sliced

25 g/1 oz bamboo shoots, chopped

3 tomatoes, skinned, seeded and chopped

60 g/2 oz/½ cup cooked peas

1 tsp sesame oil

1 Bring a large saucepan of water to the boil.

2 Add the long-grain white rice to the saucepan and cook for about 15 minutes. Drain the rice well, rinse under cold running water and drain thoroughly again.

3 Heat the peanut oil in a preheated wok or large frying pan (skillet). Add the garlic and Chinese five-spice and stir-fry for 30 seconds.

4 Add the green beans, chopped green (bell) pepper and sliced corn cobs and stir-fry the ingredients in the wok for 2 minutes.

5 Stir the bamboo shoots, tomatoes, peas and rice into the mixture in the wok and stir-fry for 1 further minute.

6 Sprinkle with sesame oil and transfer to serving dishes. Serve immediately.

VARIATION

Use a selection of vegetables of your choice in this recipe, cutting them to a similar size in order to ensure that they cook in the same amount of time.

Steamed Rice in Lotus Leaves

The fragrance of the leaves penetrates the rice, giving it a unique taste. Lotus leaves can be bought from specialist Chinese shops.

NUTRITIONAL INFORMATION

Calories . . . . . . .163 Sugars 0.1g
Protein . . . . .5g Fat 6g
Carbohydrate . . .2.1g Saturates 1g

1 HOUR   40 MINS

SERVES 4

INGREDIENTS

2 lotus leaves

4 Chinese dried mushrooms (if unavailable, use thinly sliced open-cup mushrooms)

175 g/6 oz/generous ¾ cup long-grain rice

1 cinnamon stick

6 cardamom pods

4 cloves

1 tsp salt

2 eggs

1 tbsp vegetable oil

2 spring onions (scallions), chopped

1 tbsp soy sauce

2 tbsp sherry

1 tsp sugar

1 tsp sesame oil

1 Unfold the lotus leaves carefully and cut along the fold to divide each leaf in half. Lay on a large baking sheet and pour over enough hot water to cover. Soak for about 30 minutes until softened.

2 Place the dried mushrooms in a small bowl and cover with warm water. Leave to soak for 20–25 minutes.

3 Cook the rice in a saucepan of boiling water with the cinnamon stick, cardamom pods, cloves and salt for about

10 minutes – the rice should be partially cooked. Drain thoroughly and remove the cinnamon stick. Place the rice in a bowl

4 Beat the eggs lightly. Heat the oil in a wok and cook the eggs quickly, stirring until set. Remove and set aside.

5 Drain the mushrooms, squeezing out the excess water. Remove the tough centres and chop the mushrooms. Stir into

the rice with the cooked egg, spring onions (scallions), soy sauce, sherry, sugar and sesame oil.

6 Drain the lotus leaves and divide the rice into four portions. Place a portion in the centre of each leaf and fold up to form a parcel (packet). Place in a steamer, cover and steam over simmering water for 20 minutes. To serve, cut the tops of the lotus leaves open to expose the rice inside.

Curried Rice with Pork

This rice dish is flavoured with vegetables and pork, soy sauce and curry spices with strips of omelette added as a topping.

NUTRITIONAL INFORMATION

Calories 436   Sugars 2g
Protein . . . . .30g   Fat 20g
Carbohydrate . . .37g   Saturates 5g

10 MINS   35 MINS

SERVES 4

INGREDIENTS

300 g/10½ oz/1½ cups long-grain rice

350-500 g/12 oz-1 lb 2 oz pork fillet or lean pork slices

3 tomatoes, peeled, quartered and seeded

2 eggs

4 tsp water

3 tbsp sunflower oil

1 onion, thinly sliced

1-2 garlic cloves, crushed

1 tsp medium or mild curry powder

½ tsp ground coriander

¼ tsp medium chilli powder or 1 tsp bottled sweet chilli sauce

2 tbsp soy sauce

125 g/4½ oz frozen peas, defrosted

salt and pepper

1 Cook the rice in a saucepan of boiling salted water for 15 minutes. Drain well, rinse under cold running water and drain again thoroughly.

2 Meanwhile, cut the pork into narrow strips across the grain, discarding any fat. Slice the tomatoes.

3 Beat each egg separately with 2 teaspoons cold water and salt and pepper. Heat 2 teaspoons of oil in the wok until really hot. Pour in the first egg, swirl it around and cook undisturbed until set. Remove to a plate or board and repeat with the second egg. Cut the omelettes into strips about 1 cm/½ inch wide.

4 Heat the remaining oil in the wok and when really hot add the onion and garlic and stir-fry for 1-2 minutes. Add the pork and continue to stir-fry for about 3 minutes or until almost cooked.

5 Add the curry powder, coriander, chilli powder or chilli sauce and soy sauce to the wok and cook for a further minute, stirring constantly.

6 Stir in the rice, tomatoes and peas and stir-fry for about 2 minutes until piping hot. Adjust the seasoning to taste and turn into a heated serving dish. Arrange the strips of omelette on top and serve at once.

Crab Congee

This is a typical Chinese breakfast dish although it is probably best served as a lunch or supper dish at a Western table!

NUTRITIONAL INFORMATION

Calories	327	Sugars	.......0.1g
Protein	........18g	Fat	...........7g
Carbohydrate	...50g	Saturates	.......2g

   5 MINS   1¼ HOURS

SERVES 4

I N G R E D I E N T S

225 g/8 oz/1 cup short-grain rice

1.5 litres/2¾ pints/6¼ cups
  fish stock

½ tsp salt

100 g/3½ oz Chinese sausage,
  thinly sliced

225 g/8 oz white crab meat

6 spring onions (scallions), sliced

2 tbsp chopped fresh coriander
  (cilantro)

freshly ground black pepper,
  to serve

1 Place the short-grain rice in a large preheated wok or frying pan (skillet).

2 Add the fish stock to the wok or frying pan (skillet) and bring to the boil.

3 Reduce the heat, then simmer gently for 1 hour, stirring the mixture from time to time.

4 Add the salt, sliced Chinese sausage, white crab meat, sliced spring onions (scallions) and chopped fresh coriander (cilantro) to the wok and heat through for about 5 minutes.

5 Add a little more water to the wok if the congee "porridge" is too thick, stirring well.

6 Transfer the crab congee to warm serving bowls, sprinkle with freshly ground black pepper and serve immediately.

COOK'S TIP

Always buy the freshest possible crab meat; fresh is best, although frozen or canned will work for this recipe. In the West, crabs are almost always sold ready-cooked. The crab should feel heavy for its size, and when it is shaken, there should be no sound of water inside.

Crab Fried Rice

Canned crabmeat is used in this recipe for convenience, but fresh white crabmeat could be used - quite deliciously - in its place.

NUTRITIONAL INFORMATION

Calories	225	Sugars	.........1g
Protein	........12g	Fat	...........11g
Carbohydrate	...20g	Saturates	.......2g

5 MINS   25 MINS

SERVES 4

INGREDIENTS

150 g/5½ oz/⅔ cup long-grain rice

2 tbsp peanut oil

125 g/4½ oz canned white crabmeat, drained

1 leek, sliced

150 g/5½ oz/⅔ cup bean sprouts

2 eggs, beaten

1 tbsp light soy sauce

2 tsp lime juice

1 tsp sesame oil

salt

sliced lime, to garnish

1 Cook the rice in a saucepan of boiling salted water for 15 minutes. Drain well, rinse under cold running water and drain again thoroughly.

2 Heat the peanut oil in a preheated wok until it is really hot.

3 Add the crabmeat, leek and bean sprouts to the wok and stir-fry for 2-3 minutes. Remove the mixture from the wok with a slotted spoon and set aside until required.

4 Add the eggs to the wok and cook, stirring occasionally, for 2-3 minutes, until they begin to set.

5 Stir the rice and the crabmeat, leek and bean sprout mixture into the eggs in the wok.

6 Add the soy sauce and lime juice to the mixture in the wok. Cook for 1 minute, stirring to combine, and sprinkle with the sesame oil.

7 Transfer the crab fried rice to a serving dish, garnish with the sliced lime and serve immediately.

VARIATION

Cooked lobster may be used instead of the crab for a really special dish.

Curried Rice with Tofu

Cooked rice is combined with marinated tofu (bean curd), vegetables and peanuts to make this deliciously rich curry.

NUTRITIONAL INFORMATION

Calories 598   Sugars 2g
Protein ....16g   Fat 25g
Carbohydrate ...81g   Saturates 4g

 15 MINS   15 MINS

SERVES 4

I N G R E D I E N T S

1 tsp coriander seeds

1 tsp cumin seeds

1 tsp ground cinnamon

1 tsp cloves

1 whole star anise

1 tsp cardamom pods

1 tsp white peppercorns

1 tbsp oil

6 shallots, chopped very roughly

6 garlic cloves, chopped very roughly

5-cm/2-inch piece lemon grass, sliced

4 fresh red chillies, deseeded and chopped

grated rind of 1 lime

1 tsp salt

3 tbsp sunflower oil

250 g/9 oz/1 cup marinated tofu (bean curd), cut into 2.5 cm/1 inch cubes

125 g/4½ oz green beans, cut into 2.5cm/1 inch lengths

1 kg/2 lb 4 oz/6 cups cooked rice (300 g/10½ oz/1½ cups raw weight)

3 shallots, diced finely and deep-fried

1 spring onion (scallion), chopped finely

2 tbsp chopped roast peanuts

1 tbsp lime juice

1 To make the curry paste, grind together the seeds and spices in a pestle and mortar or spice grinder.

2 Heat the sunflower oil in a preheated wok until it is really hot. Add the shallots, garlic and lemon grass and cook over a low heat until soft, about 5 minutes. Add the chillies and grind together with the dry spices. Stir in the lime rind and salt.

3 To make the curry, heat the oil in a wok or large, heavy frying pan (skillet). Cook the tofu (bean curd) over a high heat for 2 minutes to seal. Stir in the curry paste and beans. Add the rice and stir over a high heat for about 3 minutes.

4 Transfer to a warmed serving dish. Sprinkle with the deep-fried shallots, spring onion (scallion) and peanuts. Squeeze over the lime juice.

Chatuchak Fried Rice

An excellent way to use up leftover rice. Pop it in the freezer as soon as it is cool, and it will be ready to reheat at any time.

NUTRITIONAL INFORMATION

Calories 241   Sugars 5g
Protein . . . . .7g   Fat 5g
Carbohydrate . . .46g   Saturates 1g

   25 MINS   15 MINS

SERVES 4

I N G R E D I E N T S

1 tbsp sunflower oil

3 shallots, chopped finely

2 garlic cloves, crushed

1 red chilli, deseeded and chopped finely

2.5-cm/1-inch piece ginger root, shredded finely

½ green (bell) pepper, deseeded and sliced finely

150 g/5½ oz/2-3 baby aubergines (eggplants), quartered

90 g/3 oz sugar snap peas or mangetout (snow peas), trimmed and blanched

90 g/3 oz/6 baby sweetcorn, halved lengthways and blanched

1 tomato, cut into 8 pieces

90 g/3 oz/1½ cups bean sprouts

500 g/1 lb 2 oz/3 cups cooked jasmine rice

2 tbsp tomato ketchup

2 tbsp light soy sauce

T O   G A R N I S H

fresh coriander (cilantro) leaves

lime wedges

1 Heat the sunflower oil in a wok or large, heavy frying pan (skillet) over a high heat.

2 Add the shallots, garlic, chilli and ginger to the wok or frying pan (skillet). Stir until the shallots have softened.

3 Add the green (bell) pepper and baby aubergines (eggplants) and stir well.

4 Add the sugar snap peas or mangetout (snow peas), baby sweetcorn, tomato and bean sprouts. Stir-fry for 3 minutes.

5 Add the cooked jasmine rice to the wok, and lift and stir with two spoons for 4–5 minutes, until no more steam is released.

6 Stir the tomato ketchup and soy sauce into the mixture in the wok.

7 Serve the Chatuchak fried rice immediately, garnished with coriander (cilantro) leaves and lime wedges to squeeze over.

Fried Rice in Pineapple

This looks very impressive on a party buffet. Mix the remaining pineapple flesh with paw-paw (papaya) and mango for an exotic fruit salad.

NUTRITIONAL INFORMATION

Calories	197	Sugars	.........8g
Protein	.........5g	Fat	..........8g
Carbohydrate	...29g	Saturates	.......1g

  20 MINS   🕐 10 MINS

SERVES 4

INGREDIENTS

1 large pineapple

1 tbsp sunflower oil

1 garlic clove, crushed

1 small onion, diced

½ celery stick, sliced

1 tsp coriander seeds, ground

1 tsp cumin seeds, ground

150 g/5½ oz/1½ cups button
   mushrooms, sliced

250 g/9 oz/1⅓ cups cooked rice

2 tbsp light soy sauce

½ tsp sugar

½ tsp salt

25 g/1 oz/¼ cup cashew nuts

TO GARNISH

1 spring onion (scallion),
   sliced finely

fresh coriander (cilantro) leaves

mint sprig

1 Using a sharp knife, halve the pineapple lengthways and cut out the flesh to make 2 boat-shaped shells.

2 Cut the flesh into cubes and reserve 125 g/4½ oz/1 cup to use in this recipe. (Any remaining pineapple cubes can be served separately.)

3 Heat the sunflower oil in a wok or large, heavy frying pan (skillet).

4 Cook the garlic, onion and celery over a high heat, stirring constantly, for 2 minutes. Stir in the coriander and cumin seeds, and the mushrooms.

5 Add the reserved pineapple cubes and cooked rice to the wok or frying pan (skillet) and stir well.

6 Stir in the soy sauce, sugar, salt and cashew nuts.

7 Using 2 spoons, lift and stir the rice for about 4 minutes until it is thoroughly heated.

8 Spoon the rice mixture into the pineapple boats. Garnish with sliced spring onion (scallion), coriander (cilantro) leaves and a mint sprig.

Chinese Chicken Rice

This is a really colourful main meal or side dish which tastes just as good as it looks.

NUTRITIONAL INFORMATION

Calories	324	Sugars	.........4g
Protein	........24g	Fat	..........10g
Carbohydrate	...37g	Saturates	.......2g

5 MINS   25 MINS

SERVES 4

I N G R E D I E N T S

350 g/12 oz/1¾ cups long-grain white rice

1 tsp turmeric

2 tbsp sunflower oil

350 g/12 oz skinless, boneless chicken breasts or thighs, sliced

1 red (bell) pepper, deseeded and sliced

1 green (bell) pepper, deseeded and sliced

1 green chilli, deseeded and finely chopped

1 medium carrot, coarsely grated

150 g/5½ oz/1½ cups bean sprouts

6 spring onions (scallions), sliced, plus extra to garnish

2 tbsp soy sauce

salt

1 Place the rice and turmeric in a large saucepan of lightly salted water and cook until the grains of rice are just tender, about 10 minutes. Drain the rice thoroughly and press out any excess water with kitchen paper (paper towels).

2 Heat the sunflower oil in a large preheated wok or frying pan (skillet).

3 Add the strips of chicken to the wok or frying pan (skillet) and stir-fry over a high heat until the chicken is just beginning to turn a golden colour.

4 Add the sliced (bell) peppers and green chilli to the wok and stir-fry for 2–3 minutes.

5 Add the cooked rice to the wok, a little at a time, tossing well after each addition until well combined and the grains of rice are separated.

6 Add the carrot, bean sprouts and spring onions (scallions) to the wok and stir-fry for a further 2 minutes.

7 Drizzle with the soy sauce and toss to combine.

8 Transfer the Chinese chicken rice to a warm serving dish, garnish with extra spring onions (scallions), if wished and serve at once.

Fruity Coconut Rice

A pale yellow rice flavoured with coconut and spices to serve as an accompaniment – or as a main dish with added diced chicken or pork.

NUTRITIONAL INFORMATION

Calories 578   Sugars 17g
Protein ....8g   Fat 31g
Carbohydrate ....71g   Saturates 15g

5 MINS   35 MINS

SERVES 4

INGREDIENTS

90 g/3 oz creamed coconut

700 ml/1¼ pints/3 cups boiling water

1 tbsp sunflower oil (or olive oil for a stronger flavour)

1 onion, thinly sliced or chopped

250 g/9 oz/generous 1 cup long-grain rice

¼ tsp turmeric

6 whole cloves

1 cinnamon stick

½ tsp salt

60-90 g/2-3 oz/½ cup raisins or sultanas

60 g/2 oz/½ cup walnut or pecan halves, roughly chopped

2 tbsp pumpkin seeds (optional)

1 Blend the creamed coconut with half the boiling water until smooth, then stir in the remainder until well blended.

2 Heat the oil in a preheated wok, add the onion and stir-fry gently for 3-4 minutes until the onion begins to soften.

3 Rinse the rice thoroughly under cold running water, drain well and add to the wok with the turmeric. Cook for 1-2 minutes, stirring all the time.

4 Add the coconut milk, cloves, cinnamon stick and salt and bring to the boil. Cover and simmer very gently for 10 minutes.

5 Add the raisins, nuts and pumpkin seeds, if using, and mix well. Cover the wok again and continue to cook for a further 5-8 minutes or until all the liquid has been absorbed and the rice is tender. Remove from the heat and leave to stand, still tightly covered, for 5 minutes. Remove the cinnamon stick and serve.

COOK'S TIP

Add 250 g/9 oz/1 cup cooked chicken or pork cut into dice or thin slivers with the raisins to turn this into a main dish. The addition of coconut milk makes the cooked rice slightly sticky.

Green-Fried Rice

Spinach is used in this recipe to give the rice a wonderful green colouring. Tossed with the carrot strips, it is a really appealing dish.

NUTRITIONAL INFORMATION

Calories 139	Sugars 2g
Protein 3g	Fat 7g
Carbohydrate ...18g	Saturates 1g

5 MINS   20 MINS

SERVES 4

I N G R E D I E N T S

150 g/5½ oz/⅔ cup long-grain rice

2 tbsp vegetable oil

2 garlic cloves, crushed

1 tsp grated fresh root ginger

1 carrot, cut into matchsticks

1 courgette (zucchini), diced

225 g/8 oz baby spinach

2 tsp light soy sauce

2 tsp light brown sugar

1 Cook the rice in a saucepan of boiling water for about 15 minutes. Drain the rice well, rinse under cold running water and then rinse the rice thoroughly again. Set aside until required.

2 Heat the vegetable oil in a preheated wok or large, heavy-based frying pan (skillet).

3 Add the crushed garlic and grated fresh root ginger to the wok or frying pan (skillet) and stir-fry for about 30 seconds.

4 Add the carrot matchsticks and diced courgette (zucchini) to the mixture in the wok and stir-fry for about 2 minutes, so the vegetables still retain their crunch.

5 Add the baby spinach and stir-fry for 1 minute, until wilted.

6 Add the rice, soy sauce and sugar to the wok and mix together well.

7 Transfer the green-fried rice to serving dishes and serve immediately.

COOK'S TIP

Light soy sauce has more flavour than the sweeter, dark soy sauce, which gives the food a rich, reddish colour.

Chinese Vegetable Rice

This rice can either be served as a meal in itself or as an accompaniment to other vegetable recipes.

NUTRITIONAL INFORMATION

Calories	228	Sugars	.........5g
Protein	.........5g	Fat	...........7g
Carbohydrate	...37g	Saturates	.......1g

5 MINS   25 MINS

SERVES 4

I N G R E D I E N T S

350 g/12 oz/1¾ cups long-grain white rice

1 tsp turmeric

2 tbsp sunflower oil

225 g/8 oz courgettes (zucchini), sliced

1 red (bell) pepper, deseeded and sliced

1 green (bell) pepper, deseeded and sliced

1 green chilli, deseeded and finely chopped

1 medium carrot, coarsley grated

150 g/5½ oz/1½ cups bean sprouts

6 spring onions (scallions), sliced, plus extra
   to garnish (optional)

2 tbsp soy sauce

salt

1 Place the rice and turmeric in a pan of lightly salted water and bring to the boil. Reduce the heat and leave to simmer until the rice is just tender. Drain the rice thoroughly and press out any excess water with a sheet of kitchen paper (paper towels). Set aside until required.

2 Heat the sunflower oil in a large preheated wok.

3 Add the courgettes (zucchini) to the wok and stir-fry for about 2 minutes.

4 Add the (bell) peppers and chilli to the wok and stir-fry for 2–3 minutes.

5 Add the cooked rice to the mixture in the wok, a little at a time, tossing well after each addition.

6 Add the carrots, bean sprouts and spring onions (scallions) to the wok and stir-fry for a further 2 minutes.

7 Drizzle with soy sauce and serve at once, garnished with extra spring onions (scallions), if desired.

COOK'S TIP

For real luxury, add a few saffron strands infused in boiling water instead of the turmeric.

Hot & Spicy Chicken Rice

Chicken is cooked with rice and vegetables and flavoured with red curry paste, ginger, coriander and lime for a deliciously spicy dish.

NUTRITIONAL INFORMATION

Calories 350	Sugars 2g
Protein 26g	Fat 16g
Carbohydrate ...27g	Saturates 3g

10 MINS   30 MINS

SERVES 4

INGREDIENTS

250 g/9 oz/generous 1 cup white
    long-grain rice

4 tbsp vegetable oil

2 garlic cloves, chopped finely

6 shallots, sliced finely

1 red (bell) pepper, deseeded and diced

125 g/4½ oz French (green) beans,
    cut into 2.5 cm/1 inch lengths

1 tbsp red curry paste

350 g/12 oz cooked skinless, boneless
    chicken, chopped

½ tsp ground coriander seeds

1 tsp finely grated fresh ginger root

2 tbsp fish sauce

finely grated rind of 1 lime

3 tbsp lime juice

1 tbsp chopped fresh coriander
    (cilantro)

salt and pepper

TO GARNISH

lime wedges

sprigs of fresh coriander (cilantro)

1 Cook the rice in plenty of boiling, lightly salted water for 12–15 minutes until tender. Drain, rinse in cold water and drain thoroughly.

2 Heat the vegetable oil in a large preheated wok or frying pan (skillet).

3 Add the garlic and shallots to the wok or frying pan (skillet) and fry gently for 2–3 minutes until golden.

4 Add the (bell) pepper and French (green) beans and stir-fry for 2 minutes. Add the red curry paste and stir-fry for 1 minute.

5 Add the cooked rice to the wok or frying pan (skillet), then add the cooked chicken, ground coriander seeds, ginger, fish sauce, lime rind and juice, and fresh coriander (cilantro).

6 Stir-fry the mixture in the wok over a medium-high heat for about 4–5 minutes, until the rice and chicken are thoroughly reheated. Season to taste.

7 Transfer the chicken and rice mixture to a warm serving dish, garnish with lime wedges and fresh coriander (cilantro) and serve immediately.

Green Rice

The combination of fresh chopped coriander and mint makes this rice dish light and refreshing.

NUTRITIONAL INFORMATION

Calories ....582 Sugars 11g
Protein ....15g Fat 12g
Carbohydrate ...110g Saturates 4g

45 MINS 20 MINS

SERVES 4

INGREDIENTS

2 tbsp olive oil

500 g/1 lb 2 oz/2¼ cups Basmati rice, soaked for 1 hour, washed and drained

700 ml/1¼ pints/3 cups coconut milk

1 tsp salt

1 bay leaf

2 tbsp chopped fresh coriander (cilantro)

2 tbsp chopped fresh mint

2 green chillies, deseeded and chopped finely

1 Heat the olive oil in a saucepan.

2 Add the Basmati rice to the saucepan and stir with a wooden spatula until the rice becomes translucent.

3 Add the coconut milk, salt and bay leaf. Bring to the boil and cook until all the liquid is absorbed.

4 Lower the heat as much as possible, cover the saucepan tightly and cook for 10 minutes.

5 Remove the bay leaf and stir in the coriander (cilantro), mint and chopped green chillies. Fork through the rice gently and serve.

COOK'S TIP

Two segments of fresh lime would make an attractive garnish for this dish and would complement the coriander (cilantro) perfectly.

Rice with Five-Spice Chicken

This dish has a wonderful colour obtained from the turmeric and a great spicy flavour, making it very appealing all round.

NUTRITIONAL INFORMATION

Calories 412	Sugars 1g
Protein 23g	Fat 13g
Carbohydrate . . .53g	Saturates 2g

5 MINS   20 MINS

SERVES 4

I N G R E D I E N T S

1 tbsp Chinese five-spice powder

2 tbsp cornflour (cornstarch)

350 g/12 oz boneless, skinless chicken breasts, cubed

3 tbsp groundnut oil

1 onion, diced

225 g/8 oz/1 cup long-grain white rice

½ tsp turmeric

600 ml/1 pint/2½ cups chicken stock

2 tbsp snipped fresh chives

1 Place the Chinese five-spice powder and cornflour (cornstarch) in a large bowl. Add the chicken pieces and toss to coat all over.

2 Heat 2 tablespoons of the groundnut oil in a large preheated wok. Add the chicken pieces to the wok and stir-fry for 5 minutes. Using a slotted spoon, remove the chicken and set aside.

3 Add the remaining groundnut oil to the wok.

4 Add the onion to the wok and stir-fry for 1 minute.

5 Add the rice, turmeric and chicken stock to the wok and gently bring to the boil.

6 Return the chicken pieces to the wok, reduce the heat and leave to simmer for 10 minutes, or until the liquid has been absorbed and the rice is tender.

7 Add the snipped fresh chives, stir to mix and serve hot.

COOK'S TIP

Be careful when using turmeric as it can stain the hands and clothes a distinctive shade of yellow.

Rice with Crab & Mussels

Shellfish makes an ideal partner for rice. Mussels and crab add flavour and texture to this spicy dish.

NUTRITIONAL INFORMATION

Calories	336	Sugars	.........4g
Protein	........32g	Fat	..........10g
Carbohydrate	...33g	Saturates	.......1g

20 MINS   10 MINS

SERVES 4

INGREDIENTS

300 g/10½ oz/1½ cups long-grain rice

175 g/6 oz white crab meat, fresh, canned or frozen (defrosted if frozen), or 8 crab sticks, defrosted if frozen

2 tbsp sesame or sunflower oil

2.5 cm/1 inch piece ginger root, grated

4 spring onions (scallions), thinly sliced diagonally

125 g/4½ oz mangetout (snow peas), cut into 2-3 pieces

½ tsp turmeric

1 tsp ground cumin

2 x 200 g/7 oz jars mussels, well drained, or 350 g/12 oz frozen mussels, defrosted

1 x 425 g/15 oz can bean sprouts, well drained

salt and pepper

1 Cook the rice in a saucepan of boiling salted water for 15 minutes. Drain well, rinse under cold running water and drain again thoroughly.

2 Extract the crab meat, if using fresh crab (see right). Flake the crab meat or cut the crab sticks into 3 or 4 pieces.

3 Heat the oil in a preheated wok and stir-fry the ginger and spring onions (scallions) for a minute or so. Add the mangetout (snow peas) and continue to cook for a further minute. Sprinkle the turmeric, cumin and seasoning over the vegetables and mix well.

4 Add the crab meat and mussels and stir-fry for 1 minute. Stir in the cooked rice and bean sprouts and stir-fry for 2 minutes or until hot and well mixed.

5 Adjust the seasoning to taste.

COOK'S TIP

To prepare fresh crab, twist off the claws and legs, crack with a heavy knife and pick out the meat with a skewer. Discard the gills and pull out the under shell; discard the stomach sac. Pull the soft meat from the shell. Cut open the body section and prise out the meat with a skewer.

Egg Fu-Yung with Rice

In this dish, cooked rice is mixed with scrambled eggs and Chinese vegetables. It is a great way of using up leftover cooked rice.

NUTRITIONAL INFORMATION

Calories ....258 Sugars 1g
Protein ....8g Fat 16g
Carbohydrate ...21g Saturates 3g

30 MINS   25 MINS

SERVES 4

INGREDIENTS

175 g/6 oz/generous ¾ cup long-grain rice

2 Chinese dried mushrooms
(if unavailable, use thinly sliced
open-cap mushrooms)

3 eggs, beaten

3 tbsp vegetable oil

4 spring onions (scallions), sliced

½ green (bell) pepper, chopped

60 g/2 oz/⅓ cup canned bamboo shoots

60 g/2 oz/⅓ cup canned water
chestnuts, sliced

125 g/4½ oz/2 cups bean sprouts

2 tbsp light soy sauce

2 tbsp dry sherry

2 tsp sesame oil

salt and pepper

1 Cook the rice in lightly salted boiling water according to the packet instructions.

2 Place the Chinese dried mushrooms in a small bowl, cover with warm water and leave to soak for about 20–25 minutes.

3 Mix the beaten eggs with a little salt. Heat 1 tablespoon of the oil in a preheated wok or large frying pan (skillet). Add the eggs and stir until just set. Remove and set aside.

4 Drain the mushrooms and squeeze out the excess water. Remove the tough centres and chop the mushrooms.

5 Heat the remaining oil in a clean wok or frying pan (skillet). Add the mushrooms, spring onions (scallions) and green (bell) pepper, and stir-fry for 2 minutes. Add the bamboo shoots, water chestnuts and bean sprouts. Stir-fry for 1 minute.

6 Drain the rice thoroughly and add to the pan with the remaining ingredients. Mix well, heating the rice thoroughly. Season to taste with salt and pepper. Stir in the reserved eggs and serve.

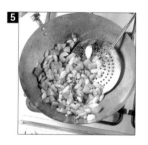

COOK'S TIP

To wash bean sprouts, place them in a bowl of cold water and swirl with your hand. Remove any long tail ends then rinse and drain thoroughly.

Stir-Fried Rice with Sausage

This is a very quick rice dish as it uses pre-cooked rice. It is therefore ideal when time is short or for a quick lunch-time dish.

NUTRITIONAL INFORMATION

Calories 383   Sugars 9g
Protein . . . . .19g   Fat 17g
Carbohydrate . . .42g   Saturates 4g

5 MINS   20 MINS

SERVES 4

INGREDIENTS

350 g/12 oz Chinese sausage

2 tbsp sunflower oil

2 tbsp soy sauce

1 onion, sliced

175 g/6 oz carrots, cut into thin sticks

175 g/6 oz/1¼ cups peas

100 g/3½ oz/¾ cup canned pineapple cubes, drained

275 g/9½ oz/4¾ cups cooked long-grain rice

1 egg, beaten

1 tbsp chopped fresh parsley

1 Using a sharp knife, thinly slice the Chinese sausage.

2 Heat the sunflower oil in a large preheated wok. Add the sausage to the wok and stir-fry for 5 minutes.

3 Stir in the soy sauce and allow to bubble for about 2–3 minutes, or until syrupy.

4 Add the onion, carrots, peas and pineapple to the wok and stir-fry for a further 3 minutes.

5 Add the cooked rice to the wok and stir-fry the mixture for about 2–3 minutes, or until the rice is completely heated through.

6 Drizzle the beaten egg over the top of the rice and cook, tossing the ingredients in the wok, until the egg sets.

7 Transfer the stir-fried rice to a large, warm serving bowl and scatter with plenty of chopped fresh parsley. Serve immediately.

COOK'S TIP

Cook extra rice and freeze it in prepration for some of the other rice dishes included in this book as it saves time and enables a meal to be prepared in minutes. Be sure to cool any leftover cooked rice quickly before freezing to avoid food poisoning.

Index